American Red Cross

Swimming and Water Safety

The following organizations provided review of the materials and/or support for the American Red Cross Swimming and Water Safety program:

A MediMedia USA Company

A MediMedia USA Company

StayWell
780 Township Line Rd.
Yardley, PA 19067

ISBN: 978-1-58480-446-8

Library of Congress Cataloging-in-Publication Data

American Red Cross swimming and water safety. – 3rd ed.
    p. cm.
  Rev. ed. of: Swimming and water safety.
  ISBN 978-1-58480-446-8
  1. Swimming. 2. Diving. 3. Aquatic sports–Safety measures. I. American Red Cross. II. Swimming and water safety.
  GV837.S933 2009
  797.028'9--dc22

                2008046036

09 10 11 12 13/9 8 7 6 5 4 3 2 1

Acknowledgments

The American Red Cross Swimming and Water Safety program and supporting materials were developed through the dedication of both employees and volunteers. Their commitment to excellence made this program possible.

The American Red Cross team for this edition included:

Jean Erdtmann
Senior Director
Program Development and Sales Support

Pat Bonifer
Director
Research and Product Development

Jennifer Deibert
Project Manager
Program Development and Sales Support

Mike Espino
Project Manager
Research and Product Development

Florence E. Fanelli
Manager
Program Development and Sales Support

Connie Harvey
Technical Manager
Program Development and Sales Support

John E. Hendrickson
Project Manager
Program Development and Sales Support

Greta Petrilla
Manager
Communication and Marketing

Greg Stockton
Project Manager
Program Development and Sales Support

Bobby Broome
Senior Associate
Program Development and Sales Support

Martha Chapin
Senior Associate
Program Management and Field Support

Lindsay Darrah
Senior Associate
Product Management and Business Planning

Kelly Fischbein
Senior Associate
Evaluation

Allanea Foreman
Senior Associate
Research and Product Development

Tom Heneghan
Senior Associate
Product Management and Business Planning

Don Lauritzen
Senior Associate
Operations and Program Management

Lindsay Oaksmith, CHES
Senior Associate
Program Development and Sales Support

John Thompson
Senior Associate
Operations and Program Management

Scott Tobias, AAI
Senior Risk Analyst
Risk Management

Erich Ericson
Associate
Program Development and Sales Support

Denise González
Associate
Operations and Program Management

Betty J. Butler
Administrative Assistant
Operations and Program Management

Guidance and support was provided by the following individuals:

Scott Conner
Senior Vice President
Preparedness and Health and Safety Services

Don Vardell
National Chair
Preparedness and Health and Safety Services

The StayWell team for this edition included:

Nancy Monahan
Senior Vice President

Paula Batt
Executive Director
Sales and Business Development

Reed Klanderud
Executive Director
Marketing and New Development

Ellen Beal
Editorial Director

Mary Ellen Curry
Director of Publication Production

Bryan Elrod
Senior Developmental Editor

Shannon Bates
Senior Production Manager

Kate Plourde
Marketing Manager

Special Acknowledgments

The American Red Cross would like to thank the following individuals who provided talent and locations for much of the photography in this manual:

Nancy Cataldo
Director of Service Center Operations
The American Red Cross of Central South Carolina
Sumter, South Carolina

Jay Fitzgerald
Head Swim Coach
Pine Crest Aquatic Center-Woodson Pool
Fort Lauderdale, Florida

Janet Gabriel
Dive Coach
Pine Crest Aquatic Center-Woodson Pool
Fort Lauderdale, Florida

Tim Godwin
Aquatics Supervisor
20th Force Support Squadron
Shaw Air Force Base, South Carolina

Peter Karl
Assistant General Manager, Aquatics
Army Navy Country Club
Arlington, Virginia

Peggy Kubala
Aquatics Director
City of Sumter
Sumter, South Carolina

Mike McGoun
Director of Aquatic Services
City of Coral Springs
Coral Springs, Florida

Briane Schonfeldt
Aquatics Supervisor
City of Irvine
Irvine, California

Jean Skinner
Fairfax County Park Authority
Fairfax, Virginia

Special thanks go to the following individuals for their assistance:

Bill Smith Design
Interior Designer

Simon Bruty
Photographer

John Healy
Production Assistant

Photo Locations

Army Navy Country Club
Arlington, Virginia

Audrey Moore Recreation Center
Fairfax County Park Authority
Annandale, Virginia

City of Sumter Aquatics Center
Parks and Recreation
Sumter, South Carolina

Coral Springs Aquatic Complex
City of Coral Springs
Parks and Recreation
Coral Springs, Florida

Mullins Park Pool
City of Coral Springs
Parks and Recreation
Coral Springs, Florida

Pine Crest Aquatic Center-Woodson Pool
Pine Crest School
Fort Lauderdale, Florida

Spring Hill Recreation Center
Fairfax County Park Authority
McLean, Virginia

University of Maryland
College Park, Maryland

William Woollett Jr. Aquatic Center
City of Irvine
Community Services
Irvine, California

Woodlands Pool
20th Force Support Squadron
Shaw Air Force Base, South Carolina

Swimming and Water Safety Manual
Table of Contents

CHAPTER 5: BASIC AQUATIC SKILLS 77

CHAPTER 6: STROKE MECHANICS 93

CHAPTER 7: STARTS AND TURNS 121

CHAPTER 8: DIVING 139

CHAPTER 9: DISABILITIES AND OTHER HEALTH CONDITIONS 161

CHAPTER 10: LIFETIME FITNESS AND TRAINING 181

CHAPTER 1
Introduction

Recreational swimming and water activities enrich our lives. Family and neighborhood ties are strengthened by weekends at the beach, vacations by mountain lakes, rides on the family boat, pool parties and just "having the neighborhood kids over to use the pool." While these activities add great value to our lives, water can potentially be a source of danger.

This chapter examines the need for water safety education and the importance of learning how to swim by exploring some of the hazards associated with aquatic activities and environments.

The Attraction to Water

People are drawn to water. Look at any waterfront and you will likely see boardwalks, beaches, bike paths, marinas and plenty of people enjoying themselves. Couples and students on spring break seek tropical beaches as vacation spots while families flock to waterparks and lake cabins. Commercial fishermen and mariners take to the water for their livelihoods. Water is an important part of our lives.

People love to swim as well. Swimmers can be found at pools and beaches all summer or in competition throughout the year. Some swimmers quietly swim their laps and mark their distance in personal notebooks or on public charts. Others join teams for water polo, diving, masters swimming or synchronized swimming.

Recreational swimming has become tremendously popular since late in the 19th century. Built in 1887, Brookline, Massachusetts was home to the first municipal pool in the United States. Today, pools are everywhere. Most hotels and motels, apartment buildings and condominiums, schools, universities and municipalities have pools (**Fig. 1-1**). Waterparks with rides, fountains, slides and artificial waves attract millions of patrons each year.

Just as the number of places for swimming has increased, so have the kinds of activities people enjoy in and on the water. Boating and waterskiing, snorkeling and scuba diving, surfing and kiteboarding, fishing and the use of personal watercraft are all increasingly popular. Likewise, many people turn to hot tubs, saunas and whirlpools for rest and relaxation.

Yet, while water can be a source of relaxation and enjoyment, it also presents a risk for drowning– a person can drown in less than 1 inch of water. Each year, young children tragically die because parents and caregivers fail to recognize or notice the danger posed by bathtubs, toilets, kiddie pools, ditches and even 5-gallon buckets of water. Many of these tragic situations could have been avoided by simply following basic water safety rules and recognizing the risks associated with all types of aquatic activities and environments.

Making Water Activities Safer

Drowning is a global public health problem. It is a leading cause of death in nearly every country. While the number of drowning-related injuries and deaths in the United States is shockingly high, the problem is much worse in the developing world. According to a World Health Organization (WHO) study, drowning rates in lower-income countries may be up to 50 times higher than in higher-income countries.

The good news is that the vast majority of drownings are preventable. A growing body of research provides evidence of a strong link between water safety education and a reduction in drowning deaths. Understanding the importance of water safety education as a public health tool, the International Life Saving Federation (ILS) issued a position statement on the importance of water safety education.

ILS Statement on Water Safety Education and Drowning Prevention

1. Death by drowning is a leading public health problem in all countries. Prevention requires public and government support.

2. The vast majority of deaths by drowning can be prevented.

3. Everyone, ideally commencing at a young age and regardless of ability and background, should have access to training in water safety, personal survival and water rescue.

Fig. 1-1

4. Knowledge and understanding of water environments and their associated hazards should be taught to everyone at the earliest possible age.

5. This awareness training should be accompanied by the provision of swimming teaching, in the safest manner possible and to at least a basic level of skill that provides the capacity for survival after unexpected and sudden immersion in water.

6. Acquisition of more advanced water safety knowledge and swimming skills, to include water rescue and competitive swimming, should be encouraged as these enhance aquatic safety.

7. Water hazards should be reduced wherever possible, particularly where swimming and water safety education take place.

8. Trained lifeguards should provide prevention, rescue and treatment where recreational swimming and water safety education take place.

9. Wherever possible, organizations with drowning-prevention expertise, based in high-income countries, should provide assistance to lower-income countries.

10. Accessible and affordable training in water safety and swimming skills should, ideally, be made available for everyone, particularly children, in all countries, to a level consistent with the ILS International Water Safety and Swimming Education Guidelines. (Source: International Life Saving Federation, 2007)

The Red Cross and Water Safety

The issue of drowning is not a new one. The American Red Cross became involved in swimming and water safety largely because of one person, Wilbert E. Longfellow, otherwise known as Commodore Longfellow. Longfellow, the founder of American Red Cross water safety education, once said, "Water can be a good friend or a deadly enemy." In the early 1900s, Longfellow was one of the first to become concerned with the number of drownings in the United States. As Commodore in Chief of New York City's newly formed U.S. Volunteer Life Savings Corps, Longfellow helped promote lifeguarding across the Northeast.

Seeing the need for a nationwide program of swimming and lifesaving instruction, Longfellow presented a plan for the "waterproofing of America" to the Red Cross in 1912. Soon after, the Red Cross Life Saving Corps (forerunner of the present-day Red Cross Water Safety courses) came into being. Longfellow was appointed to organize the new lifesaving program and was awarded Red Cross Lifesaving Certificate Number One and the lifesaving emblem that has since been earned and proudly worn by millions of people (**Fig. 1-2**).

Longfellow worked with intense devotion and great enthusiasm in support of the nationwide Red Cross Water Safety program. The results of his efforts were astonishing. The nation's drowning rate was cut dramatically–from 8.8 people per 100,000 in 1914 to 4.8 in 1947–and there was a tremendous upsurge in the popularity of swimming, boating and other water activities. It reached the point to where an estimated 80 million Americans were participating in some form of aquatic recreation. Thanks to the dedication and untiring efforts of those who followed his example and continued his work, the Red Cross has led the way in helping the nation stay safe in and around the water.

Fig. 1-2

The Red Cross Swimming and Water Safety Program

It is the mission of the Red Cross to prevent, prepare for and respond to emergencies. Today, the Red Cross Swimming and Water Safety program helps fulfill that mission by teaching people to be safe in, on and around the water through water safety courses, water-orientation classes for infants and toddlers and comprehensive Learn-to-Swim courses for individuals of different ages and abilities. Red Cross Learn-to-Swim courses are structured in a logical progression for aquatic skill development. As participants develop these skills, they become safer and better swimmers.

Parent and Child Aquatics

Red Cross Parent and Child Aquatics courses can help young children become comfortable in and around the water so that when the time comes, they are ready to learn how to swim. These courses are not designed to teach children to become good swimmers or even to survive in water on their own. They are intended to lay the foundation for future aquatic skills. One of the most valuable benefits of Parent and Child Aquatics is that it teaches parents about water safety and how to safely handle their children in and around the water (**Fig. 1-3**). Through this philosophy and practice, the Red Cross Parent and Child

Aquatics courses comply with and complement the American Academy of Pediatrics statement, which recommends that formal swimming lessons not begin until after a child's 4th birthday. As many families have experienced, these young children may still benefit from early aquatic experiences.

Preschool Aquatics

Red Cross Preschool Aquatics courses are targeted to children about 4 and 5 years old. The Preschool Aquatics program consists of three levels that teach fundamental water safety and aquatic skills. The program aims to meet the safety and developmental needs of this age group. The Preschool Aquatics program allows participants to move seamlessly into Learn-to-Swim courses as they get older and progress through the levels.

Learn-to-Swim

Red Cross Learn-to-Swim consists of six comprehensive levels that teach people of all ages and abilities how to swim skillfully and safely. The program gives participants a positive learning experience. Each level includes training in basic water safety, such as knowing when and how to call for help and helping a swimmer in distress. All aquatic and safety skills are taught in a logical progression. The objective is to teach people to swim and to be safe in, on and around the water.

Fig. 1-3

Elements of a Good Swim Instruction Program

Good swim instruction programs, including Red Cross Parent and Child Aquatics, Preschool Aquatics and Learn-to-Swim courses, have the following elements:

- The facility is clean and well maintained.
- The pool chemistry is properly balanced.
- The water temperature is conducive for teaching (83° to 86° F).
- Trained lifeguards supervise all classes.
- The program has clearly defined objectives, expectations, schedules and pricing.
- The program coordinator is accessible and knowledgeable.
- Instructors are professional and well trained by a nationally recognized training agency, such as the Red Cross.
- Instructors communicate regularly with parents and provide progress reports and other relevant information (**Fig. 1-4**).
- The instructor-to-participant ratio is appropriate.
- Participants are active and engaged throughout each lesson.
- Instructors are in the water when teaching unless it is appropriate to be on the deck (**Fig. 1-5**).
- Participants make progress over time.

Your Responsibilities

Standards and laws have been developed regarding the design of swimming pools and spas, including the types and use of pool barriers or fences. The U.S. Consumer Product Safety Commission (CPSC) offers a free publication on guidelines on home pool barriers, which can be downloaded from their Web site (*www.cpsc.gov*). Additionally, the Virginia Graeme Baker Pool and Spa Safety Act was signed into law in 2007. This legislation encourages states to institute pool safety laws designed to protect adults and especially children from the dangers of certain types and designs of pool and spa drains.

If our neighborhoods are to be safe from water hazards, everyone in the community must do his and her part to keep neighborhoods safe from water hazards. Homeowners should be aware that any body of water on their property—everything

Fig. 1-4

from ponds and canals to beachfronts—could represent an attractive play area for unsupervised children and should take action to prevent or minimize unauthorized and unsupervised access to these areas. Docks, boats and other types of water recreation equipment are equally enticing.

Fig. 1-5

Parents must educate their children about the water hazards in their community and practice water safety at all times. The importance of wearing life jackets, enrolling in a boating safety course and refraining from alcohol while operating watercraft cannot be understated. Visit the National Safe Boating Council Web site (*www.safeboatingcouncil.org*) for more information on boating safety education. Above all, always designate a responsible individual to provide constant supervision whenever children are in or around water—even a momentary distraction can result in tragedy.

Home Swimming Pools

Home swimming pools, also referred to as residential swimming pools, are an attractive feature for many homeowners. They create a beautiful environment that offers years of fun and activity for families. However, home swimming pools also can be a significant threat to young children. These pools pose both a risk to the children living in the home and to children living in the surrounding neighborhood. Children outside the home can gain access to poorly secured or unsupervised pools in the neighborhood. If left unsupervised, even for a brief moment, children inside the home can sneak into backyard pools if access is not secured.

A swimmer in distress can easily go unnoticed at pool parties when inattentive or distracted adults supervise the children. Even worse, some pool parties fail to designate a person whose sole job is to provide constant supervision whenever children are in and around the water. Additionally, the drains of some home pools, spas and hot tubs create a dangerous entrapment hazard to swimmers that can cause drowning or serious injury by trapping a swimmer against the drain opening.

Recreational Pools, Beaches and Waterparks

Even if there are lifeguards present, a responsible adult should always monitor children at recreational pools (pools that are part of a public or private recreational facility), beaches and waterparks, which are often very crowded. Beaches can have strong currents, heavy waves, cooler temperatures, aquatic life or other hazards that can make swimming more difficult. Swimming in wave pools can be challenging, even for the experienced swimmer. Waterslides and other waterpark attractions can be dangerous if the rules are not closely followed (**Fig. 1-6**).

Fig. 1-6

Fig. 1-7

Natural Bodies of Water

Nearly every community has a canal, pond, creek, stream, river, lake, drainage basin, reservoir, wetlands area or shoreline that can be easily accessed. In many communities, these areas frequently are features of public parks (**Fig. 1-7**). Often, these unsupervised or unsecured bodies of water represent an enticing play area for adventurous children who may decide to swim on their own or fall in while playing nearby. When they are not part of a designated swimming area, natural bodies of water pose many potential hazards and should never be considered safe. Even for children or adults who have good swimming skills, these bodies of water contain elements, such as cold water, dams, aquatic life, currents, steep drop-offs and entrapment hazards that can make swimming dangerous.

Environmental Issues

Environmental factors can create water hazards where they are not expected. Heavy rainfall, wildland fires and drought can lead to changes in how much water flows into certain areas. Washes, aqueducts, drainage canals, culverts and ditches can suddenly swell with water after heavy rains and flooding. Additionally, storms, snowmelt or runoff can create strong currents, making the shoreline near any moving water dangerous. Natural disasters, such as hurricanes, tornadoes or wildland fires, may also create new water hazards. For example, abandoned or destroyed homes or motels after a natural disaster may leave access to some pools unsupervised or unrestricted.

Boating

Boating is a rewarding pastime that allows families to spend time together. Millions of people enjoy recreational boating safely every day. It is a sobering fact that more people die in recreational boating accidents every year than in airplane crashes or train wrecks. Boating emergencies often occur suddenly and in many cases involve alcohol use and inexperience. In crowded waters, collisions with other watercraft are possible. Due to their speed and unique handling characteristics, personal watercraft can be quite dangerous, especially to young and inexperienced operators. Additionally, underwater hazards, dams, locks, commercial vessels and sudden weather changes are elements frequently encountered while boating that can lead to an emergency. In most cases, wearing a life jacket can mean the difference between life and death in a boating emergency. In all cases, there is never

FLOODS

Every year, floods threaten the lives and homes of many families across the country. Floods are among the most common water hazards that occur in the United States and can affect small communities as well as large towns and cities.

Some floods build gradually over a period of days. However, flash floods can develop within minutes or hours without any obvious signs of rain. They often produce powerful and destructive walls of water and debris. Overland flooding, which occurs outside of rivers and streams, can wreak havoc on communities. Even small creeks and streams can flood. All states are at risk for flooding so everyone should be aware of flood hazards in their area. This is especially important for those who live near water, downstream from dams or in low-lying areas.

The first step you can take to protect your family and home is to know your flood risk. Call your emergency management office or planning and zoning department for information on your area's flood risk. Next, prepare for floods by developing a disaster plan before flooding or other disasters strike and making a disaster supplies kit. Your disaster plan should include information on how to turn off electricity, gas and water (if authorities advise turning them off) and identify where you could go if you are told to evacuate.

Because most homeowner's insurance policies do not cover damages caused by floods, every homeowner should consider purchasing a separate policy under the National Flood Insurance Program (NFIP). Insurance policies and other valuable items that could be damaged by

flooding should be kept in a safe deposit box. Keeping an up-to-date written, photographed or videotaped inventory and receipts for the contents of your home is important because it can help avoid delays in filing an insurance claim in the event of a flood loss.

Talk to your local building departments to determine your area's required level of flood protection. People who live in areas where flooding is likely should take steps to floodproof their homes. *Floodproofing* means remodeling or rebuilding a home using materials and methods that will prevent or minimize damage from future floods. Elevating key items that flood waters can damage, such as the furnace and electrical panels, and constructing barriers or sealing the walls of the home with waterproofing compounds to help prevent floodwaters from entering are examples of floodproofing.

Everyone who lives in areas prone to flooding should pay attention to local radio and TV stations if it has been raining for any length of time. A flash flood **WATCH** means that flooding is possible; a flash flood **WARNING** means that flash flooding is occurring. In any case, the way to stay safe is to head for higher ground and stay away from the water.

If emergency officials advise you to evacuate, do so immediately. Never drive in flooded areas. Even 6 inches of water can reach the bottom of many vehicles causing drivers to lose control and raising the risk for stalling. If floodwaters rise around your vehicle, abandon your vehicle and move to higher ground.

---

a substitution for boating safety education and experience (**Fig. 1-8**).

Drownproofing and Young Children: A Dangerous Myth

Participation in any swim lesson program cannot "drownproof" your child. Despite claims to the contrary, no young child is drownproof or

water safe. Young children are, by nature, wildly curious, unpredictable and vary greatly in their size, physical abilities and motor skills and may be clumsy at times. An infant or a toddler who falls into the water can become disoriented and scared and may not correctly remember techniques for self-rescue. Although some young children are quite skilled at swimming, due to

Fig. 1-8

their age and maturity, you cannot rely on young children to rescue themselves, especially in adverse situations.

According to the Centers for Disease Control and Prevention (CDC), in 2005, drowning was the number one cause of accidental death and the second-leading cause of death for children ages 1 to 4. The majority of these deaths occur in home pools. The CPSC reports that the vast majority of children who drown in home pools were not expected to be in or around the pool. This means that most children who drown in home pools

do so by entering the water accidentally and without their parents' or guardian's knowledge. Do not test your child's swimming ability by allowing this situation to occur! For anyone who has the responsibility of a home pool, the best way to keep children safe from drowning is to provide layers of protection: securing the pool with appropriate barriers, keeping young children under active supervision at all times, enrolling children in a Red Cross Learn-to-Swim program and ensuring everyone in the home knows how to respond in an aquatic emergency (**Fig. 1-9**). It is every parent's duty to educate his or her

Fig. 1-9

children on the dangers associated with water and continuously remind them to stay away from water hazards. Make sure that everyone in the family is water smart!

Efforts Toward Sun Safety Education

For many, having fun in the water goes hand-in-hand with fun in the sun, but too much sun is no fun! Overexposure to ultraviolet (UV) rays can lead to skin cancer, eye damage and immune suppression. The thinning of the ozone layer has resulted in more UV radiation reaching the Earth's surface. At the same time, skin cancer has become the most common type of cancer in the United States, making up more than half of all new cases. In time, the Earth's natural processes will work to restore the ozone layer, but not until the last half of the 21st century. This is especially troubling for children who still have most of their lives to live in a world with increased levels of UV radiation.

Children need sun protection education since unprotected exposure to the sun during youth puts them at increased lifetime risk for skin cancer. Organizations, such as the U.S. Environmental Protection Agency (EPA), the CDC and the Red Cross, have undertaken efforts to increase public awareness on the dangers of overexposure to UV radiation. The EPA SunWise School Program is one such effort. The components of the SunWise Program are available to partner schools and organizations free of charge. Encourage your child's school, recreation center, pool, camp or other organization to implement sun-safe policies and adopt the SunWise Program so your children can grow up SunWise.

Summary

The chapters that follow provide advice and guidance for making every aquatic experience safe and enjoyable. The early chapters focus on practical steps to take to prevent, prepare for and respond to emergencies whenever you are in, on or around a wide variety of aquatic environments. The middle chapters explain the why's and the how's of skills that make people safer, more proficient and even more highly skilled in all types of aquatic settings. Finally, the later chapters emphasize how aquatics can benefit nearly everyone—no matter your physical ability or level of fitness.

Participation in aquatics can be a rewarding, lifelong activity. This book gives the basic information everyone needs to know before heading out to the water for the first time or the next time. Whether you are reading this book to improve your strokes or your lap time; learn how to stay safe, stay in shape or teach a class; or to find what class is right for you, there is something in it for everyone. Enjoy!

CHAPTER 2
Water Safety—Prevention

Staying safe in and around the water is no accident—it takes knowledge and forethought. Whether it is a day at the beach, boating, visiting a waterpark or going to a neighborhood pool party, do not let the good times distract your focus. Water safety takes deliberate action.

This chapter addresses safety issues for swimming and aquatic activities that take place in, on and around water by looking at the main environments where these activities take place. This chapter also will discuss the importance of sun safety and some of the responsibilities associated with pool ownership.

Planning for Safety

Staying Smart Around the Water

In most cases, aquatic emergencies occur when they are least expected. Most people do not realize that a great number of people who drown never intended to go in the water in the first place. The best thing anyone can do to stay safe in, on and around the water is to learn to swim well. It is also important to establish and follow water safety rules. This is just as true for a day of swimming at the beach as it is for a pleasant dip in the backyard pool–whether you are in the water or out. Be aware that aquatic emergencies do not always happen when people are swimming. A hike along the shores of a mountain stream or canoe–camping trip can turn out disastrous if basic water safety rules are not followed. Everyone should follow the general swimming safety tips listed below whenever they are in, on or around any body of water. Parents, families and activity leaders also can use these tips to help make their own set of water safety rules.

- Swim only in areas supervised by a lifeguard (**Fig. 2-1**).
- Always swim with a buddy; never swim alone.
- Read and obey all rules and posted signs.
- Only swim in designated areas.

- Have young children or inexperienced swimmers take extra precautions, such as wearing a U.S. Coast Guard-approved life jacket, when around the water and staying within arm's reach of a designated water watcher.
- Designate a responsible individual(s) as the person to watch over children whenever they are in, on or around any body of water, even if a lifeguard is present.
- Watch out for the "dangerous too's": too tired, too cold, too far from safety, too much sun and too much strenuous activity.
- Set specific swimming rules for each individual in a family or a group based on swimming ability (for example, inexperienced swimmers should stay in water less than chest deep).
- Make sure swimmers know about the water environment and any potential hazards, such as deep and shallow areas, currents, obstructions and the locations of entry and exit points. The more informed people are, the more aware they will be of hazards as well as safe practices.
- Identify potential water hazards within the community and make certain that children stay away from them.
- Know how to prevent, recognize and respond to emergencies.

Fig. 2-1

- Use a feetfirst entry when entering the water.
- Enter headfirst only when the area is clearly marked for diving and has no obstructions.
- Do not mix alcohol with boating, swimming or diving. Alcohol impairs judgment, balance and coordination; impacts the ability to operate watercraft safely; affects swimming and diving skills; and reduces the body's ability to stay warm.
- Take a boating safety course before operating any watercraft.
- Be especially cautious near moving water, cold water and ice.
- Be prepared. Aquatic emergencies happen quickly and suddenly. Whenever possible have a telephone or mobile phone nearby.

Sun Safety

Everyone enjoys spending time outside on a warm, sunny day, but spending too much time in the sun without taking steps to protect yourself from the sun's damaging rays is a case of too much of a good thing. While some groups are at lower risk for developing skin cancer specifically, overexposure to the sun should be of concern to everyone, regardless of age, location or skin color. However, because sunburns in childhood can result in health problems later in life, children are especially at risk. The consequences of overexposure are severe. Too much unprotected exposure to the sun can lead to eye damage, cataracts, immune system suppression, premature aging of the skin and, most seriously, skin cancer. Fortunately, it is easy to protect yourself from overexposure by being SunWise.

Ultraviolet Radiation

Energy from the sun is called solar radiation. Solar radiation reaches the Earth in a range of wavelengths or rays, including ultraviolet (UV), infrared, visible light, gamma ray and x-ray (**Fig. 2-2**). Some of these rays are blocked by the atmosphere, while others make it to the Earth's surface. Problems from too much sun come from overexposure to certain types of this radiation. There are two types of rays to be concerned about: ultraviolet A (UVA) rays and ultraviolet B (UVB) rays. UVA rays, also found in tanning salons, can cause premature aging of the skin and contribute to the development of skin cancer. UVB rays are the burn-producing rays.

Fig. 2-2

Overexposure to UVB rays is thought to be the most common cause of skin cancer.

The ozone layer of the atmosphere acts to shield the planet from dangerous UV rays, but it is not as thick as it used to be. This means that more and more UV rays are able to reach the surface. According to the Environmental Protection Agency (EPA), excess amounts of certain manmade chemicals have contributed to this thinning. Even though efforts have been made to stop the production of ozone-layer depleting chemicals, scientists predict that normal ozone-layer levels will not return until around 2065. Consequently, children growing up in this timeframe will live most of their lives with increased levels of UV radiation.

Effects from Overexposure
Skin Cancers

Skin cancer is the most common type of cancer in the United States and it is reaching epidemic proportions. The statistics are alarming. According to the American Academy of Dermatology, current estimates are that one in five Americans will develop skin cancer in their lifetime.

Melanoma is the most serious form of skin cancer. Melanoma is also one of the fastest growing types of cancer in the United States. Worse yet, many dermatologists think that sunburns suffered in childhood may lead to melanomas later in life.

Non-melanoma skin cancers are other types of skin cancer that can be caused by overexposure to UV radiation. There are two primary types of non-melanoma skin cancers: basal cell carcinomas and squamous cell carcinomas. Even though they are less deadly than melanomas, non-melanoma skin cancers can be disfiguring and cause more serious health problems if left untreated.

Cataracts and Other Eye Damage

Cataracts are a form of eye damage resulting in clouded vision. Without medical care, cataracts can result in blindness. Research has shown that UV radiation increases the likelihood of certain types of cataracts. Other kinds of eye damage from too much sun include skin cancer around the eyes and degeneration of the macula (the part of the retina where visual perception is most acute).

Immune Suppression

Overexposure to UV radiation also can suppress the body's immune system and the skin's natural defenses. This can result in problems with certain immunizations, increased sensitivity to sunlight and adverse reactions to certain medications.

Other Damage

Other damage from UV radiation includes actinic keratoses and premature aging of the skin. Actinic keratoses are skin growths that occur on body areas exposed to the sun, especially the face, hands, forearms and the "V" of the neck. Chronic exposure to the sun also can cause premature aging, which can make the skin wrinkled and leathery.

Be SunWise

The good news is that skin cancer is the most preventable type of cancer. Everyone can take steps to avoid the damaging effects from UV radiation. However, staying safe from the sun is more than just putting on sunscreen when at the

Fig. 2-3

beach. Everyday exposure to the sun's harmful rays is dangerous too. Taking steps to reduce exposure to the sun each and every day is the best defense against skin cancer and the other negative effects of the sun. The EPA recommends the following steps to stay SunWise:

- Do not burn. Five or more sunburns significantly increases your risk of developing skin cancer.
- Avoid suntanning and tanning beds. UV light from tanning beds and the sun causes skin cancer and wrinkling. If you want to look like you have been in the sun, consider using a sunless self-tanning product, but continue to use sunscreen with it.
- Generously apply sunscreen. Apply ample amounts of sunscreen to all exposed skin using a sun protection factor (SPF) of at least 15 that provides broad-spectrum protection from both UVA and UVB rays. Reapply every 2 hours, even on cloudy days, and after swimming or sweating (**Fig. 2-3**).
- Wear protective clothing, such as a long-sleeved shirt, long pants, a wide-brimmed hat and sunglasses, when possible.
- Seek shade when appropriate remembering that the sun's UV rays are strongest between 10 A.M. and 4 P.M. Follow the shadow rule when in the sun: Watch Your Shadow. No Shadow, Seek Shade!
- Use extra caution near water, snow and sand. Water, snow and sand reflect the damaging rays of the sun, which can increase your chance of sunburn.
- Pay attention to the UV Index. The UV Index provides important information to help you plan your outdoor activities in ways that prevent overexposure to the sun.
- Get vitamin D safely through a diet that includes vitamin supplements and foods fortified with vitamin D. Do not seek the sun for your vitamin D.

And remember, early detection of melanoma can save your life. Carefully examine **ALL** of your skin once a month. A new or changing mole in an adult should be evaluated by a dermatologist.

The UV Index

Developed by the National Weather Service and the EPA, the UV Index is issued daily in selected cities across the United States. The UV Index is

THE UV INDEX

UV Index Number	Exposure Level
2 or less	Low
3–5	Moderate
6–7	High
8–10	Very High
11+	Extreme

a forecast of the expected risk of overexposure to the sun. UV intensity levels are listed on a scale of 1 to 11+. On a day with an intensity level of 1, there is a low risk of overexposure and on an 11+ day there is an extreme risk.

Recreational Water Illness

Swimming and other aquatic activities should occur only in areas with good water quality. Many guarded beaches are tested regularly for pollution and disease-causing organisms. In some areas, water-quality flags let swimmers know water conditions. For example, blue flags indicate good swimming conditions and red flags indicate a potential water-quality problem. Also, swimmers should avoid natural bodies of water for 24 hours after heavy rains. Runoff can contaminate a natural body of water with toxic substances after heavy rains and flooding.

A recreational water illness (RWI) is an illness that comes from contact with contaminated water. These illnesses are most commonly spread when swimmers swallow or breathe in water particles containing germs. RWIs can be found in waterparks, swimming pools, hot tubs and spas, rivers, lakes and oceans. Diarrhea is the most common symptom of RWIs, but they can also cause infections in the skin, ears, eyes, chest and lungs.

To avoid RWIs—

- Check for clean, clear pool water. The main drain on the bottom of the pool should be clearly visible.

- Check the pool. Pool tiles should not be sticky or slippery and slides should be smooth.
- Check for odors. A clean pool has very little odor—a strong chemical smell may indicate a problem.
- Check with the staff. Ask them about water quality, health inspections and water-quality training.

The Centers for Disease Control and Prevention (CDC) recommends that all swimmers follow the six "PLEAs" that promote safe, healthy swimming.

1. Please do not swim when you have diarrhea. You can spread germs in the water and make other people sick. This is especially important for children in diapers.
2. Please do not swallow pool water. In fact, avoid getting water in your mouth altogether.
3. Please practice good hygiene. Take a shower before swimming and wash your hands after using the toilet or changing diapers (**Fig. 2-4**).
4. Please take children on bathroom breaks or check diapers often. Waiting to hear "I have to go" may mean that it is too late.
5. Please change diapers in a bathroom or a diaper-changing area and not poolside. Germs can

Fig. 2-4

spread to surfaces and objects in and around the pool and cause illness.

6. Please wash your child thoroughly (especially the buttocks) with soap and water before swimming.

Watching Children Around Water

Drowning is the second-leading cause of death for children ages 1 to 4. Anyone watching children who are in, on or around water must understand that drowning happens quickly and suddenly. Any source of water is a potential drowning hazard, especially for young children and weak swimmers. Parents, adults and caregivers should follow these guidelines whenever they are near water with children:

- Know each child's swimming ability and set specific rules for each child based on swimming ability.
- Maintain constant supervision, keeping an eye on the children at all times. Provide constant and vigilant supervision whenever children are around any source of water (such as pools, rivers, lakes, bathtubs, toilets and even buckets of water) no matter how well the child can swim and no matter how shallow the water. This is also true if you are in boat, on a dock or just near the shore. If a child is in distress, provide assistance by notifying a lifeguard, if one is available. If no lifeguard is available, provide assistance consistent with your level of training.
- Stay within an arm's reach of any weak or inexperienced swimmer who is in the water (**Fig. 2-5**).
- Do not rely on substitutes. The use of water wings, swim rings, inflatable toys and other items designed for water recreation cannot replace parental supervision, nor should they be counted on as lifesaving devices. These devices can suddenly shift position, lose air or slip out from underneath, leaving the child in a dangerous situation.

SWIMMER'S EAR

Moisture that remains in the S-shaped ear canal after swimming can promote the growth of organisms that cause infection. This type of chronic irritation is called "swimmer's ear." People can get swimmer's ear in chlorinated and non-chlorinated pool water as well as fresh water. Whether or not swimmers get this irritation depends on many factors, including how long swimmers stay in the water and how deep they swim. Swimmer's ear often goes away without treatment. People should see a doctor if their ears feel painful, swollen or "full" or if they notice even mild hearing loss. These symptoms could be signs of a more serious inner ear infection that can cause long-term damage to the ear.

Tips to Prevent Swimmer's Ear

- Get the water out of the ears after swimming. Tilt the head and jump energetically several times or use a towel to gently wipe (do not rub) the outer ear. A hair dryer on a low setting can also help. When using a hair dryer, gently pull down the ear lobe and blow warm air into the ear from several inches away.

- Use over-the-counter eardrops that contain one or more agents to evaporate the water, kill the organisms and moisturize the ear canal. Ask a health-care professional to recommend a brand.

- Wear a swim cap or wet suit hood, especially for activities, such as surfing, that involve frequent submersions.

- Avoid wax-type earplugs. They may damage the ear canal and make infection more likely. Silicone earplugs provide better protection. Do not use any earplugs when surface diving.

- Ask a health-care professional how to flush out the ears using warm water and an ear syringe.

- Do not scratch, touch or put anything into the ears because these actions can introduce bacteria into the ear canal and remove protective earwax.

- Young children who have ear tubes should only participate in swimming activities approved by their health care providers.

Fig. 2-5

- Caution children never to hyperventilate before or during any swimming activity and do not allow competitive, repetitive or prolonged underwater swimming or breath-holding.

- Prevent access to community and landscape water features, such as small ponds and waterfalls.

- Empty kiddie pools immediately after use.

- If there are small children in the home, use safety locks on toilets and keep bathroom doors closed and toilet-bowl covers down.

- Empty cleaning buckets immediately after use.

- When visiting another home, check the site for potential water hazards and always supervise children.

- Do not allow children to swim outdoors during inclement weather conditions, especially prior to and during storms with lightning and high winds.

- Contact your local American Red Cross chapter for further information on enrolling in Learn-to-Swim programs; water safety courses; adult, child and infant cardiopulmonary resuscitation (CPR) courses; and first aid courses.

  ○ Teach everyone in the family to swim by enrolling them in Red Cross Learn-to-Swim courses. Providing early aquatic experiences to a child is a gift that will have lifelong rewards.

  ○ Urge family members to enroll in a Red Cross water safety course. A water safety course encourages safe practices and provides lifelong safety skills (**Fig. 2-6**).

  ○ Learn first aid and CPR. Parents and other guardians, such as grandparents, older siblings and babysitters, should take a CPR and first aid course. Knowing these skills can be important around the water.

Refer to **Chapter 3** for basic information on how to respond to an aquatic emergency.

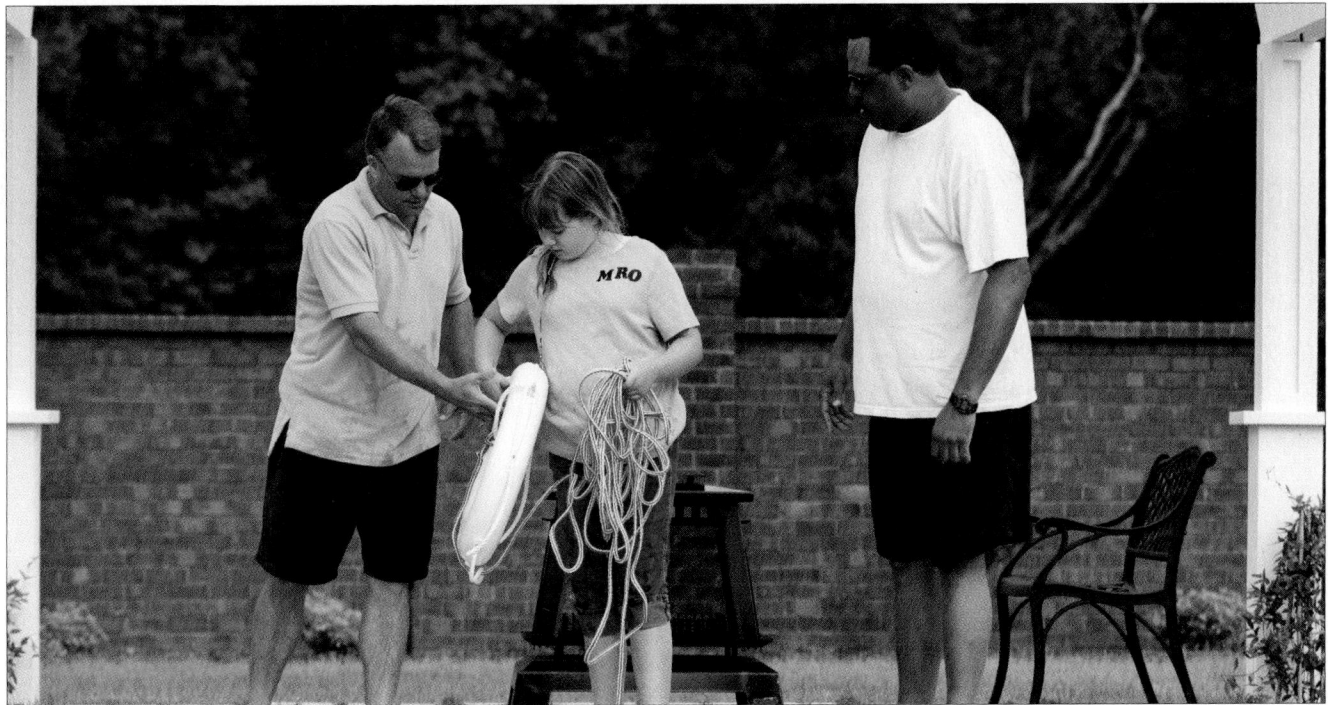
Fig. 2-6

Hyperventilation and Extended Breath-Holding

Do not hyperventilate! Hyperventilation is a dangerous technique that some swimmers use to try to stay under water longer. This technique involves taking a series of deep breaths and forcefully blowing them out. Hyperventilation reduces the carbon dioxide in the blood, which delays the demand for the body to take a breath (it does not give you more oxygen or help your body to use the oxygen it has more efficiently). This happens because the level of carbon dioxide in the blood is what signals the body to take each breath. A person who hyperventilates and then swims under water could pass out before the brain signals it is time to breathe. By the time someone notices the swimmer is under water, it could be too late. Make sure that everyone understands that underwater activities should never be competitive or repetitive. Prolonged underwater swimming for distance and breath-holding for time are extremely dangerous. Caution everyone never to hyperventilate before or during any swimming activity.

Life Jackets

Life jackets, also known as personal flotation devices (PFDs), are not just for boats. Unless under direct supervision in a designated swimming area, young children and weak swimmers should wear life jackets whenever they are in, on or around the water. People who cannot swim well should wear a life jacket whenever they are near the water as well. Even in public pools or waterparks, people with little or no swimming ability should wear one. All life jackets should be U.S. Coast Guard approved and in good condition. If the life jacket is U.S. Coast Guard approved, it will be marked on the device.

Because most boating emergencies happen suddenly, everyone on a boat should ALWAYS wear a life jacket. Local laws may even require wearing one. Put your life jacket on at the dock and do not take it off until you return, because it is difficult to put a life jacket on while in the water (**Fig. 2-7**)! It is also a good idea to practice putting one on to be sure that the life jacket fits correctly and is worn properly. Practice swimming with it in shallow water. Even good swimmers should wear a life jacket in any situation where there is a chance of falling or being thrown into the water, especially if the water is cold. Most states require that life jackets be worn for anyone being towed on water skis, tubes or similar devices, and while operating or riding on a personal watercraft (PWC).

Fig. 2-7

TYPES OF PERSONAL FLOTATION DEVICES

Type	Description	Advantages	Disadvantages
Type I (off-shore life jackets)	■ Designed for boating on all waters, especially open, rough or remote waters where rescue may be delayed ■ Designed to turn *most* unconscious wearers in the water to a face-up position	■ Offers the most flotation ■ May help prevent hypothermia ■ Comes in highly visible colors ■ Has reflective material for search and rescue	Bulky in and out of water
Type II (near-shore life jackets)	■ Designed for calm, inland water or where there is a good chance of quick rescue ■ Will turn *some* unconscious wearers to a face-up position in the water	■ Requires little maintenance ■ Good flotation ■ Good for nonswimmers ■ Less bulky than off-shore style	Not recommended for long hours on rough water
Type III (flotation aids)	■ Often used for general boating in calm inland waters or for specialized activity as marked on the device, such as waterskiing, hunting, fishing, canoeing or kayaking ■ Designed so wearer may have to tilt their head back to avoid turning face-down in the water	■ Designed for general boating and designated activities marked on the device ■ Available in many styles, including vests and flotation coats ■ More comfortable for active water sports than types I and II	■ May not turn unconscious wearer face-up—the wearer may have to tilt the head back to avoid turning face-down in water ■ Not recommended for extended survival in rough water ■ Must be water-tested by inexperienced swimmers before boating activity
Type IV (throwable devices)	■ Designed to be thrown to a person in the water and grasped and held by the user until rescued—not designed to be worn ■ Does not take the place of wearing a life jacket	■ May be thrown from boat or land ■ Provide backup to wearable life jackets ■ Some styles may be used as seat cushions	■ Not for unconscious persons ■ Not suitable for inexperienced swimmers or children
Type V (restricted-use life jackets)	Intended for specific activities, such as whitewater rafting, and may be worn instead of another life jacket only if used according to the approval condition(s) on its label	■ Designed for specific activities ■ Continuous wear prevents users from being caught without protection; most accidents occur suddenly	Less safe than other life jacket types if used for activities other than those specified on label

Fig. 2-8

There are several types and many styles of life jackets and all life jackets have ratings for their buoyancy and purposes (**Fig. 2-8**). Swimming ability, activity and water conditions help determine which type to use. Certain types of life jackets are made to turn an unconscious person in the water from a face-down position to a vertical or slightly tipped-back position. Other flotation devices, such as buoyant cushions and ring buoys, do not take the place of life jackets, but may be good throwing aids in an emergency. New inflatable life jackets are also available. These jackets offer comfort, safety and style and are a good alternative to the traditional life jackets—there is no excuse for not wearing a life jacket!

The U.S. Coast Guard has categorized life jackets into five types. The four wearable types may have permanent flotation or may be inflatable.

When choosing a life jacket—

- Make sure it is the right type for the activity.
- Make sure it is U.S. Coast Guard approved.
- Make sure it fits the intended user. Check the label on the life jacket for weight limits.
- Check buckles and straps for proper function. Discard any life jacket with torn fabric or straps that have pulled loose.
- Put it on and practice swimming with it.

Water wings, swim rings, inflatable toys and other items designed for water recreation are not substitutes for U.S. Coast Guard-approved life jackets or adult supervision. These devices enable swimmers to go beyond their ability. For those with little or no swimming skill, a fall off one of these devices could lead to a drowning situation. Additionally, the materials used for these devices deteriorate in sun and rough pool surfaces, leading to deflation and leaks.

Safety at Public Pools, Designated Swimming Areas and Waterparks

Public Pools

The term "public pool" refers to any pool used for recreational swimming by any segment of the population. This includes wading pools, hot tubs, lap pools or any other type of swimming pool intended for public use. Pools that are part of recreational facilities, exercise and fitness facilities and private clubs or organizations are all public pools. Other examples include pools owned and operated by apartment buildings, mobile home communities, condominium or home associations and hotels or motels.

Some public pools may be supervised by lifeguards and others may not. In either case, children at these facilities still require the supervision of a designated person (**Fig. 2-9**). Parents, guardians and activity leaders should create rules and expectations before visiting any public pool. Anyone visiting a public pool should follow these safety tips:

- Read and obey all posted pool rules.
- Designate a person to supervise children at all times. Remember, if you bring children to a public pool, they are your responsibility.
- Know the depth of the water throughout the pool and enforce "no diving" rules in any water less than 9-feet deep.
- Check for the availability of and know how to use any safety equipment, such as a reaching pole, ring buoy and telephone. (Refer to **Chapter 3** for basic information on how to respond to an aquatic emergency.)
- Do not play with safety equipment.
- Take breaks from water activities. This gives swimmers and those supervising them an opportunity to rest.
- Do not swim in a pool that is overly crowded or with swimmers who are not following the rules.

Fig. 2-9

- Do not bring any glass or breakable objects onto the pool deck.
- Check the pool area for obvious hazards (slippery decks, debris on the pool bottom, malfunctioning equipment, drop-offs or cracks in the deck).
- Check to see that fences are in good repair and that gates are self-closing and self-latching. Do not prop gates open or leave furniture near the pool fence that would allow children to climb the fence.

- Check for a well-maintained area.
- Check the water conditions. The water should be clear and clean without debris. The drain or the bottom of the pool should be visible at the deepest point. If the drain or bottom is not visible, do not enter the water.

Designated Swimming Areas

Many natural bodies of water have designated areas for swimming (**Fig. 2-10**). Like public pools,

Fig. 2-10

lifeguards may or may not staff these areas. Many of the same safety precautions for public pools should be taken at designated swimming areas in natural bodies of water as well.

Even when a lifeguard is present, swimming at a designated swimming area that is part of a natural body of water requires more caution. In an ocean, river, lake or other natural body of water, swimmers may encounter potentially dangerous conditions that do not exist in a pool, such as currents, waves, submerged objects and inclement weather. It is important to recognize that in many of these swimming areas, conditions can change from hour to hour.

Before swimming in a new area, become familiar with its conditions and hazards. Check with lifeguards or park rangers to find out what to look for. Look for the following safety features before swimming in a designated area at any natural body of water (**Fig. 2-11**):

- Lifeguard on duty
- Clearly posted rules
- Clean water that is regularly tested
- Clean, well-maintained beaches and deck areas

- Nonslip surfaces on decks, boardwalks, shower facilities and other surrounding areas
- Free of electrical equipment or power lines
- Safety equipment
- Buoyed lines to separate shallow and deep water, if possible
- Firm bottom with gentle slope and no sudden drop-offs
- No submerged objects, such as logs and rocks
- Well-constructed rafts, piers and/or docks
- Free of dangerous currents and waves
- Free of dangerous aquatic life
- Signals for different wave conditions
- Surfboards, boats, personal watercraft and other types of equipment dangerous to swimmers are prohibited

Waves and currents are always a concern at ocean beaches and large lakes. Many guarded beaches use flags to signal weather and/or surf conditions (**Fig. 2-12**). Always heed these warnings and any other posted signs. A yellow flag means the swimmers should be cautious when swimming because of currents and/or other conditions. A red flag means that the area is too dangerous for swimming and is closed.

Fig. 2-11

Fig. 2-12

Waterparks

A waterpark is an aquatic amusement park. Waterparks have become increasingly common and are a favorite source of recreation for many families (**Fig. 2-13**). Modern waterparks offer a wide selection of special attractions including tube rides, wave pools and slow-moving and rapid rivers. Speed slides, mat rides, drops, swirling rides and children's play areas are other examples of common waterpark attractions. While most waterparks go to great lengths to maintain safety, accidents can still happen.

The potential for injury exists whenever the body is moving quickly. Fast slides and rides are common at waterparks. Excited kids often run between activities and up stairs. As a result, slips and falls on hard surfaces are common. Failing to maintain proper body position, which can be hard for some individuals, may lead to serious

Fig. 2-13

accidents on some rides. On other attractions, a collision with another rider is possible.

Follow these guidelines to stay safe at waterparks:

- As is true whenever children are in, on or around water, make sure a responsible individual maintains constant supervision.
- Young children or inexperienced swimmers should wear a U.S. Coast Guard-approved life jacket whenever they are in, on or around water. Some waterparks may prohibit the use of life jackets on some attractions.
- Dress appropriately. In some cases, this may mean wearing water shoes. Take efforts to make sure you and others stay protected from the sun.
- Stay with a buddy—never swim alone.
- Follow all posted rules. Speak with waterpark staff if you are unsure about any rules or procedures.
- Recognize that water depth and procedures change between attractions.
- Get into the correct position before starting down a water slide—face up and feet first. On speed slides, cross the legs to help prevent injuries.
- Do not let children hold onto or be held by others when using water slides.
- Do not go in the water if you have diarrhea and do not let anyone in your group who has diarrhea go in the water, especially children in diapers.
- Shower before entering a waterpark attraction and make sure young children are clean.
- Make sure young children have several opportunities to use the bathroom throughout the day.
- Change diapers away from the pool or any waterpark attraction.

Summer Camps

Water activities are a major attraction of many summer camps. Before enrolling a child, check to see that the camp has the necessary state permits. State regulations often address aquatic safety. Because codes vary from state to state, it is also appropriate to determine if the camp follows the aquatic safety standards of a national organization, such as the American Camping Association (ACA), the Boy Scouts of America or the YMCA of the USA. Also, check to see if the applicable standards are being followed. For example, look for an accreditation from the ACA. Observe the condition of the pool, waterfront or any other aquatic features and find out how they

are supervised. Trained and qualified staff should teach and supervise all aquatic activities, such as swimming, boating, waterskiing and scuba diving.

The aquatic activity areas should be well designed and maintained, free of obvious hazards and closely supervised by adequate numbers of alert, trained staff. All safety, boating and other aquatic equipment should be in good condition. The camp should have a system that ensures that supervisors can quickly account for all swimmers at all times, such as roll calls, buddy checks or buddy tags, and have prompt access to emergency medical personnel and facilities (**Fig. 2-14**). All campers should be classified by swimming ability and provided instructional and recreational activities consistent with their abilities. For example, nonswimmers are not permitted in deep water other than during special instructional situations. A system should be in place so that the staff can easily identify a camper's swimming ability, such as color-coded tags or swim caps. The camp should request information on any temporary or chronic medical conditions that require special precautions in or on the water.

Group Trips

The most important thing for staying safe on group outings on and around the water is to only swim in designated areas under the supervision of a lifeguard. Also, designate a responsible individual to supervise the swimmers at all times. If you are on a canoe trip or hiking in a remote area, help may be far away if an aquatic emergency occurs.

Group leaders should talk to the group to set expectations and specify what will be accepted as appropriate and inappropriate behavior before the trip begins. In some cases, it may be necessary to pretest swimming skills to find out a child's swimming ability. Trips involving open water, swift water, remote areas and activities, such as extended-day backcountry camping, whitewater canoeing, kayaking, rafting and open-water crossings, require special training and planning. Do not take a group, especially children, on one of these trips unless you are properly trained.

Safety at Pools and Spas
Home Pools
Whether it is an above-ground or in-ground pool, lap pool, hot tub or spa, owning a pool is

Fig. 2-14

a tremendous responsibility. Drownings at home pools and spas are a problem in every state, but in warm weather states, where pools are more common, the problem is serious. In Arizona, California and Florida, drowning is the leading cause of accidental death in and around the home for children under the age of 5. Nationwide, drowning is the second-leading cause of accidental death for this age group. The vast majority of these fatalities take place in home pools and spas.

These figures from a U.S. Consumer Product Safety Commission (CPSC) comprehensive study on pool accidents in Florida, Arizona and California show just how dangerous home pools and spas can be:

- 75 percent of children involved in home pool submersion or drowning accidents were between the ages of 1 to 3 years; 65 percent of these were boys.

- Most children involved in submersion or drowning accidents were being supervised by one or both parents at the time of the incident.
  - 46 percent of these children were last seen in the house.
  - 65 percent of these incidents took place in pools owned by the child's family.
  - 33 percent happened in pools owned by friends or relatives.
  - 75 percent had been missing or out of sight for 5 minutes or less.
  - 69 percent of these incidents took place when the children were not expected to be in the pool area.

These statistics suggest that a good number of pool drownings happen suddenly and without notice. By the time someone notices a child is missing, it may already be too late. The key to preventing home pool drownings is to have layers of protection. This includes placing barriers around your pool to prevent access, using pool alarms, making sure everyone in the home knows how to swim, closely supervising your child and being prepared in case of an emergency. The CPSC recommends the following guidelines for pool, hot tub and non-portable spa owners:

- Pool fence gates should be self-closing and self-latching and open outward, away from the pool. The latch should be out of a small child's reach (**Fig. 2-15**).

Fig. 2-15

- Pool barriers should be at least 4 feet high and enclose the entire pool area. They should not have any features that could be used as a hand- or foothold.

- Solid barriers should not have any features other than normal construction joinery.

- For most fence designs, spacing between vertical members should not exceed 1¾ inches. The opening on chain link fences should not exceed 1¼ inches.

- Horizontal fence support structures that are less than 45 inches apart should be on the pool side of the fence. On fences with horizontal support structures that are greater than 45 inches apart, the horizontal support structures can be on either side of the fence.

- Aboveground pools should have a barrier mounted on top of the pool structure that encloses the entire pool. Steps or ladders to the pool should be removable or enclosed by a locked barrier, so that the pool surface is inaccessible. A *power safety cover*–a motor powered barrier that can be placed over the water area– can also be used to secure the pool area.

- The space under a pool barrier should not exceed 4 inches.

- Any openings in the barrier should not allow a 4-inch sphere to pass through.

- It is preferable that the house should not form any side of the barrier. However, in situations where a house does form one side of the barrier, the doors leading from the house to the pool should be locked and protected with alarms that produce a sound when a door is unexpectedly opened. Alarms should continuously sound for 30 seconds and begin within 7 seconds after the door is opened.

- Keep rescue equipment by the pool and be sure a telephone or mobile phone is poolside and emergency numbers are posted (**Fig. 2-16**).

- If a child is missing, always look in the pool first. Seconds count in preventing death or disability.

- Pool alarms can be used as an added precaution. Underwater pool alarms generally perform better and can be used in conjunction with pool covers. CPSC advises that consumers use remote alarm receivers so that the alarm can be heard inside the house or in other places away from the pool.

- The pool area should be properly illuminated.

Fig. 2-16

Local building codes, regulations and statutes for pools and spas differ from state to state. Many states have pool fence laws. Pool and spa owners should check with the local authorities to find out specific building codes and owner responsibilities. The publication, *Safety Barrier Guidelines for Home Pools* (Pub. No. 362) is available at no charge from the CPSC Web site (*www.cpsc.gov*).

Pool and Spa Entrapment Hazards

Between 1990 and 2004, there were 130 confirmed cases of pool or spa drain entrapments. In a pool or spa drain entrapment or entanglement, a part of a person's body gets stuck to a pool drain, causing death or severe injury. This can happen when a person's hair is sucked into or entangled in a poorly designed drain. Sometimes children playing with an open drain put a hand or foot inside it and become trapped. This can also happen when unsuspecting swimmers sit on top of powerful drains with missing covers, which can lead to serious injury including disembowelment. Drain entrapments and entanglements typically result from inadequately designed drainage systems and/or the use of ineffective drain covers.

In 2007, the Virginia Graeme Baker Pool and Spa Safety Act was signed into law. The legislation provides incentives for states to adopt comprehensive pool safety laws that will protect swimmers from dangerous pool and spa drains. Every pool owner should make sure that their pool is free of drain entrapment or entanglement hazards by installing anti-entrapment drain covers and protection from dangerous drain suction, such as safety release systems. Pool and spa owners should check with the CPSC, Association of Pool and Spa Professionals, National Swimming Pool Foundation or the local authorities to find out more about safe pool drainage systems.

Additional Responsibilities

Pools owners should—

- Teach children not to go near the water without an adult; the pool area is off limits without adult supervision.

- Provide supervision for children at all times.

- Post the rules for the pool and enforce them without exception. For example, never allow anyone to swim alone, do not allow bottles or glass around the pool, do not allow running or pushing and do not allow diving unless the pool meets the safety standards.

- Post depth markers and "No Diving" signs, as appropriate. Use a buoyed line to show where the depth changes from shallow to deep. Limit nonswimmer activity to shallow water.

- Completely remove pool covers prior to pool use and completely secure them in place immediately after use.

- Never leave furniture or toys near the fence that would enable a child to climb over the fence.

- Keep toys that are not in use away from the pool and out of sight. Toys can attract young children into the pool.

- Have an emergency action plan to address potential emergencies.

- Learn Red Cross first aid and CPR. Insist that babysitters, grandparents and others who care for children know these lifesaving skills.

- Post first aid and CPR instructions near the pool.

- Keep the pool water clean and clear. Water should be chemically treated and tested regularly. If it is not possible to clearly see a 6-inch disk at the bottom of the deep end, close the pool. Contact a local pool store or health department for information and instruction.

- Store pool chemicals—chlorine, soda ash, muriatic acid, test kits—in childproof containers and out of children's reach. Clearly label the chemicals. Follow manufacturer's directions and safety instructions.

- Make sure the homeowner's insurance policy covers the pool.

At a minimum, pool owners should have the following equipment easily accessible:

- Reaching equipment, such as a reaching pole

- Throwing equipment, such as a ring buoy with a line attached

- Flotation devices, such as a rescue tube

- Extra life jackets

- First aid kit

- Telephone or mobile phone with emergency numbers posted near the phone

Risks of Diving

Injuries occurring from diving are quite common and can be very severe. Serious diving accidents may result in head injuries, paraplegia (paralysis from the waist down) or quadriplegia (total paralysis from the neck down).

Most diving injuries take place in water 5 feet deep or less. Many involve the use of alcohol or other drugs. Diving into open water that is shallow, diving from the deck into the shallow end of a pool, diving into aboveground pools and unsupervised diving from starting blocks cause most diving accidents. Only dive in areas that are safe for diving. At public pools, follow all posted diving rules and only dive in areas designated for diving. No swimmer can be completely safe in inadequately supervised or improperly maintained swimming areas—some areas simply are not safe for diving!

Diving Safety

Inground home pools come in many sizes and shapes. However, not all home pool designs are

MAKE A SAFETY POST

A safety post that holds reaching and throwing equipment, such as a ring buoy or a heaving jug and a reaching pole, is essential for any home pool or private pond used for boating or ice-skating.

Materials needed:

- 4" × 4" post, 6 feet long
- Screw-in hanging hook that is large enough to hold the throwing equipment
- Throwing equipment, such as a ring buoy or 1-gallon plastic jug with top
- 40 to 50 feet of lightweight rope
- Reaching equipment, such as a reaching pole 10 to 12 feet long
- Clips to secure the reaching equipment or two 6-ounce cans open on both ends and nails

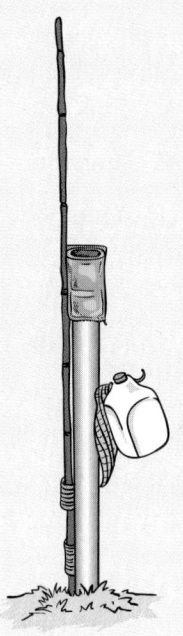

- Safety poster or first aid booklet (optional)
- First aid kit
- Emergency contact information
- Plastic zipper bag

Procedure

Screw in the hanging hook about 1 foot from the top of the post. Secure the clips or nail the two open-ended cans, one about 1 foot above the other, no lower than 2½ feet from the bottom of the post. Set the post 2 feet in the ground near the water where swimmers, boaters or skaters might get into trouble. Purchase a commercially made ring buoy with a line or make a heaving jug by putting a ½ inch of water or sand in a plastic jug and screwing the top on tightly. (If the jug has a snap-on top, secure it with very strong glue.) Tie the rope to the handle of the jug. Hang the ring buoy and line or jug and rope on the hanging screw. Secure the reaching pole with the clips or by putting the reaching pole through the open-ended cans. A safety poster, first aid kit, first aid booklet and emergency contact information can be put into the plastic zipper bag and attached to the top of the post, if desired.

---

safe or appropriate for diving. Pool depth, bottom shape and other features of certain home pool designs create hazards for diving. The same is true for many hotel, motel, apartment and other public pools. Pool owners must determine where and if swimmers are allowed to dive into their pools. No one should ever dive or allow anyone to dive into an unfamiliar pool without first determining if it is safe for diving.

The two common home pool designs are the hopper-bottom pool and the spoon-shaped pool. A hopper-bottom pool has a bottom that angles sharply up on all four sides from the deepest point (**Fig. 2-17, A and B**). Thus, the safe diving envelope (the area safe to dive into) is much smaller than it appears. Diving into a hopper-bottom pool may be like diving into a funnel. If the depth markers

give only the depth at the deepest point, a diver may think the area for safe diving is larger than it actually is.

The spoon-shaped pool also may present risks to safe diving because the distance from the end of the diving board or the side of the pool to the slope of the bottom is greatly reduced (**Fig. 2-18, A and B**). The bottom contour of the spoon-shaped pool may give a false sense of depth and bottom area throughout the deep end. Because of these design features, the average home pool is not long enough or deep enough for safe springboard diving. It is the diving board manufacturer's responsibility to determine the necessary water envelope for safe diving.

Because most head, neck and back injuries in home pools come from dives into shallow water,

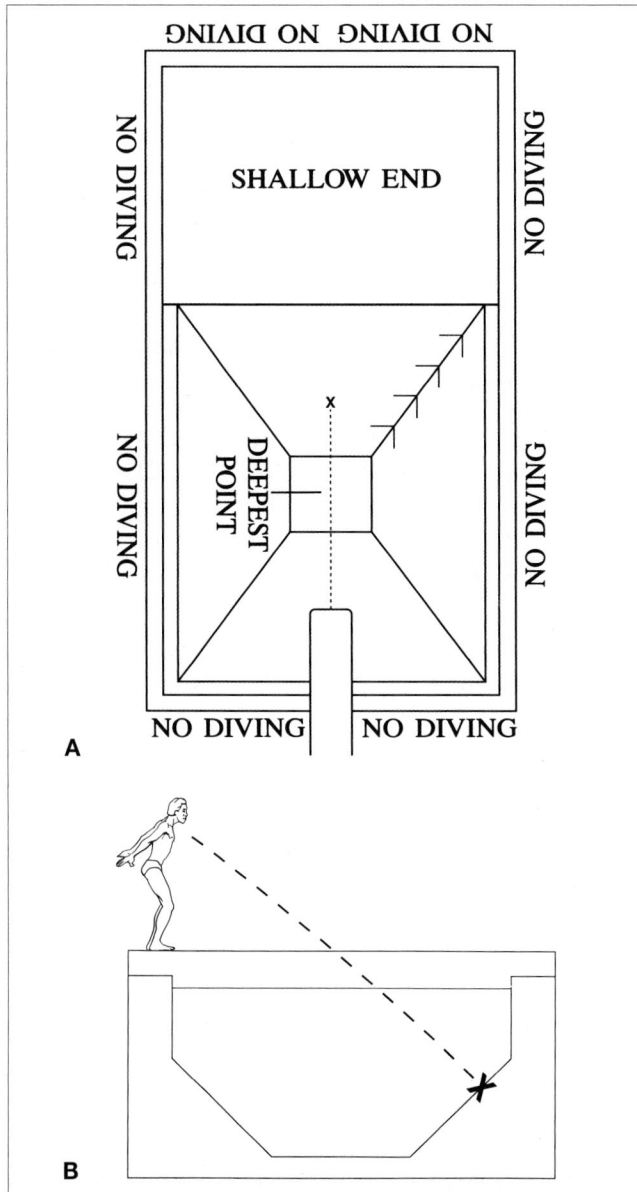

Fig. 2-17, A and B

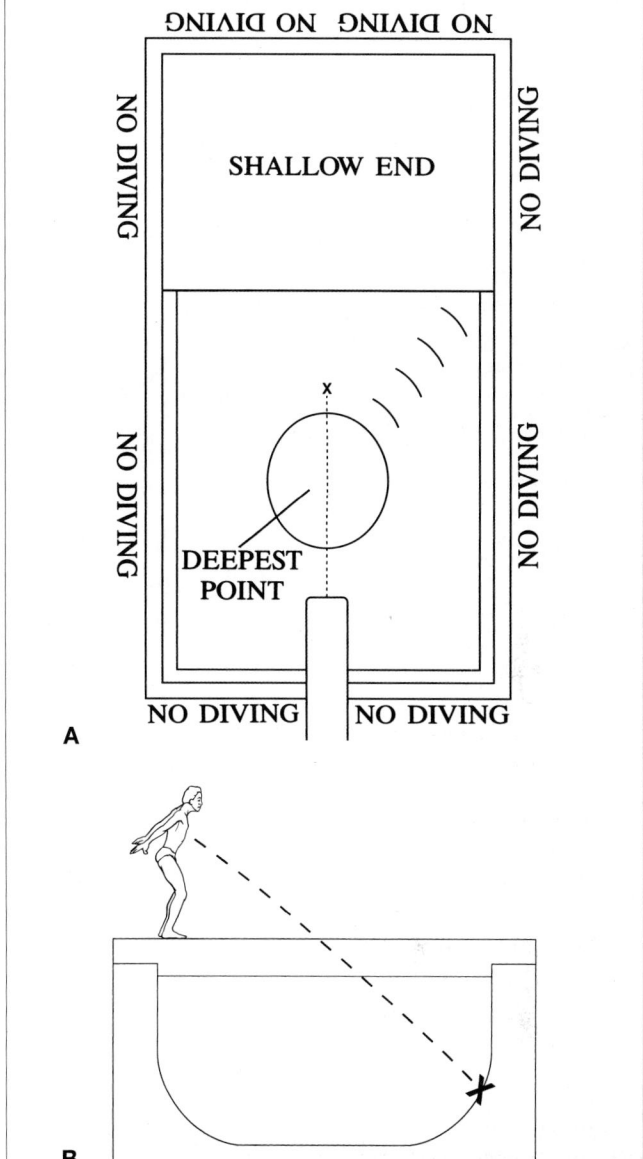

Fig. 2-18, A and B

the Red Cross recommends that pool owners take these precautions:

- Consult the Association of Pool and Spa Professionals (APSP), state law and local building codes for pool dimension guidelines to help establish rules for a pool to ensure safe diving activities. For example:
  - Prohibit all dives into shallow water.
  - Only allow shallow angle dives from the edge of the pool into deep water.

- Diving from a diving board should only occur if there is a safe diving envelope (the area of water in front of, below and to the sides of a diving board that is deep enough that a diver will not strike the bottom, regardless of the depth of the water or the design of the pool).

- Clearly mark the location of the breakpoint between shallow and deep water with a buoyed line, a contrasting stripe on the bottom 12 inches before the breakpoint and mark the deck with signs that indicate the depth.

- Place "No Diving" signs on the deck near shallow water and on the fence or wall around the swimming pool or on a stand at the entry to the swimming pool area (**Fig. 2-19**).
- Prohibit elevated entry from any object not specifically designed for diving such as chairs, fences or balconies.

Aboveground Pools

No one should ever dive into an aboveground pool. People have been seriously injured by diving from the deck, the rim or a structure above the edge into aboveground pools. Swimmers should use the ladder to enter or ease feetfirst into any aboveground pool.

Pool Parties

- Make sure that the parents or guardians of all invited guests are aware that the party is a pool party.

- If possible, have a lifeguard on duty. Contact the local parks and recreation department or local swimming pools to get names of Red Cross-trained lifeguards who are willing to lifeguard at private parties. It is the host's responsibility to provide all appropriate rescue equipment and check the certifications of all lifeguards hired. It is the lifeguard's responsibility to have current certification.

- If not hiring a lifeguard, identify or appoint water watchers. A water watcher is a responsible individual with a specific job to supervise the pool when it is in use. Each water watcher must understand and accept responsibility for monitoring the pool and should be trained in first aid, CPR and water safety.

Fig. 2-19

- Establish rules for safety, such as—
  - No diving into shallow water.
  - No running on the deck.
  - No glass in the pool area.
- If the swimming portion of the party goes on for more than 1 hour, set rest breaks. This allows guests the opportunity to rest and warm up and provides a break for the lifeguard or water watcher.
- Do not serve alcoholic beverages to guests who are or will be supervising or participating in water activities.

Check with the homeowner's insurance company to determine the limits of coverage. Additional coverage for the event may be required.

Spas and Hot Tubs

Spas and hot tubs in the home or at a facility are typically not guarded. Never spend time in a spa or hot tub alone. According to the APSP, the maximum safe water temperature for spas is 104° F (40° C). Soaking too long at too high a temperature can raise body temperature over safe limits.

Follow these spa and hot tub safety tips:

- Always shower or bathe before entering a spa.
- Spas should be chemically treated and tested regularly. High water temperature can foster bacteria and parasite growth. Check with the health department or a local pool or spa store for information.
- Time spent in a spa should be limited to 15 minutes or less.
- Do not exceed the maximum amount of allowable bathers.
- Never use a spa or hot tub when drinking alcohol.
- Do not let children of any age use a spa unsupervised.
- Do not allow anyone to sit or play near the drain.
- Children under 5 years of age should not use a spa. Young children are more prone to overheating because their bodies have not developed enough to handle extreme temperatures.
- Pregnant women or people taking medications or who have a chronic medical condition, such as high or low blood pressure, heart disease, epilepsy or diabetes, should not use a spa or hot tub without their health care provider's approval.

Following is a checklist of questions to ask before hiring a lifeguard to guard a private pool. Make sure to go over the list completely and ask for proof of certification prior to the date of hire.

- Do you have current American Red Cross Lifeguarding certification (or equivalent)?
- Do you have current CPR/AED certification? If so, through what training agency?
- Do you have a current first aid certification? If so, through what training agency?
- Do you have a current list of references?

- Do you have a current job history list?
- What do you charge per hour?
- Are there any specific pieces of safety equipment we need to provide for you (rescue tube, ring buoy, reaching pole, backboard with head immobilizer, first aid kit)?
- How do you enforce pool rules?
- Do you have a list of rules you require while lifeguarding?
- Are there any accommodations we need to make for you?

- Know the location of the emergency cut-off switch.
- When not in use, securely cover a hot tub to prevent anyone from falling in.
- Post the emergency telephone number for the emergency medical services (EMS) system by the telephone. Keep a telephone or mobile phone near the spa.

Safety Around the Home

Water safety is more than just trying to stay safe by the pool. Anywhere there is water there is a risk of drowning. Every year many children drown in bathtubs, buckets of water and other containers of water. Young children are curious and their interests and abilities change from day to day. Do not leave a young child unattended near any source of water, even for a moment. Parents and anyone with young children in the home should use physical barriers to prevent access to any water in the home. Shut the bathroom door, keep the toilet lid locked and empty bathtubs and any buckets of water. Do not rely on bathtub floating aids to protect your child, and never, ever leave a child in a bathtub alone–always stay within arm's reach.

Safety In, On and Around Natural Bodies of Water

Many people enjoy swimming in natural bodies of water, including lakes, rivers and oceans. Such environments can be safe when under the supervision of a lifeguard or designated as a swimming area by the proper authorities. However, if these elements are not in place, always assume that these areas are too dangerous for swimming.

While pools are a source of danger for younger children, a good number of drowning accidents involving older children take place in, on or around natural bodies of water. This is one of the main reasons why swimming in these environments should only take place in designated swim areas under the supervision of a lifeguard. Easy access to natural water environments combined with the growing independence of older children and adolescents can make these environments especially dangerous to children who are old enough to explore on their own (**Fig. 2-20**).

Fig. 2-20

Fig. 2-21

Other factors, such as social or cultural values regarding the importance of swimming skills and the lack of familiarity with swimming and aquatic activities, may also contribute to this problem.

Many older children involved in aquatic emergencies never intended to swim in the first place. Understanding the hazards and features associated with natural bodies of water is important even if swimming is not intended. One reason these accidents happen is because the children playing in, on or around these bodies of water do not know or fail to appreciate how dangerous they can be. Every parent and child should know the dangers associated with all types of bodies of water. Parents should make specific rules about how children should behave when they are near the bodies of water in their community—or even their own backyard (**Fig. 2-21**).

Weather Conditions

Weather conditions can make the natural water environment more dangerous. This is true at an ocean beach, in a boat, on the dock or just being near the shore. Always check the weather before heading out to an aquatic environment, even for a trip to the pool. Leave the water at the first sound of thunder or sight of lightning. If possible, get to an enclosed area during an electrical storm. Do not stay in an open area, under a tree or near anything metal. The National Lightning Safety Institute recommends waiting at least 30 minutes after the last sound of thunder is heard before resuming activity in the water (**Fig. 2-22**).

Even at a designated swim area, the water may be dangerous after a storm. Heavy rains and flooding can cause strong currents. The clarity and depth of the water may change, and new unseen obstacles may become hazards. Runoff also can contaminate a natural body of water with toxic substances after heavy rains and flooding.

Rivers, Streams and Creeks

The water in rivers, streams and creeks is constantly flowing downstream. Take great care around these currents, which are often unpredictable and fast moving. Currents can abruptly change in direction and intensity due to changes below the surface. The current may not be visible on the water surface even though it may be strong below the surface.

National Oceanic and Atmospheric Administration (NOAA)

Fig. 2-22

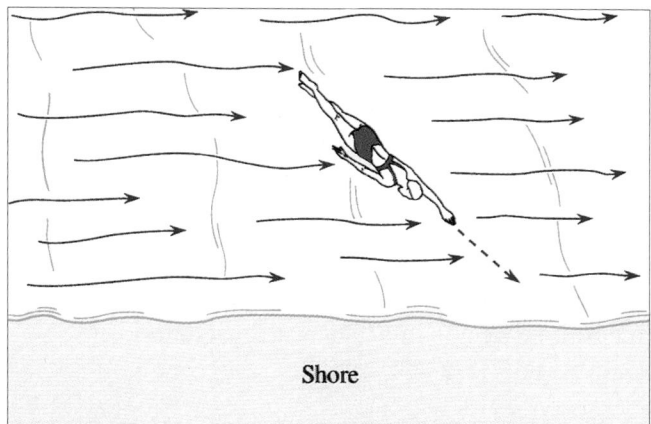

Fig. 2-23

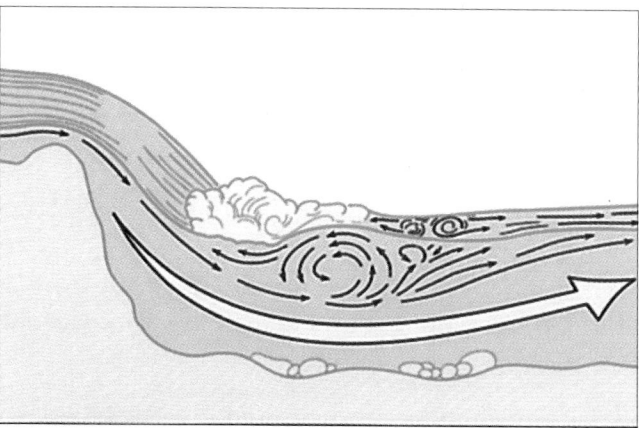

Fig. 2-24

Because the water is moving, anyone caught in a current may have a difficult time getting to shore or may be carried downstream. Moving water can exert tremendous forces on any object in its path. This force increases exponentially with the speed of the current. A current flowing at the rate of 2 miles per hour can exert pressure up to 33 pounds per square inch. A current at the rate of 8 miles per hour can exert a whopping 538 pounds per square inch! Do not allow yourself to get caught between the force of the water and an immovable object—you will become trapped.

Although tubing is quite popular and often thought of as safe, this activity can be very dangerous. All "whitewater" activities require expert instruction. Anyone accidentally caught in a current should roll onto his or her back and float downstream feetfirst, back paddle with the arms and try to steer away from the main current. Once out of the main current, the goal is to swim or wade directly toward shore. Because of the force of the current, this will result in a slightly downstream path (**Fig. 2-23**).

Strainers

A strainer is an obstacle in a current that acts like a kitchen colander. Strainers usually result from downed trees or shrubs resulting in a snarl of tree limbs and branches. As the current forces water through these obstacles, anything upstream will become entrapped.

Avoid strainers at all costs. Anyone approaching a strainer should try to swim toward the object headfirst, grab any part of the strainer at the surface of the water and try to kick and climb up and over the top.

Foot Entrapments

The bottom surface of many rivers, streams and creeks is covered with rocks and other submerged objects that can easily trap a person's feet. When combined with the powerful forces of moving water, anyone whose foot is caught can be pushed under water and pinned down, even in shallow water.

Never try to stand up in moving water. If caught in a current, try to float downstream feetfirst on your back and steer out of the main current.

Hydraulics and Dams

Hydraulics are vertical whirlpools that happen as water flows over an object, such as a low-head dam or waterfall, causing a strong downward force that may trap a swimmer (**Fig. 2-24**).

Whitewater rapids are often filled with dangerous hydraulics. A fixed-crest/low-head dam is a barrier built across a river, stream or creek to control the flow of water (**Fig. 2-25**). Some of the most harmless looking low-head dams are often

Fig. 2-25

the most dangerous. Low-head dams with a thin line of whitewater across the surface can contain powerful hydraulic forces. No matter how small the hydraulic appears, the reverse flow of the water can trap and hold a person under water.

It is difficult and sometimes impossible to escape from a hydraulic. Anyone caught in a hydraulic should resist fighting the current and try to swim to the bottom and get into the downstream current and then reach the surface.

Dams are common on rivers and in large lakes or ponds. When the floodgates open, the water level can rise quickly below the dam, making a wall of water. If the dam is part of a hydroelectric power plant, the current made when the gates are open can pull anyone or anything above the dam into danger, including boats. The area downstream of dams also is dangerous. Recirculating water currents caused by the movement of water over or through the dam can draw objects back toward the dam.

No dam is ever safe. When you are in, on or around the water, stay away from dams. The chances of surviving an aquatic emergency involving a dam are slim.

Oceans

Ocean waves and currents are always a safety concern. Even at guarded beaches, wave activity can be dangerous. Do not swim at unguarded ocean beaches or in areas not designated for swimming (**Fig. 2-26**).

Even in designated swimming areas, waves at ocean beaches can become quite large. The stronger the wind, the amount of time it blows and the longer distance it travels across the water's surface, the bigger the wave. In the open ocean during strong winds that travel in the same direction for long distances, waves can reach heights of well over 20 feet.

Breaking waves are tremendously powerful and capable of moving large objects and can knock

Photo courtesy of Shutterstock Images LLC

Fig. 2-26

anyone down. Differences in bottom conditions and wave height create changes in how waves break. In some situations, the weight of the wave and power of the crashing water can hold a person under water–1 cubic foot of water weighs 62 pounds! Breaking waves near rocky shores are especially dangerous. Slippery conditions nearby can make it easy to fall into the water. Anyone caught in breaking waves near a rocky shore can suffer severe injuries or even die.

The action of breaking waves against the beach or coastline creates currents. A current that runs parallel to the shore is called a longshore current. Longshore currents can transport beach sediment, debris or swimmers rapidly away from the original point of entry. Anyone caught in a longshore current should try to swim toward shore while moving along with the current.

Another result of wave action is rip currents. Rip currents, sometimes referred to as rip tides, move water away from the shore or beach and out to sea beyond the breaking waves. A narrow strip of choppy, turbulent water that moves differently from the water on either side of it is a common rip current indicator. Rip currents often occur if a sandbar has formed off shore. A band of water a few feet wide may rush back from the beach through a gap in the sandbar made by breaking waves. Rip currents typically break apart just past the line of breaking waves and are usually no more than 80 feet wide.

One of the dangers of rip currents is that they are very fast. Often times faster than a human can swim. Under gentle surf conditions, there may be more frequent, less intense rip currents. In periods of high-wave activity however, rip currents tend to form fewer but stronger currents. The United States Lifesaving Association estimates that each year more than 100 people die due to rip currents on our nation's beaches. Rip currents account for more than 80 percent of rescues performed by surf beach lifeguards.

Because rip currents can be very strong and carry a person away from shore, anyone near a beach needs to be careful. Even though most rip currents break apart near the shore, they can still take a person into deep water or a frightening distance from the shore. In rare cases, rip currents can sometimes push a person hundreds of feet beyond

the surf zone. Rip currents can be a challenge to even the strongest and most experienced swimmers. If caught in a rip current, swim parallel to the shore until free of the current. Once free, turn and swim toward shore (**Fig. 2-27**). A swimmer also can just let the rip current take them out to sea, then swim back after the current breaks apart. If you are too exhausted to swim to shore, signal a lifeguard by calling and waving for help. No matter what the case, the most important thing to remember if ever caught in a rip current is not to panic.

Tides

Tidal currents are a cycle of ocean water movements that first surge toward shore, called

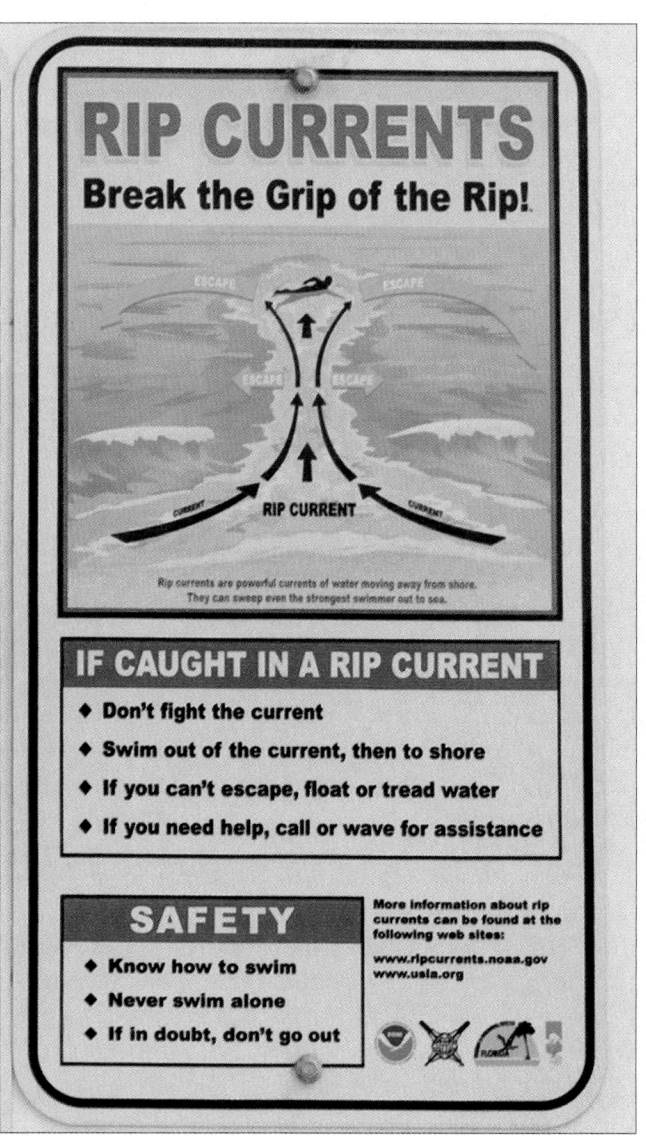

Fig. 2-27

flood tides, then away from shore, called ebb tides. The period in between tides when water is neither moving toward nor away from shore is called slack water. Tides are caused by the gravitational forces of the sun, the moon and the Earth's rotation. The movement of the moon however, has the strongest influence on tidal currents.

Tidal currents are strongest during a new or full moon, called spring tides. When the moon is in its first or third phases, tidal currents are weak, called neap tides. Tidal currents near inlets, estuaries and bays can be very strong and should be avoided.

Lakes and Ponds

Lakes and ponds are common features of many communities. In many cases, lake and pond water is murky, which makes it difficult to see below the surface. In such murky conditions, it may be hard to notice a distressed or submerged swimmer. It also may be difficult to determine the depth of the water or safety of the bottom surface, making these areas unsafe for diving. The bottom of lakes and ponds often contain hidden hazards, such as rocks, plants or weeds, sunken logs or broken glass that can cause serious injury and/or entrapment. Conditions in these bodies of water change constantly.

Aquatic Life

There is aquatic life in almost all natural bodies of water. Weeds, grass and kelp often grow thickly in open water and can entangle a swimmer. If you find yourself caught up in any aquatic plant life, avoid quick movements, which may only entangle you more. Anyone in this situation should try to stay horizontal at the surface and swim slowly and gently out of the plants, preferably along with a current. Always stay clear of any patch of plants near the surface.

Aquatic animals seldom pose a danger to swimmers. In the ocean, however, Portuguese man-of-war, jellyfish or other types of marine life can pose a threat to swimmers (**Fig. 2-28**). A sting can be very painful and may cause illness or even death if the affected area is large. Swimmers may not see the tentacles of stinging jellyfish below the surface, and they may extend far from what is seen on the surface. A sting can even be caused by

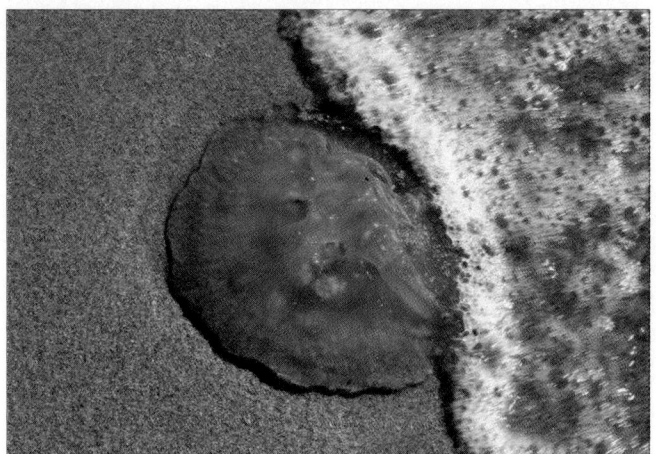

Fig. 2-28

stepping on a dead jellyfish or Portuguese man-of-war while walking on the beach. The stinging cells remain active hours after death.

First aid care for stings from these animals is simple. First, rinse the skin with seawater—not fresh water. Do not use ice, and do not rub the skin. Soothe the skin by soaking it in vinegar or isopropyl alcohol. If these materials are not available, use a baking soda paste. Call for emergency medical help if the victim—

- Does not know what caused the sting.
- Has ever had an allergic reaction to a sting from marine life or insects.
- Is stung on the face or neck.
- Develops any problem that seems serious, such as trouble breathing.

In some ocean areas, there are sea urchins with spines that can break off in the foot and cause a painful wound. Another danger comes from stinging coral. Stingrays and other marine animals also have stings that may be dangerous. Before going into any ocean, find out what local marine life may be dangerous, how to avoid it and how to care for any injuries. Warning signs of hazardous marine life may be posted at supervised beaches. When entering the ocean, shuffle the feet to stir up marine life resting on the bottom to avoid stepping on anything that could cause harm.

The chance of a shark attack is relatively small. Because the consequences are severe, the risk should always be minimized whenever possible. The chances of interacting with a shark can be reduced by following this advice:

- Always stay in groups. Sharks are more likely to attack a solitary individual than a group.

- Avoid being in the water at night, dawn or dusk, when sharks are most active and not easily seen.

- Do not enter the water if bleeding from an open wound or if menstruating–sharks are attracted to blood and their sense of smell is acute.

- Do not wear shiny jewelry, because the reflected light resembles fish scales.

- Do not enter the water in areas where there are signs of baitfish, especially those used by sport or commercial fishermen. Feeding areas or areas where sewage, runoff or rivers flow into the sea are also dangerous. Diving sea birds are good indicators of these areas.

- Use extra caution when waters are murky and avoid brightly colored clothing–sharks see contrast particularly well.

- Refrain from excess splashing and do not allow pets in the water because of their erratic movements.

- Exercise caution when occupying the area between sandbars or near steep drop-offs–these are favorite hangouts for sharks.

- Do not enter the water if sharks are known to be present and evacuate the water swiftly but calmly if sharks are seen while there.

- Do not harass a shark.

Alligators, snapping turtles, snakes and leeches inhabit certain freshwater areas. Alligators are very dangerous, especially to small children, and can be found in freshwater in some southern states, such as Florida, Louisiana, Georgia and Texas. Avoid snapping turtles; their bites can cause severe injury. Do not go into water known to be inhabited by alligators or snapping turtles and stay away from the shore. Snakes rarely pose a threat. Leave them alone and swim away slowly. Swimmers usually will not see a leech but may come out of the water and find one on their skin. They can be pulled off slowly and are not harmful.

Safety Around Cold Water and Ice
Exposure to Cold Water

Cold water is always a danger. Falling off a pier, breaking through ice on a lake or being thrown into the water as a boat swerves are accidents that can suddenly put a person in cold water (**Fig. 2-29**). Exposure to cold water leads to the danger of hypothermia. Hypothermia is a life-threatening condition in which cold or cool temperatures cause the body to lose heat faster than it can produce it.

Here is what happens when a person falls into cold water:

- The temperature of the skin and of the blood in the arms and legs drops quickly.

- At first, the victim may have trouble breathing and then may slowly become unable to use the arms and legs.

- The temperature of the heart, brain and other vital organs gradually drops.

- Shivering begins.

- The victim may become unable to think clearly.

- The victim may become unconscious. If the temperature drops more, death from heart failure is possible, but drowning may occur first.

Preventing Hypothermia

Protect against hypothermia in the following ways:

- Whenever near cold water–whether playing, working, hunting or fishing–remember that cold water is dangerous, even if you do not intend to go in.

- Only engage in aquatic activities when and where it is possible to get help quickly in an emergency.

Fig. 2-29

- Always wear a U.S. Coast Guard-approved life jacket while boating in cold water.

- In cooler weather, wear rain gear, a warm hat and layers of clothes or insulated clothes. Avoid cotton and wear fabrics containing wool or synthetic blends instead. Winter clothes can help you float and stay warm if you fall into the water.

- Wear a wet suit for skin diving, surfing and kayaking or other activities that take place in the open water or involve repeated submersion.

- If you are in a remote area, carry matches in a waterproof container. It may be necessary to build a fire to warm up after a fall into cold water.

- Do not drink alcohol for the sensation of warmth. Alcohol increases loss of body heat.

Ice Safety

Outdoor ice sports and activities can be safe and enjoyable, but there is no such thing as 100 percent safe ice (**Fig. 2-30**). Anyone who spends time near the ice should first determine the ice conditions, and then take precautions to stay safe.

Ice that forms over open water when the following conditions are present may be unsafe:

Fig. 2-30

- Springs or fast-moving water

- Wind and wave action

- Waterfowl and schooling fish

- Decomposing material in the water

- Water bubblers (devices designed to keep the water near boat docks from freezing thick)

- Discharge from an industrial site or power production facility

- Objects protruding through the ice, such as tree stumps

Preventing Ice Accidents

Follow these guidelines to avoid accidents when on or near ice:

- Check the ice thickness before going out. To be safe, ice should be solid and at least 4 inches thick. Remember, the ice may not be the same thickness over the entire area of a lake or pond.

- Only walk on solid, 4-inch-thick ice. It is generally safe, but it is not thick enough for snowmobiles, all-terrain vehicles or other vehicles. Test ice thickness by using a chisel, cordless drill or ice auger.

- Wear a life jacket under your outer layer but NOT if you will be traveling inside a vehicle, such as a car or truck. It may be difficult to exit the car if it falls through the ice and a life jacket worn under the clothes cannot be easily removed in an emergency.

- Be safe—the more people on the ice, the thicker it should be.

- Use ice on smaller, shallower and slower-moving bodies of water for ice activities, it is usually more solid.

- Look for objects sticking up through the ice and mark them as hazards.

- Do not go out on ice that has recently frozen, thawed and then frozen again. This happens in the spring and early winter as temperatures change often. Wait until the outside temperature has been below freezing long enough that at least 4 inches of solid ice forms over the entire area.

- Always stay with at least one other person. (Remember, more people require thicker ice for safety.)

- Let someone on shore know where you are and when you will return.

- Wear warm clothes.

- Have something at hand to throw or extend to a person who needs help—a life jacket, a rope with a weighted end, a long tree branch, a wooden pole or a plastic jug with a line attached.

Ice "Claws"

Whenever someone falls through the ice, it usually comes as a surprise. The shock of the cold causes many to panic. Adding to this problem is the fact that the ability to move the arms and legs reduces almost immediately after falling into icy water. As a result, any effort to get out of the water becomes even more difficult. Ice rescue picks or ice "claws" can be an invaluable piece of equipment in this situation. These handles with sharp metal spikes can help a person climb back onto the ice after falling in. Ice rescue picks can be purchased at many outdoor recreation stores. Keep them readily available whenever on the ice.

Safety for Boating and Other Water Activities

Boating Safety

Boating is a very popular pastime. According to U.S. Coast Guard statistics, in 2007, there were nearly 13 million registered boats in the United States and more than 77 million Americans are involved in recreational boating each year. Recreational boating includes, but is not limited to, the following types of vessels:

- Open motorboats
- Personal watercraft
- Cabin motorboats
- Sailboats
- Canoes/kayaks

Boating can be a safe and enjoyable pastime, but it is important to know the dangers. Each year hundreds of people die and thousands more are injured in boating accidents. Do not become one of these statistics—follow the basic rules of boating safety:

1. Always wear a life jacket. Most boating fatalities occur from drowning. In 90 percent of all drownings associated with a boating accident, the victim was not wearing a life jacket. Collisions with another vessel or an object are the most common types of boating accidents. Boating collisions happen unexpectedly, with very little warning. A person involved in a boating accident could suffer a head injury or be thrown into cold or dangerous water. A life jacket can help a person stay alive until help arrives. Always wearing a life jacket is the only way to stay safe in a boat, no matter how big or small the vessel (**Fig. 2-31**). Put it on at the dock and do not take it off until safe ashore.

Fig. 2-31

2. Take a boating safety course. Training in boating safety is not just for those with large boats. More than 65 percent of all boating accidents involve smaller open motorboats and personal watercraft. As personal watercraft become more and more popular, the accidents involving them are becoming more frequent. Many states have minimum age and training requirements for these powerful watercraft. Additionally, accidents involving canoes and kayaks are on the rise. Most boating accidents are caused by operator error. To stay safe, boaters need to be trained in the fundamentals of boating safety including how to handle their vessel under different conditions. There is a different set of "rules of the road" for the water. Boaters need to know and understand which vessel needs to "give-way" or "stand-on" when approaching. This is especially important when large boats with limited steerage and high speeds are involved. Because of the great distances required to maneuver, large boats may not be able to avoid a collision with a smaller vessel. Additionally, all the navigable waters are marked by different sets of lights, buoys and signs that boaters need to understand in order to find the safest route. Boating safety courses are offered through some local Red Cross chapters, U.S. Coast Guard Auxiliary, United States Power Squadrons and local state boating authorities. Check with the American Canoe Association or U.S. Sailing for information on safe boat handling for canoes, kayaks and sailboats, respectively.

3. Do not drink alcohol. According to the U.S. Coast Guard's 2007 Boating Statistics, alcohol was the leading contributing factor in fatal boating accidents. Alcohol was involved in nearly 21 percent of all boating fatalities. Alcohol affects balance and judgment, makes it harder to swim and stay warm, slows reflexes and impairs vision. Boating and alcohol never mix.

4. Make a float plan and have a way to communicate. Before leaving the shore, leave the details of your boating trip with a responsible person on land who will take action if you fail to return or check in on time. It is also important to have a reliable way to communicate with the shore and other boats in case of an emergency. At the very least, carry a mobile phone. However, a mobile phone can only place calls to shore. In many boating emergencies, a nearby boat may be able to provide assistance and can respond quickly. In many situations, it also may be helpful to contact bridge operators or harbor officials who may not be easily reached by phone. A marine VHF radio is a two-way communication device that allows boaters to contact other boaters. All marine rescue personnel and commercial ships use marine VHF radios. Many of these devices can provide rescue personnel with an exact location. In many locations, the U.S. Coast Guard monitors VHF channel 16 at all times–24 hours a day, everyday. If possible, all boat owners should install and use marine VHF radios.

5. Pay attention to weather forecasts and understand local water conditions and hazards. In many open-water environments, the weather and water conditions can change rapidly. Changing tides can cause dramatic changes in water depth. Sand bars, currents, aquatic life and bottom conditions are constantly changing and creating new hazards. Local knowledge is often necessary to avoid these hazards. Certain areas may become crowded with commercial traffic. In some aquatic environments, it may be necessary to pass under a drawbridge or go through a lock. Check with the U.S. Coast Guard, U.S. Army Corps of Engineers, marina staff and local authorities to identify the hazards and conditions in your area. Always make sure you "know before you go." Bad weather is always dangerous, but it can be deadly for boats far away from shore. Large waves, high winds and changing currents can all make travel difficult and can possibly lead to capsizing. Always check the weather before leaving and keep an eye on the weather throughout the day. Boats equipped with a marine VHF radio

Fig. 2-32

can monitor local weather forecasts. Changes in cloud cover or sky color, a sudden drop in temperature, abrupt change in wind speed or direction or a falling barometer are all signs of incoming weather changes.

If you are caught in severe weather–

- Slow down and maintain enough speed to steadily move forward and still stay in control.

- Make sure everyone on board is adequately dressed and wearing a properly fitted life jacket.

- Turn on the boat's navigation lights.

- Head into waves at a 45-degree angle. Personal watercraft should approach waves at a 90-degree angle.

- Have passengers sit low in the boat or on the floor of the boat near the centerline.

- Anchor the boat, if necessary and it is safe to do so.

To prevent yourself or passengers from falling overboard–

- Do not lean out. Keep centered in the boat with your center of gravity low in the boat. Always keep your shoulders between the gunwales on small boats.

- Do not move about the boat. If you must move, maintain three points of contact (**Fig. 2-32**).

- Sit only where appropriate. Do not sit on the gunwales, bow, seatbacks or any other area not designed for seating.

- Do not stand up in small boats.

Personal Watercraft
- Riders should wear U.S. Coast Guard-approved life jackets.

- A personal watercraft, such as a jet ski, is a type of boat. Know the local laws and regulations. Some states have special laws governing the use of personal watercraft that address operation, life jacket use, registration and licensing requirements; education; environmental restrictions; required safety equipment; and minimum ages.

- Operate personal watercraft with courtesy and common sense. Pay attention to surroundings and follow the traffic pattern of the waterway. Obey no-wake and speed zones.

- Use extreme caution around swimmers, surfers and other boaters. Run personal watercraft at a slow speed until the craft is away from shore, swimming areas and docks. Avoid passing close to other boats and jumping wakes. This behavior is dangerous and often illegal.

- Ride with a buddy. Always ride in groups of two or three. You never know when an emergency might occur.

- Riders should always attach the engine cut-off lanyard to themselves and the personal watercraft during operation.

- Develop a float plan before leaving the shore.

Tubing and Rafting
- Always wear a U.S. Coast Guard-approved life jacket.

- Do not drink alcohol while tubing or rafting.

- Do not overload the raft.

- Do not go rafting after a heavy rain or if flash flood warnings are posted.

- When rafting with a tour company, make sure the guides are qualified. Check with the local

Fig. 2-33

chamber of commerce for listings of accredited tour guides and companies (**Fig. 2-33**).

- Develop a float plan.

- Check the conditions beforehand and make sure that you have the training and experience for those conditions.

Fishing and Hunting

In most fishing- and hunting-related accidents, the victim never intended to get in the water. When fishing or hunting near water or from a boat–

- Always wear a U.S. Coast Guard-approved life jacket.

- Dress properly for the weather and have some type of reaching device nearby.

- Watch footing when walking next to water.

- Guard against losing balance when in a boat by keeping a wide base of support and low center of gravity and using hands to balance.

- Do not drink alcohol. Alcohol is a cause of many hunting and fishing mishaps.

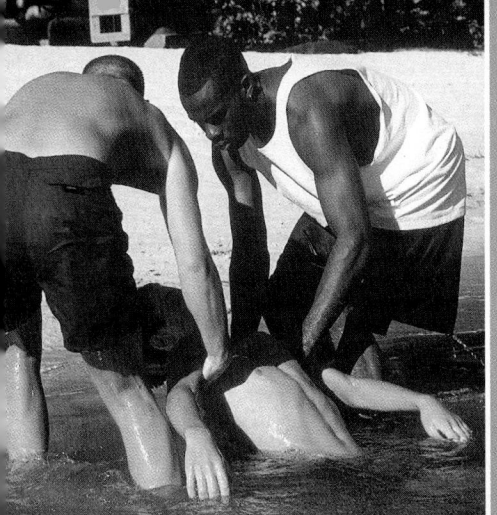

CHAPTER 3
Water Safety—Recognition and Response

Anyone who participates in aquatic activities should know how to recognize and respond to an aquatic emergency. Learning basic skills for self-rescue and for helping someone who is in trouble in the water is important for everybody, because most people live, work or play near water. In fact, knowing how to respond to an aquatic emergency is just as important as knowing how to prevent one.

By focusing on the steps necessary for recognizing and responding to an aquatic emergency as well as tips and procedures for self-rescue, this chapter outlines the information necessary to handle most aquatic emergencies.

Emergency Action Steps

In the excitement of an emergency, it is easy to become frightened or confused about what to do. Remember to stay calm—you can help. In any emergency situation, follow the three action steps.

CHECK–CALL–CARE

1. Check Check the scene and the victim.
- Check the scene for unsafe conditions that would prevent you from helping.

2. Call Call 9-1-1 or the local emergency number.

3. Care Care for the victim.
- Care for the conditions found.
- Make the victim comfortable until emergency medical services (EMS) personnel arrive and take over.

Recognizing an Emergency

An emergency can happen to anyone in or around the water, regardless of swimming ability. For example, a strong swimmer can get into trouble in the water because of sudden illness or injury. A nonswimmer playing in shallow water can be knocked down by a wave or pulled into deeper water by a rip current. The key to recognizing an emergency is staying alert and knowing the signals that indicate an emergency is happening.

Use all your senses when observing others in and around the water. A swimmer may be acting oddly or a scream or sudden splash may be heard. Sometimes an unusual odor, such as a strong chlorine odor, could indicate a problem. Whenever around an aquatic environment, stay alert for anything that seems unusual.

Being able to recognize a person who is having trouble in the water may help save that person's life. Most people who are in trouble in the water cannot or do not call for help. They spend their energy just trying to keep their heads above water to get a breath. A person who is experiencing a medical or other type of emergency might slip underwater quickly and never resurface.

There are two types of drowning victims. An active drowning victim is in a vertical position but unable to move forward or tread water. Normally, an active drowning victim will try to press down with the arms at the side in an instinctive attempt to keep the head above the water (**Fig. 3-1**). All energy is going into the struggle to breathe, and the person cannot call for help. A passive drowning victim is not moving and will be floating face-down on the bottom or near the surface of the water (**Fig. 3-2**).

A swimmer in distress may be too tired to get to shore, the side of the pool or a boat, but is still afloat and able to breathe. A distressed swimmer may be calling for help and/or floating, treading water or clinging to a line for support. Someone who is trying to swim but making little or no forward progress may be in distress (**Fig. 3-3**). If not helped, a swimmer in distress may soon become a drowning victim.

Table 3-1 compares the behaviors of distressed swimmers and drowning victims with those of swimmers.

Deciding to Act

Once you recognize an emergency, the next step is to decide to act and how to act. This is not always as simple as it sounds. Often people are slow to act in an emergency because they are not sure exactly what to do or they think someone else will act. If you are in an emergency situation, your decision to act may save someone's life.

Once you have decided to act, proceed safely. Make sure the scene is safe—do not go rushing into a dangerous situation and become a victim yourself. If the victim is in the water, first decide whether he or she needs help getting out of the water then act based on your training. Never enter the water to help a victim unless you are trained to do so. The first goal is for the responder to stay safe. If it can be done safely, the next step is to help get the victim out of the water.

If the victim is out of the water, quickly try to determine what help the victim needs and check for any dangers to yourself or others helping. Look for any other victims. Look for bystanders who can help give first aid or call for help. If the victim is in the water, remember that the first goal is for the responder to stay safe. If it can be done safely, the next step is to help get the victim out of the water.

Fig. 3-1

Fig. 3-2

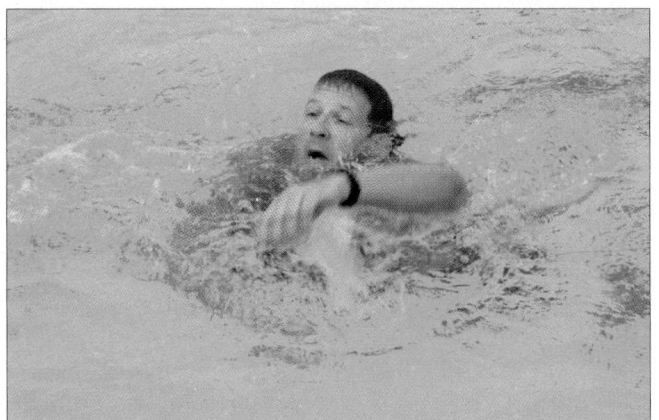

Fig. 3-3

Calling for Help

If the victim is unconscious, send someone else to call EMS personnel and care for the victim. If the victim is conscious, first try to safely get the victim out of the water and then determine the help and care needed.

If the victim is not in the water and there is an emergency, call EMS personnel immediately. If in doubt about whether the victim needs professional help, do not hesitate—call EMS

TABLE 3-1.	Comparing Behaviors of Distressed Swimmers and Drowning Victims with Swimmers			
Behaviors	**Swimmer**	**Distressed Swimmer**	**Active Drowning Victim**	**Passive Drowning Victim**
Breathing	Rhythmic breathing	Can continue breathing and may call for help	Struggles to breathe; cannot call out for help	Not breathing
Arm and Leg Action	Relatively coordinated	Floating, sculling or treading water; may wave for help	Arms to sides alternately moving up and pressing down; no supporting kick	None
Body Position	Horizontal	Horizontal or diagonal, depending on means of support	Vertical	Horizontal or vertical; face-down, face-up or submerged
Locomotion	Recognizable	Little or no forward progress; less and less able to support self	None; has only 20–60 seconds before submerging	None

Fig. 3-4

personnel (**Fig. 3-4**). If there are other bystanders, ask someone else at the scene to call. If possible, send two people to make the call. Tell the callers to report back what the dispatcher said. The following conditions and situations are serious and require a call to EMS personnel:

- Any drowning or nonfatal submersion (near-drowning) situation
- Injury to the head, neck or back
- Trouble breathing
- Persistent chest or abdominal pain or pressure
- Unconsciousness
- Severe bleeding, vomiting blood or passing blood
- Seizure, severe headache or slurred speech
- Poisoning
- Possible broken bones
- Multiple injuries

Anyone calling EMS personnel should stay on the phone after giving all the information to

the dispatcher, in case there are any questions. Make sure that the dispatcher has all the correct information to get the right type of help to the scene quickly. Anyone calling for help should be prepared to tell the dispatcher the following:

- The location of the emergency (exact address, city or town, nearby intersections or landmarks, name of the facility)
- The telephone number of the phone being used
- The caller's name
- What happened
- The number of victims
- The type of help being given so far

Do not hang up first when calling for help. In many cases, the dispatcher may need more information or may be able to help by giving first aid directions.

The Emergency Medical Services System

The EMS system is a network of professionals linked together to provide the best care for victims in all emergencies, both in and out of the water. The system begins when someone sees an emergency and decides to take action by calling 9-1-1 or the local emergency number. This action allows the EMS dispatcher to take down information about the emergency and provide it to the trained professionals who will respond to the scene. These professionals may include police or fire personnel, special rescue squads or an ambulance with emergency medical technicians (EMTs) (**Fig. 3-5**).

Once on the scene, these professionals will take over the care of the victim, including transportation to a hospital or other facility for the best medical care. Your role in this system is to recognize the emergency, decide to act, call EMS personnel for help and give assistance consistent with your knowledge until EMS personnel arrive and take over.

Emergency Action Plan

Emergency action plans are detailed plans that describe how everyone should act in an emergency. An emergency action plan should be established for any body of water around or near the home, such as a pool, pond or canal.

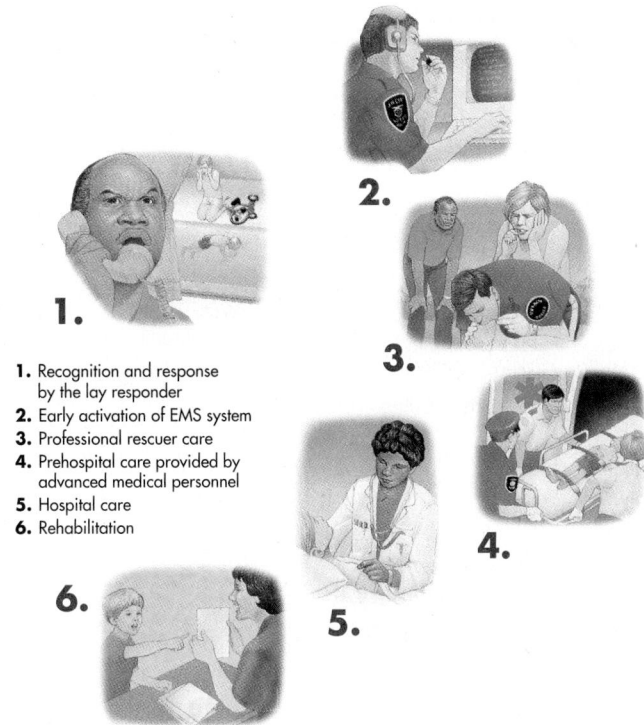

1. Recognition and response by the lay responder
2. Early activation of EMS system
3. Professional rescuer care
4. Prehospital care provided by advanced medical personnel
5. Hospital care
6. Rehabilitation

Fig. 3-5

Only swim in supervised areas where emergency action plans have been established. If there is an emergency, follow the lifeguard's instructions.

To create an emergency action plan—

- Identify types of emergencies that could occur, such as someone falling into the pool or other body of water.
- Identify rescue equipment available, such as a nearby telephone, ring buoy with a line attached and reaching pole.
- Create an emergency contact list that includes telephone numbers for EMS personnel and names of the nearest cross streets to the home.

The basic elements of an emergency action plan include the following:

- An emergency signal. Blow a whistle or horn or wave a flag to alert swimmers that they should leave the water immediately. At a home pool or other body of water near the home, the signal will tell family members and neighbors that there is an emergency and help is needed quickly.
- Safety equipment. For the home pool or other body of water near the home, safety equipment includes a telephone and rescue equipment. Keep all safety equipment near the water. Make a safety

post for the emergency equipment and set it close to the water. The safety post should have a throwing or other device, such as a reaching pole for assists, along with a well-stocked first aid kit. (Refer to **Chapter 2** for more information on making a safety post.)

- Emergency procedures. Develop and post procedures for what to do in a water emergency. Emergency procedures must be carefully planned and should outline:
  ○ Steps a responder should take to remove the victim from danger, without putting the responder in danger.
  ○ Who is responsible for calling 9-1-1 or the local emergency number and how and where the call is made. Remember to take the use of mobile phones into account.
  ○ How EMS personnel are directed to the specific scene of the emergency. For example, appoint someone to meet EMS personnel at the street.
  ○ Who should be contacted, such as the victim's immediate family members and health care provider.

Anyone with a home pool or who lives near any body of water should teach family and guests the procedures in the emergency action plan. Neighbors should also know those procedures to provide assistance, if necessary.

Responding in an Emergency

The most important thing you can do in an aquatic emergency situation is to keep yourself safe. In most cases, only trained professionals should enter the water to perform a rescue, such as a rescue in deep water or when the victim is far from shore.

Self-Rescue
Muscle Cramps

Muscle cramps can occur when muscles become tired or cold from swimming or other activity. A cramp is an involuntary muscle contraction, usually in the arm, foot or calf. A person with a muscle cramp in shallow water should—

- Try to relax the muscle by stopping the activity and begin floating or changing the swimming stroke.

LEARN FIRST AID, CPR AND AED

More than 300,000 Americans die every year from sudden cardiac arrest that occurs outside a hospital or emergency room. People who suffer heart attacks or other emergencies have a better chance of surviving when those around them know how to respond in an emergency. Unfortunately, many people do not know how to provide or are uncomfortable providing even basic first aid in these difficult situations. The Red Cross urges everyone to learn first aid, cardiopulmonary resuscitation (CPR) and the use of an automated external defibrillator (AED).

Red Cross first aid, CPR and AED programs are designed to give you the confidence to respond in an emergency situation with skills that can save a life. By taking a Red Cross course, you learn from the best. Red Cross materials are developed in collaboration with leading educational and medical authorities and incorporate the latest science in first aid, CPR and emergency cardiovascular care. Courses are taught by certified instructors and, upon successful completion, participants earn nationally recognized certificates. Spanish-language courses are also available.

While the importance of being trained in CPR and the use of AEDs cannot be underestimated, even those who do not have formal training can help victims who suffer cardiac arrest. The Red Cross encourages people who are unwilling, unable, untrained or unsure how to perform full CPR (cycles of chest compressions and rescue breaths) to instead perform compression-only CPR. This means giving continuous chest compressions (at the rate of 100 compressions per minute) without rescue breaths.

The Red Cross offers a *First Aid and CPR for Everyone* kit that teaches compression-only CPR. The *First Aid and CPR for Everyone* kit is a portable practice tool that can be used at home, in the office, in classrooms or anywhere it is convenient for people to practice their skills. It features an illustrated guide to demonstrate hand placement on the chest and a compression practice tool to help measure just the right amount of pressure needed to properly administer chest compressions.

Remember, the most important thing bystanders can do in an emergency is to call 9-1-1 or the local emergency number. Those who know how to perform first aid and CPR or use an AED can take steps to save a life.

To enroll in a first aid, CPR and AED class or to order a *First Aid and CPR for Everyone* kit, contact your local Red Cross or visit *www.redcross.org*.

- Change the position of the limb to stretch the cramped muscle and massage the area to help relieve the cramp.

For a muscle cramp in deep water–

- Take a deep breath, roll forward face-down and float.
- Extend the leg and flex the ankle or toes.
- Massage the cramp (**Fig. 3-6**).

Abdominal cramps, although rare, can happen if a person is tired and cold. A person with an abdominal cramp should try to relax and maintain the position in the water until the cramp passes.

Exhaustion

Exhaustion simply means that a person no longer has the energy to keep swimming or floating. Exhaustion can occur–

- In reaction to cold water.
- After being in the sun too long.
- From swimming when very tired.
- From swimming too long and too hard.
- From being dehydrated.
- From any combination of these factors.

Fatigue early in the season when the water is cold can be a serious problem. Exhaustion is more

Fig. 3-6

likely for swimmers who swim too much before they are really in shape. Exhaustion is also more likely to overtake those who do not know which strokes to use to conserve energy. For example, the elementary backstroke takes relatively little energy when compared with a front crawl.

Prevent exhaustion by resting often while swimming or doing other water activities. Younger, inexperienced swimmers, who may become exhausted before they realize they are in danger, should be especially careful.

Falling into Water

Water emergencies often happen to people who did not intend to go into the water in the first place. In most cases, people who fall in end up in the water fully clothed. There are some advantages to keeping clothes on in this case. Many types of clothing will actually aid floating and provide protection against cold water. If shoes are light enough to allow swimming comfortably, leave them on. If they are too heavy, assume a jellyfish float position and remove them. Refer to **Chapter 5** for more information on basic aquatic skills that can be used in this and other types of aquatic emergencies.

Submerged Vehicle

When a vehicle plunges into the water, an occupant's first response is usually to frantically try to open the doors. Because the external water pressure makes opening the doors difficult, occupants may begin to panic, believing that they are unable to help themselves. In a submerged vehicle emergency, remain calm and remember the following guidelines:

- Wearing a seat belt will reduce the chances of injury when the vehicle hits the water.
- Tests indicate that even a heavy vehicle will float for up to 45 seconds after it enters the water. During this time, release the seat belt, try to open the nearest window and exit immediately through that window.
- If the vehicle begins to sink, move to the higher end to breathe the trapped air. Do not try to open the door to exit.
- Use one of three routes to escape:
  - Open a window.
  - Open an undamaged door when the water pressure is equal inside and out (when the vehicle is nearly full of water–you may need to open the vehicle's vents to do this).
  - Break or push out a window when the water pressure is equal inside and out (when the vehicle is nearly full of water).

Water and cars do not mix. Never drive into flooded areas or on unsafe ice. Anyone who witnesses a vehicle plunging into the water should get immediate assistance by calling 9-1-1 or the local emergency number.

Capsized Boat

If the boat you are in capsizes and it is floating, stay with the boat. Most boats will assist in keeping you floating, which reduces energy loss from being in the water. If you are not wearing a life jacket, put it on immediately. If possible, climb on top of the overturned boat. It is important to get as much of your body as possible out of the water if the water is cold.

If you can right the boat, try to reboard. Use the ladder or swim platform on larger boats. If the weight in the boat is distributed correctly, climb up over the transom (back of the boat) being very careful not to injure yourself on the boat's propeller or outboard engine. On smaller boats, pull yourself over the middle and lie across it. Once the boat is stabilized, roll your legs into the boat. Many small boats, such as canoes, kayaks and rowboats, can be rowed to shore even when filled with water. In the event of an emergency, canoes and kayaks should have painters (short lengths of rope attached to the ends of the canoe or kayak) and end loops, and other boats should have a rope ladder or dock line available, as well as rescue equipment.

If you cannot right the boat, stay with it and wait for rescue. Staying with your boat will help you conserve energy and make you more visible to rescue personnel. Other boaters nearby may be able to assist you. If you filed a float plan and do not return on time, someone will notice when you are missing and look for your boat.

- If the boat sinks or floats away, do not panic. If it is safe to do so, stay in place.
- Make sure your life jacket is securely fastened, remain calm and wait for help.
- If a life jacket is not available, look for any other buoyant items, such as coolers, oars, paddles or decoys, to use as flotation aids instead.
- If no flotation aids are available, then you may need to use survival floating or swimming.

Survival Floating in Warm Water

This survival floating technique is performed face-down. Use this method in warm water if it is not possible to reach safety and it is necessary to wait for help or to rest while making the way to safety.

To survival float—

1. Hold your breath then put your face in the water. Allow the arms and legs to hang freely. Rest in this position for a few seconds (**Fig. 3-7, A**).

2. To take another breath, slowly lift the arms to about shoulder height and move the arms forward. Separate the legs, moving one leg forward and one leg back.

3. Gently press down with the arms while bringing the legs together. This movement lifts the mouth above the water, allowing you to take a breath (**Fig. 3-7, B**).

4. Return to the resting position. Repeat these steps to take additional breaths.

Survival Swimming in Warm Water

Survival swimming should be used together with the survival float in a warm water emergency only. A considerable distance can be covered while using a minimal amount of energy with this stroke. Remember that swimming long distances to safety should only be used as a last resort.

1. After taking a breath, bend forward at the waist and bring the hands up alongside the head (**Fig. 3-8, A**).

2. Separate the legs into the stride position and extend the arms forward then bring the legs together again to propel yourself diagonally toward the surface (**Fig. 3-8, B**).

Fig. 3-7, A

Fig. 3-7, B

Fig. 3-8, A

Fig. 3-8, B

3. Sweep the arms out and back to the thighs and glide near and almost parallel to the surface.

4. When a breath is needed, bend the legs and draw them toward the torso and bring the hands up alongside the head once again. Pull hard with the arms and then quickly return to the survival float position. This can help prevent the body from sinking for those who do not float well.

5. Extend the arms forward and separate the legs to the stride position once again. Tilt the head back and prepare to breathe out, as in survival floating.

6. Repeat steps 1 through 5.

A person who is not very buoyant must perform these movements slightly faster to prevent sinking before the breath.

Self-Rescue with Clothes

A person may be able to swim toward safety by inflating the pants or by trapping air in the shoulders of a shirt or jacket. Once filled with air, the shirt or pants can be used as a flotation aid.

To inflate a shirt or jacket by blowing air into it–

1. Tuck the shirt in or tie the shirttail ends together around the waist.

2. Unbutton the collar button, take a deep breath, bend your head forward into the water, pull the

shirt or jacket up to the face and blow into the shirt (**Fig. 3-9**).

3. Keep the front of the shirt or jacket under water and hold the collar closed.

4. Repeat the steps above to reinflate the shirt or jacket if necessary.

To inflate a shirt or jacket by striking air into it–

1. Fasten the buttons or close the zipper up to the neck.

2. Hold the bottom of the shirt or jacket out with one hand, keeping it just under the surface of the water, and lean back slightly.

3. From above the surface of the water, strike the water with the free hand (palm down) and drive

Fig. 3-9

it down, pulling air to a point below the shirttail or jacket (**Fig. 3-10, A**).

4. Keep the front of the shirt or jacket under water and hold the collar and the shirttail closed (**Fig. 3-10, B**).

5. Repeat the steps above to reinflate the shirt or jacket if necessary.

To inflate pants–

1. Take a deep breath, lean forward into the water and reach down and remove your shoes.

2. Loosen the waistband and belt.

3. Take another deep breath, lean forward and reach down and take off your pants one leg at a time without turning them inside out. Bring your face to the water and take a breath whenever necessary.

4. Once the pants are off, tie both legs together at the cuff or tie a knot in each leg as close as possible to the bottom of the leg then zip or button the pants to the waist.

5. Hold the back of the waistband under water with one hand and, while keeping the pants on the surface of the water, strike the water to force air into to the open waistband with the other hand. Strike the water with the palm of the free hand and follow through into the open waistband below the surface (**Fig 3-11, A**). You can also inflate the pants by submerging them and then blowing air into the open waistband below the surface of the water.

6. Once the pants are inflated, gather the waistband together with your hands or by

tightening the belt and then slip your head in between the pant legs where they are tied together (**Fig. 3-11, B**). If the pant legs are tied separately, reach one arm over and between the two pant legs for support.

7. Repeat the steps above to reinflate the pants if necessary.

Falling into Cold Water with a Life Jacket

In a cold water emergency, it is essential to decide whether to try to reach safety or float and wait for help because people cannot swim as far in cold water as in warm water. Anyone who has fallen into cold water should try to swim to safety if it is possible to do so with only a few strokes. Strokes with an underwater arm recovery can help maintain heat when swimming in cold water. Floating in place until help arrives is the best way to survive a cold water emergency in open water or when a great distance from the shore.

After falling into cold water while wearing a life jacket–

- Keep the face and head above the surface. In the event of a boating accident, try to climb up onto the capsized boat to get more of the body out of the water.

- Keep all clothes on, especially a hat. Even wet clothes help retain body heat.

- If caught in a current, float on the back and go downstream feetfirst until breathing is slowed.

Fig. 3-10, A

Fig. 3-10, B

Fig. 3-11, A

Fig. 3-11, B

Breathe normally for a few seconds before starting to swim to shore.

- Try to swim to safety if the current is carrying you toward some danger.

- If you are not in immediate danger but far from shore, stay still and let the life jacket provide support until help arrives. To stay warmer, assume the heat escape lessening posture as described in the next section.

Treading water chills the body faster than staying still with a life jacket on in the water. In cold water, tread water only if it is necessary.

Heat Escape Lessening Posture

The heat escape lessening posture (HELP) can increase the chances of survival by reducing the amount of body surface area that is directly exposed to cold water. In this position, the chest and knees are in contact with each other rather than being in contact with cold water.

1. Draw the knees up to the chest.

2. Keep the face forward and out of the water.

3. Hold the upper arms at the sides and fold the lower arms against or across the chest (**Fig. 3-12**).

Do not use the HELP position in swift river currents or whitewater.

Huddle

The huddle position is much like the HELP position. In this position, the body surface area is in contact with other bodies rather than with cold water. Use this position when two or more people are in the water together.

- With two people, put your arms around one another so that your chests are together.

Fig. 3-12

Fig. 3-13

- With three or more people, put your arms over one another's shoulders so that the sides of your chests are together (**Fig. 3-13**).

- Sandwich a child or elderly person between adults.

Falling into Cold Water without a Life Jacket

- Look around for a log or anything floating for support. If near a capsized boat, climb or hold onto it.

- Move as much of the body as possible out of the water. Keep the face and head above the water. Turn your back toward waves to help keep water out of the face.

- Keep all clothes on, especially a hat. Try to inflate clothing with air for flotation.

- Do not splash around trying to warm up. Splashing increases blood circulation in the arms and legs and will drain energy, resulting in heat loss.

- Swim to shore only if you are close enough to reach the shore safely. Factors that determine whether you should attempt to swim to shore include swimming ability, amount of insulation and water conditions. Because cold water reduces the distance a person can swim, be careful not to underestimate the distance to shore. Keep in mind that in emergencies it is often hard to judge distance. When the water is 50° F (10° C) or colder, even a good swimmer may have difficulty reaching shore.

Benefits of Winter Clothes

People who fall into the water wearing winter clothes, especially heavy boots or waders, usually panic because they think they will sink immediately. But winter clothes can actually help a person float. Snowmobile suits and other heavy winter clothes trap air and can help a person float. Winter clothes also help delay hypothermia. Tight-fitting foam vests and flotation jackets with foam insulation can double the survival time. If a person falls into the water wearing a snowmobile suit or other heavy winter clothes, air will be trapped in the clothes and will help the person float.

If you fall into cold water with heavy winter clothes–

- Simply lie back.

- Spread the arms and legs.

- Perform a "winging" motion with the arms to move toward safety (**Fig. 3-14**).

If you fall into the water wearing hip boots, waders or rubber boots, relax, bend the knees and the trapped air in the boots will bring you back to the surface quickly.

Moving Water Self-Rescue

If you fall into moving water–

1. Float downstream on your back with your feet in front to fend off obstacles and avoid entrapping the feet or legs.

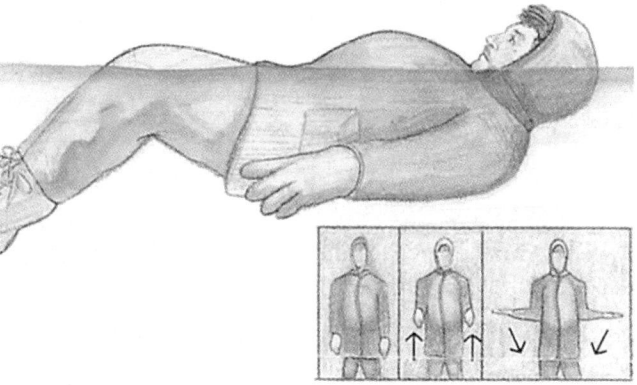

Fig. 3-14

Fig. 3-15

2. Use your arms to back paddle to slow down and steer out of the main current.

3. Swim toward shore when out of the main current or as soon as it is safe to do so.

4. Do not stand up–this can entrap your foot with the full force of the water holding you in place. Only a modest amount of water volume and velocity can exert significant force on a leg, arm or body caught in a current.

5. Hold on to a boat, if capsized, and stay upstream of the craft (**Fig. 3-15**). Try to swim with the boat to shore. Let go of the boat if necessary.

Falling Through the Ice

If you fall through the ice–

- Resist the urge to try to climb out onto the ice. It is likely to be weak in the area where the fall took place.

- Quickly get into a floating position on the stomach. Bend your knees to help trap air in pant legs and boots.

- Reach forward onto the broken ice, but do not push down on it. Use a breaststroke or other kick to push farther onto the ice.

- Do not stand up once on the ice. Crawl or roll away from the break area, with arms and legs spread out as far as possible.

- Have someone throw or extend something if needed. Remember not to stand on the ice.

Once Ashore

Hypothermia is still a risk even after reaching safety. Call 9-1-1 or the local emergency number after someone has been in cold water for any length of time.

Helping Others
Out-of-Water Assists

Help a person in trouble in the water by using an out-of-water assist, such as a reaching or throwing assist. Out-of-water assists are safer for the responder. Wherever possible, start the rescue by talking to the victim. Let him or her know help is coming. Use gestures if it is too noisy or if the victim is too far away to hear. Tell the victim what he or she can do to help with the rescue, such as grasping a line, rescue buoy or any other floating device. Ask the victim to move toward safety by kicking or stroking. Some people have reached safety by themselves with the calm and encouraging assistance of someone calling to them from shore.

Reaching Assists

If the victim is close enough, use a reaching assist to help him or her out of the water. Use any available object that will extend your reach, such as a pole, an oar or paddle, a tree branch, a shirt, a belt or a towel (**Fig. 3-16**). Community pools and recreational areas, as well as hotel and motel pools, often have reaching equipment beside the water, such as a shepherd's crook (an aluminum or fiberglass pole with a large hook on one end). When using a rigid object such as a pole or oar, sweep it toward the victim from the side until it makes contact with an arm or hand. When using a shirt or towel, lie down and flip it into the victim's hands.

If there is equipment available–

1. Brace yourself on a pool deck, pier surface or shoreline.

2. Extend the object to the victim.

3. When the victim grasps the object, slowly and carefully pull him or her to safety. Keep your body low and lean back to avoid being pulled into the water.

If no equipment is available–

1. Brace yourself on the pool deck or pier surface.

2. Reach with an arm and grasp the victim.

3. Pull the victim to safety (**Fig. 3-17**).

If you are already in the water–

1. Hold onto a pool ladder, overflow trough (gutter), piling or another secure object with one hand.

2. Extend a free hand or one leg to the victim. Do not let go of the secure object or swim out to the victim (**Fig. 3-18**).

3. Pull the victim to safety.

Throwing Assists

One way to rescue a conscious victim who is out of reach is to use a throwing assist. Use a throwing assist with anything that will provide the victim support. A floating object with a line attached is best. The victim can grasp the object and then be pulled to safety by a responder on shore or in a boat. However, lines and floats can also be used alone. Suitable throwing objects include a heaving line, ring buoy, throw bag,

Fig. 3-16

Fig. 3-17

Fig. 3-18

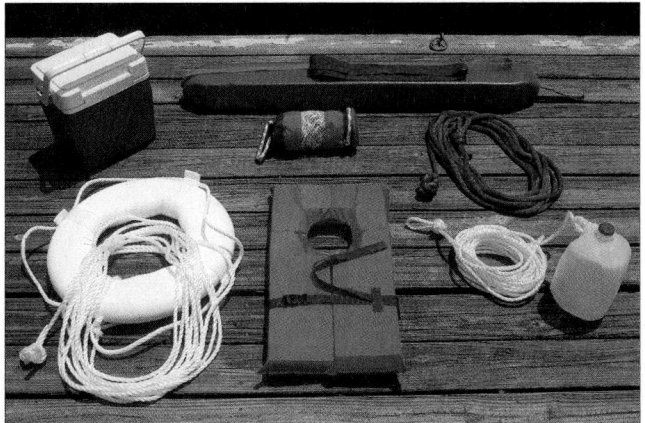

Fig. 3-19

rescue tube or homemade device (**Fig. 3-19**). Use any floating object at hand, such as a picnic jug or inner tube. Keep a throwing object with a coiled line in a prominent location that is accessible to the water so that anyone can quickly grasp it to throw to someone in trouble. All boats should have rescue equipment for throwing assists onboard.

To perform a throwing assist, follow these guidelines:

- Get into a stride position: The leg opposite the throwing arm is forward. This helps maintain balance during the throw.
- Step on the end of the line with the forward foot. Avoid stepping on the coiled line with the other foot (**Fig 3-20, A**).
- Shout to get the victim's attention. Make eye contact and tell the victim that you will now throw the object and he or she should grab it.
- Bend the knees and throw the object to the victim. Try to throw the object upwind or upstream, just over the victim's head, so the line drops within reach (**Fig 3-20, B**).
- When the victim has grasped the object or the line, slowly pull him or her to safety. Keep weight low and back. Lean away from the water while bringing the victim to safety (**Fig 3-20, C**).
- If the object does not reach the victim, quickly pull the line back in and throw it again. Try to keep the line from tangling, but do not waste time trying to coil it. If the object is a throw bag, partially fill the bag with some water and throw it again.

Fig. 3-20, A

Fig. 3-20, B

Fig. 3-20, C

WATER RESCUE EQUIPMENT

Aquatic emergencies often happen with little warning. This is why lifeguards must have special rescue equipment readily available. The same is true for anyone spending time in, on and around the water. At home pools and other areas where no lifeguards are present, one or more of the following types of rescue equipment should be close at hand.

- Throwing equipment. A responder can throw one of these devices to a victim and pull them to safety. Specific types of throwing equipment include ropes, throw bags, ropes with buoys attached and rescue rings/buoys.

- Reaching equipment. A responder can use a reaching pole or shepherd's crook to pull a victim to safety.

- Flotation devices. Young children and weak swimmers can wear life jackets and U.S. Coast Guard-approved flotation aids can be used for reaching or throwing assists.

In addition to life jackets and throwing, reaching and flotation devices designed for use with boats, certain types of recreational boats require some additional rescue equipment. Visuals distress signals such as flags, flares or lights; fire extinguishers; and sound producing devices, such as an air horn or an athletic whistle, are a good idea for all boats and required for some. Check with the U.S. Coast Guard for specific regulations on safety equipment for recreational boating. Additionally, anyone spending time on the water should have communication equipment such as a marine VHF radio or a mobile phone. Larger boats should have a ladder to help a person who needs to reboard.

No one in, on or around water should take their safety for granted. Before taking part in any aquatic activity, consider all potential hazards and do your best to prevent or avoid them. Make sure that you are prepared by purchasing appropriate rescue equipment to use in emergency situations.

In most cases, only trained professionals should enter the water to perform a rescue. Always remember, "Reach or throw, don't go!"

If the throwing assist does not work and the water is shallow enough for wading, try a wading assist with equipment.

Helping Someone Who Has Fallen Through Ice

Never go out onto the ice in an attempt to rescue a person who has fallen through the ice. Because a person has just fallen through it, the ice is probably unsafe. Any responder who rushes out onto the ice is likely to become a victim. Instead, follow these guidelines:

1. Send someone to call EMS personnel immediately. Trained responders may be needed to get the person out of the ice. Even in the event of a successful rescue, a person who has fallen through the ice will probably need medical care.

2. From a secure place on land, try a reaching or throwing assist. Use anything at hand that the person can grasp for support, such as a tree branch, pole, life jacket or weighted rope (**Fig. 3-21**). Act quickly. Within 1 minute, the victim's hands may be too numb to grasp the object.

3. If it is possible to do it safely, pull the victim to shore and treat the person for hypothermia. If it is not possible, talk to the victim and make sure he or she is as secure as possible until help arrives.

In-Water Assists
Wading Assist with Equipment

If the water is less than chest deep, wade into the water to assist the person using a rescue tube, ring

Fig. 3-21

buoy, kickboard or a life jacket. A tree branch, pole, air mattress or paddle also can be used (**Fig. 3-22, A and B**). If a current or soft bottom makes wading dangerous, do not enter the water. If possible, wear a life jacket when attempting a wading assist with equipment.

1. Take a buoyant object to extend out to the victim.
2. Wade into the water and extend the object to the victim.
3. When the victim grasps the object, tell him or her to hold onto the object tightly for support and pull him or her to safety. Keep the object between yourself and the victim to help prevent the victim from grasping the responder.

A victim who has been lying motionless and face-down in the water for several seconds is probably unconscious.

1. If the water is less than chest deep, wade into the water carefully with some kind of flotation equipment and turn the person face-up.
2. Bring him or her to the side of the pool or to the shoreline.
3. Remove the victim from the water.

Submerged Victim

If a victim is discovered on or near the bottom of the pool in deep water, call for trained help immediately. If the victim is in shallow water that is less than chest deep—

1. Wade into the water carefully with some kind of flotation equipment and reach down and grasp the victim.
2. Pull the victim to the surface.
3. Turn the victim face-up and bring him or her to safety.
4. Remove the victim from the water.
5. Provide emergency care.

Helping Victims from the Water
Walking Assist

If the victim is in shallow water, he or she may be able to walk with some support. In this situation, use the walking assist.

1. Place one of the victim's arms around the neck and across the shoulder of the responder.
2. Grasp the wrist of the arm that is across the responder's shoulder, and wrap the free arm around the victim's back or waist.

Fig. 3-22, A

Fig. 3-22, B

3. Maintain a firm grasp, and help the victim walk out of the water (**Fig. 3-23**).

Beach Drag

Use the beach drag for a victim in shallow water on a sloping shore or beach who cannot walk with support. This method works well with a heavy or unconscious victim.

1. Stand behind the victim, and grasp him or her under the armpits. Support the victim's head with the forearms, when possible.

2. While walking backward slowly, drag the victim toward the shore (**Fig. 3-24**).

3. Remove the victim completely from the water or at least to a point where the head and shoulders are out of the water.

Use a two-person beach drag if another person is present to help (**Fig. 3-25**).

Injuries to the Head, Neck or Back

Headfirst entries into shallow water and other unsafe activities can cause injuries to the head, neck or back. Usually a head, neck or back injury is caused by hitting the bottom or an object in the water. In this situation, movement can cause more injury and increase the risk of paralysis. In this type of aquatic emergency, the goal is to keep the spine from moving until help arrives.

If you are unsure whether a victim has a head, neck or back injury, think about what the victim was doing and what happened to cause the injury. The following are situations in which head, neck or back injury is possible:

- Any headfirst entry into shallow water

- Any fall onto land from a height greater than the victim's height

- Any injury involving a diving board or waterslide

- Entering water from a height, such as a bank or cliff

Signals of a possible head, neck or back injury include:

Fig. 3-23

Fig. 3-24

- Head, neck or back pain
- Loss of balance
- Difficulty breathing
- Loss of movement in the arms and legs or below the injury site

Fig. 3-25

- Tingling or loss of sensation in the arms, legs, hands or feet

- Bumps, bruises or depressions on the head, neck or back

- Altered consciousness or seizures

- Fluid or blood in the ears

If you suspect someone has a head, neck or back injury, have someone call 9-1-1 or the local emergency number immediately. Give care with the assumption that there is a head, neck or back injury anytime one is suspected. If the victim is in the water, the goal is to prevent any further movement of the head or neck and to move the victim to safety. Always check first whether a lifeguard or other trained professional is present before touching or moving a victim who may have a head, neck or back injury.

General Guidelines for Care

A victim's head, neck or back can be stabilized in several ways while the victim is still in the water. The details of these methods are described in the next section. Follow these general guidelines for a victim with suspected head, neck or back injury:

- Be sure someone has called 9-1-1 or the local emergency number. If other people are available, ask someone to help.

- Minimize movement of the victim's head, neck and back. This technique is called in-line stabilization.

- Position the victim face-up at the surface of the water. Keep the victim's face out of the water, allowing him or her to breathe.

- Support the victim with his or her head, neck and back immobilized until help arrives.

Hip and Shoulder Support

This method helps limit movement to the head, neck and back. Use it for a victim who is face-up. Support the victim at the hips and shoulders to keep the face out of the water.

1. Slide into the water and approach the victim from the side, and lower yourself to about shoulder depth.

Fig. 3-26

2. Slide one arm under the victim's shoulders and the other under the hips (**Fig. 3-26**).

3. Hold the victim's body horizontal in the water, keeping the face out of the water.

Head Splint

This method provides better stabilization than the hip and shoulder support. Use it for a victim who is face-down at or near the surface in the water. The victim must be turned face-up to breathe.

1. Slide into the water and approach the victim from the side.

2. Grasp the victim's arms midway between the shoulder and elbow (your right hand on the victim's right arm and your left hand on the victim's left arm). Gently move the victim's arms up alongside the head.

3. Squeeze the victim's arms against his or her head (**Fig. 3-27, A**).

4. Glide the victim slowly forward. Lower yourself to shoulder depth then continue moving forward and slowly roll the victim toward you, until he or she is face-up (**Fig. 3-27, B**).

5. Position the victim's head in the crook of your arm, with the head in line with the body (**Fig. 3-27, C**).

6. Hold the victim in this position with the face out of the water until help arrives.

Head and Chin Support

The head and chin support is used for face-down or face-up victims at or near the surface of the water. Do not use this technique on a victim who is face-down in water less than 3 feet deep.

To perform the head and chin support for a victim in shallow water at or near the surface–

1. Slide into the water and approach the victim from the side.

2. Lower your body to shoulder depth, place one forearm along the length of the victim's breastbone and the other forearm along the victim's spine.

Fig. 3-27, A

Fig. 3-27, B

Fig. 3-27, C

Fig. 3-28, A

Fig. 3-28, B

Fig. 3-28, C

Fig. 3-28, D

Fig. 3-28, E

3. Use the hands to gently hold the victim's head and neck in line with the body. Place one hand on the victim's lower jaw and the other hand on the back of the lower part of the head (**Fig. 3-28, A and B**). Be careful not to touch the back of the neck.

4. Squeeze the forearms together, clamping the victim's chest and back. Continue to support the victim's head and neck.

   - If the victim is face-down, use the head and chin support to stabilize the spine and slowly move the victim forward to help lift the victim's legs. Turn the victim toward your body as you submerge (**Fig. 3-28, C**).

   - Roll under the victim while turning the victim over (**Fig. 3-28, D**). Avoid twisting the victim's body. The victim should be face-up when you surface on the other side (**Fig. 3-28, E**).

5. Hold the victim face-up in the water until help arrives.

CHAPTER 4
Hydrodynamics

What does physics have to do with being a good swimmer? Good question! The simple answer is that swimming involves the science of matter and energy, also known as physics. Researchers have spent years trying to learn–and continue to study– how the human body moves through the water, leading to new ways to move more efficiently through water. This is why it is important to understand basic hydrodynamic principles.

This chapter relates some main principles of physics to swimming and the aquatic environment. In doing so, it describes the principles related to being in and moving through the water. This chapter also includes exercises to help people understand and get a "feel" for certain hydrodynamic principles.

Why Some Things Float

Archimedes' Principle

Imagine three containers of the same size and shape. Each weighs 1 pound and can hold 10 pounds of water. Leave the first container empty and seal it, then put it in water and see what happens. It bobs high in the water with most of the container visible above the surface of the water. Next, try putting 8 pounds of pebbles in the second container then seal it and put it in water. This container also floats, but much lower in the water than the other container—most of it will be submerged. Finally, put 11 pounds of pebbles into the third container, seal it and put it in water. This container will sink even if it has air inside.

The effect shown on all three containers demonstrates what is called Archimedes' principle. This principle states that a body in water is buoyed up by a force equal to the weight of the water displaced (**Fig. 4-1**). If someone tried to lift the third container while it was still under water, it would seem to weigh only 2 pounds. The container weighs 1 pound plus 11 pounds of pebbles minus 10 pounds of displaced water equals 2 pounds.

Archimedes' principle explains why most people float. Consider three different people: one with a large amount of body fat, another with less body fat and a third with very little body fat but who is heavily muscled. These bodies will act similarly to the containers because the bodies displace water. This principle can be easily seen when someone sits in a bathtub and the water level goes up. (In fact, this is reportedly what Archimedes was doing when he discovered this famous principle.) When the weight of the water displaced is more than the person's body weight, flotation occurs. When flotation occurs, the force of buoyancy is greater than the force of gravity.

Buoyancy

Buoyancy—the upward force that water exerts on an object—causes many swimmers to weigh less than the water displaced. These swimmers can spend most of their energy producing forward movement rather than supporting themselves. This is especially valuable for persons with limited physical abilities. It may be easier for these individuals to move around in water because the buoyancy of water helps support the body.

The amount of buoyancy exerted on a body is primarily determined by a body's specific gravity. *Specific gravity* is the ratio of the weight of a body to the weight of the water it displaces. Think back to the containers. Recall that the first two containers floated at different heights in the water even though buoyancy pushed them both up. Although they both displaced the same amount of water, they had different weights or specific gravities, which caused them to float differently.

Pure water has a specific gravity of 1. The specific gravity of other objects is the ratio of their density to that of water—an object's density divided by the density of water. Objects with a specific gravity that is less than 1 float. Objects with a specific gravity that is greater than 1 sink.

The first container, which weighs only 1 pound but displaces 10 pounds of water, has a specific gravity of 0.1. This container floats high on the surface of the water because its specific gravity value is much lower than that of water. The second container, which weighs 9 pounds (the container weighs 1 pound plus 8 pounds of pebbles) but displaces 10 pounds of water, has a specific gravity of 0.9. This object floats just above the surface of the water because its specific gravity value is only slightly lower than that of water. Because its specific gravity value is greater than 1, the third container sinks. This container

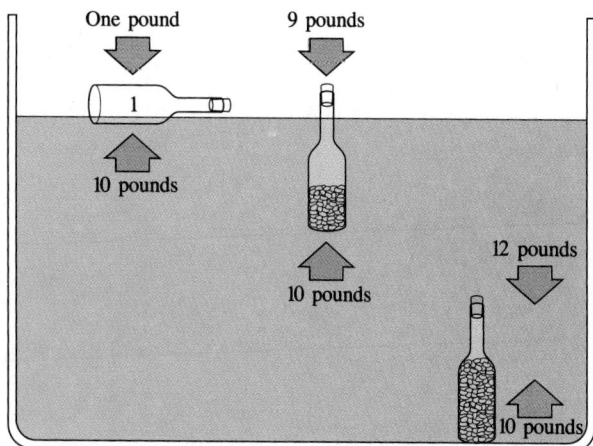

Fig. 4-1

Fig. 4-2

weighs 12 pounds (the container weights 1 pound plus 11 pounds of pebbles) but displaces 10 pounds of water so it has a specific gravity of 1.2.

What does all this mean for swimming? For one thing, it explains why some people can float easily while others cannot (**Fig. 4-2**). Specific gravity among humans varies greatly because people have different amounts of muscle mass, body fat and bone density. Adipose tissue (body fat) has a specific gravity that is less than 1.0 and promotes floating. Bone and muscle tissue, on the other hand, have specific gravity values that are slightly greater than 1.0 and promote sinking.

Most people tend to float at or near the surface of the water depending on their specific gravity value. Those with more body fat float more easily. People with lots of muscle, a heavy bone structure and little body fat do not float easily and may even sink. In general, children are more buoyant than adults are because they do not have as much muscle mass and their bones are less dense. The average female in the United States has 21 to 24 percent body fat. The average male has 15 to 20 percent body fat. This means that females, as a group, tend to float more easily than males. However, many males have an easy time floating and many females have trouble staying near the surface.

Although the ability to float motionless on the water's surface depends on body composition, individuals can make adjustments to improve their buoyancy. Inhaling deeply and holding a

breath lowers specific gravity and enhances the ability to float—although some individuals cannot float, even with a full breath of air. Wearing a life jacket also increases buoyancy because it displaces a large amount of water with only a minimal increase in weight. People who tend to sink might have to use additional techniques, such as sculling with the arms or kicking slightly, to keep at the surface. People who float more easily than others may need more time to develop underwater skills.

THE EFFECTS OF WEARING CLOTHES IN WATER

Entering the water unexpectedly and fully clothed can be quite frightening. This experience can leave people with the impression that clothing will pull them underwater. Clothing that is weighted down with water adds weight to the body, which results in a higher specific gravity. Unless people take action, it may become more difficult for them to float. Swimming while wearing heavy clothes that are weighted down requires a great deal of energy and expends a great deal of heat.

Yet, if people end up in the water unexpectedly and fully clothed, there are advantages to keeping the clothes on. Clothing can provide protection against hypothermia, marine life, fuel spills and sunlight. Many types of winter clothes, such as snowsuits, can actually trap air and can help a person float.

Those who have had training can inflate their clothing with air to make it easier to float. People involved in any aquatic activities (such as learning to swim, boating or fishing) should experience being in water while wearing clothes and know how to use clothing to their advantage.

Chapter 3 provides detailed descriptions of how people can inflate clothes to provide additional buoyancy as well as the steps they can take if they accidentally fall into water.

Here is a simple way to check for buoyancy:

1. Move into a tuck float position (**Fig. 4-3**). Lean over and tuck your knees up into your chest. Hold your knees against your chest until the body stops rising or sinking.

2. Recover to a standing position.

3. Take a large breath of air, hold it and return to the tuck float position.

4. Recover to a standing position.

5. Return to the tuck float position, then slowly let air out through your mouth and nose.

6. Recover to a standing position.

7. Move into a back float with your arms at your side.

8. Recover to a standing position.

A person whose back rose above the surface during step 1 will normally float easily. A person whose back rose during step 3 is likely to float in a diagonal position. Swimmers whose body drifted down during the exhale in step 5 may be likely to sink while trying to float motionlessly. A person who is more buoyant will assume a more horizontal position in step 7.

The water also can make a difference in how a person floats. Saltwater has more buoyant force because it has a higher, specific gravity than freshwater. Floating in the ocean may be easier for people who have trouble floating in freshwater. A person who floats easily in freshwater will float even higher in the ocean.

Fig. 4-3

Center of Mass and Center of Buoyancy

Specific gravity is not the only factor affecting how a body floats in the water. Two other factors affect the position of a floating body: the center of mass (sometimes called the center of gravity) and the center of buoyancy.

The *center of buoyancy* is a theoretical point in a body where the entire buoyancy of that body can be considered to be concentrated. Likewise, the *center of mass* is a theoretical point in a body where the entire mass of that body can be considered to be concentrated. If you were to try to balance a body on a seesaw, the pivot point would have to be directly below the center of mass. In other words, the supporting upward force exerted on the body by the pivot point would have to go through the center of mass in order for balance to occur.

Two large forces act on the body when a person is floating. One force is the downward force of gravity. The other force is the upward force of buoyancy. In reality, both forces occur all over the body. To help understand how these forces affect floating, however, we can assume that the center of mass is the location of all downward force and that the center of buoyancy is the location of all upward force. When the center of mass is directly below the center of buoyancy, a person is able to float in a stable position. This happens because the two forces act on the body along the exact same line. If the center of mass is not directly below the center of buoyancy, the body will rotate until it achieves this alignment.

When standing with arms down along the side, the center of mass is located near the hips and the center of buoyancy is located in the chest for most people (**Fig. 4-4**). In the water, each person's natural floating position (vertical, diagonal or horizontal) depends upon the location of the center of mass relative to the center of buoyancy (**Fig. 4-5**). The relationship of these two centers changes, however, as people change their body shape or position. Moving the center of mass and the center of buoyancy so that they are closer together increases stability during a horizontal float by minimizing the tendency of the body to rotate. To move those centers closer together, a person has to move as much body tissue with a

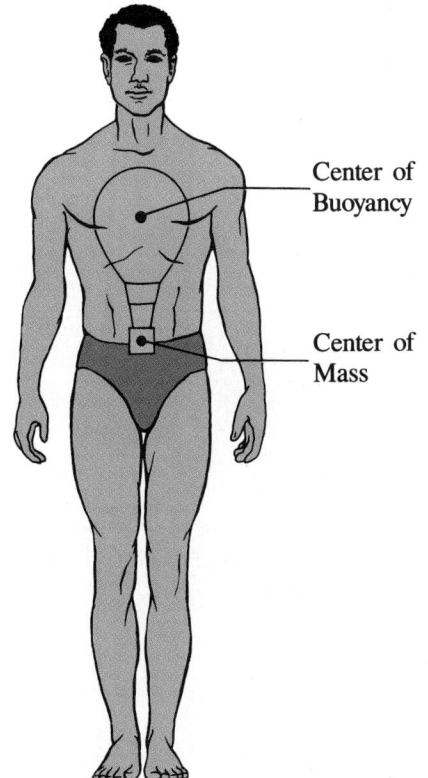

Fig. 4-4

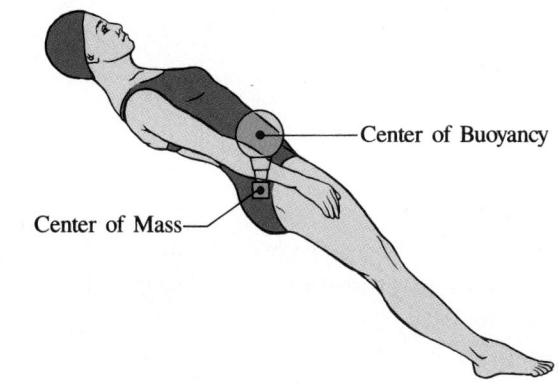

Fig. 4-5

Fig. 4-6

specific gravity of less than 1 (e.g., fat, air in the lungs) toward the feet and move as much body tissue that has a specific gravity of greater than 1 (e.g., bones, muscle) as far toward the head as possible.

The following steps demonstrate how to change the relationship between the center of mass and the center of buoyancy:

1. Float on the back with your arms at your side.

2. Move your arms above your head.

3. Flex the wrists so your hands (or fingers) are out of water.

4. Bend the knees (**Fig. 4-6**).

THE PRESSURE OF WATER

Water is heavy. Every cubic foot of water weighs about 62 pounds. Because water is much heavier than air, breathing takes more effort when the chest is surrounded by water. Swimmers must inhale more deeply (attempt to expand the lungs more) to compensate. Efficient air exchange, or "breath control," is an essential and relatively easy skill for swimmers to master. Activities such as blowing bubbles, bobbing, floating and rhythmic breathing all help swimmers develop good breathing habits.

When swimmers submerge even a small depth, there is a large amount of water above them. As they swim deeper, more water pushes against the body. The weight of the water results in more pressure around the body. Swimmers typically feel this increased pressure first in the ears, which they can try to equalize by blowing through the nose while pinching or blocking the nose. This process increases the pressure on the inside of the ear to help balance the added pressure on the outside of the ear.

Even though swimmers may only feel the increased pressure on the ears, their entire body is actually experiencing this increased pressure. This is not harmful as long as swimmers do not dive too deeply.

Resistance to Movement in the Water

Water is more dense and thick than air. Due to these characteristics, people experience much more resistance to movement in the water than on land. This resistance is called drag. Drag from the body's shape or form, wave action and surface friction slows people down when they swim.

Form drag is the resistance related to a swimmer's shape and body position when moving through the water. Form drag has the most impact on a swimmer's total resistance to movement in the water. Overwhelmingly, form drag is the one factor that all swimmers can control to improve their efficiency when swimming.

To reduce form drag while swimming on the surface, the entire body should be as close as possible to a horizontal straight line at the surface of the water. Swimmers will create much less resistance by keeping their hips and legs at the same level as their head and chest than by allowing them to drop to a lower position in the water. Because most people's hips and legs naturally float lower in the water, it is critical to control the center of mass with a neutral head position (the head is neither too high nor looking forward).

A tight, narrow body shape is equally important for reducing the amount of resistance because a broad body shape needs to push aside more water to move forward. A tight, narrow shape reduces the amount of frontal surface area that is pushing through the water by having a pointed, rather than blunt, front end. This streamlined position in the water reduces the frontal surface area and form drag. To attain a streamlined position, swimmers need to narrow their shape from their fingers to their toes (**Fig. 4-7**). Avoiding excessive side-to-side or up-and-down body motion also helps reduce form drag.

Swimmers' movements through the water create waves that add resistance to forward progress. Swimmers cannot prevent those waves from occurring, but they can reduce resistance caused by the waves they produce by paying strict attention to skill and technique. For example, making smooth, even strokes and limiting the amount of splash made from arm strokes help reduce wave drag. Turbulence caused by other

Fig. 4-7

swimmers and water activity can also cause drag, although lane lines at pools help reduce this turbulence. Wave drag is also reduced, but not completely eliminated, when swimmers' move underwater, such as during starts and turns and in underwater swimming.

Each swimmer's body surface causes friction, which produces resistance to movement through the water (frictional drag). Wearing loose clothing while swimming dramatically increases this type of drag. Competitive swimmers wear swimming caps and smooth, tight-fitting swimwear or racing suits to reduce frictional drag. Some competitors even go so far as to shave their body hair to reduce frictional drag.

The following activities demonstrate how resistance affects swimming:

Fig. 4-8

Activity 1
1. Wear a T-shirt while swimming. Notice the slower speed (**Fig. 4-8**).

Activity 2
1. Stand in chest-deep water. With your elbows at your side and palms facing down, bring your hands together and apart several times.
2. Repeat with your thumbs up and palms facing each other.

In step 2 there was a greater resistance, and therefore the movement was more difficult. In water aerobics, resistance exercises take advantage of this principle.

Activity 3
1. Push off on the surface of the water in a streamlined position (arms extended overhead, hands clasped together with your arms against the ears, the legs extended together behind and toes pointed) and glide as far as possible.
2. Push off underwater in a streamlined position (arms extended overhead, hands clasped together with your arms against the ears, the legs extended together behind and toes pointed) and glide as far as possible.
3. Push off underwater with your hands apart and glide as far as possible.
4. Push off underwater in a streamlined position then flex your feet, pointing the toes downward.
5. Push off underwater with your arms in a streamlined position, but with your legs apart, and glide as far as possible.
6. Push off underwater with both arms and legs separated and glide as far as possible (**Fig. 4-9, A**).
7. Push off underwater in a streamlined position then separate your legs and move your arms so that they point straight down.

Each step in this activity increases drag. In the first step, you are in position to glide the farthest (**Fig. 4-9, B**).

Creating Movement in the Water
Research and analysis of stroke mechanics shows that swim strokes contain two types of propulsive forces that cause forward movement: drag and lift. For the last few decades, many thought that lift force played the major role in propulsion. However, recent research has demonstrated that drag propulsion is actually the dominant form of propulsion in swimming. This new awareness

Fig. 4-9, A

Fig. 4-9, B

Goggles and masks are pieces of equipment designed to improve visibility while swimming. Each type of equipment serves a specific purpose.

Goggles

Goggles, which only cover the eye socket, improve visibility at the surface of the water. They are not made for underwater swimming. There is no way to equalize the pressure inside the goggles with the increasing water pressure outside the body. The air volume inside the goggles tends to compress. This compression tends to "pull" the eyeball out of the eye socket to effectively reduce the trapped air volume. If swimmers spend time below the surface of the water wearing goggles, they may pop blood vessels in their eyes. Goggles should not be worn for underwater swimming.

Face Masks

Face masks used for snorkeling and diving are intended to improve visibility at and below the surface of the water. These protective devices encase the eyes and the nose. As the outside water pressure increases with depth, divers wearing face masks can exhale through the nose, which forces additional air into the space behind the lens and increases pressure. Once swimmers and divers exhale enough air into the space behind the lens, they equalize the pressure inside the mask to the pressure outside.

means that swimmers who want to improve the efficiency and effectiveness of their stroke should focus on maximizing the drag propulsive forces.

Drag Propulsion

Drag propulsion is based on one of Isaac Newton's three laws of motion: *the law of action and reaction.* This law states that for every action there is an equal and opposite reaction. An example of the law of action and reaction is the backward push of a paddle blade moving a canoe forward. This pushing motion is referred to as drag, or paddle, propulsion. In swimming, the limbs act as paddles to push water backward and move swimmers forward. A swimmer's hands and forearms should be facing towards the feet in order to create the greatest drag propulsive force **(Fig. 4-10)**.

Fig. 4-10

To experience drag propulsion, try the following exercise.

Activity 1

1. Stand in chest-deep water.
2. With arms in front and palms and forearms facing down, press downward with your arms.
3. With arms in front and palms angled slightly inward, press downward with your arms.
4. With arms in front and palms angled slightly outward, press downward with your arms.

The first time the arms are pressed down, the swimmer will feel the most resistance from the water. This motion results in the most propulsion because the swimmer pushes against the greatest amount of water when the arms and hands are in this position.

Drag propulsion can also be experienced by swimming the front crawl while paying special attention to the arm stroke. To experience this, focus on moving the arms directly from the head to the toe with minimal sideways motion.

In the aquatics environment, the law of action and reaction is not just limited to stroke mechanics. The law of action and reaction also applies to a person diving from a diving board. In this situation, the board reacts to the force of the feet acting against it and gives divers the lift they need to take off for the dive (**Fig. 4-11, A and B**).

To experience this law, try the following exercise.

Activity 2

1. Stand at the end of the diving board.
2. Push down on the end of the board (jump).
3. The board lifts your body into the air.

Lift Propulsion

While drag propulsion plays the dominant role in forward movement, lift propulsive forces help

Fig. 4-11, A

Fig. 4-11, B

in overall propulsion. The basic principle behind lift propulsion as it relates to swimming is that as fluid moves around an object, the individual particles within the fluid speed up or slow down to stay parallel with the particles on either side of the object. The faster moving particles tend to lift the object as they try to remain parallel with the slower moving particles on the other side of the object. Lift propulsion is the natural result of several movements involved in swimming. Sculling is an example of how certain movements of the arms and hands can manipulate the flow of water to achieve lift. When sculling, swimmers keep the hands pitched at a slight angle and press them toward the body. During this motion, the water that passes over the top of the hand must cover a greater distance than the water on the other side of the hand. As a result, the water flowing over the top of the hand speeds up to remain parallel with the slower moving water on the other side. Lift propulsion can also take place when the hands and feet move outward away from the body and then back inward toward the body or as the hands and feet move deep in the water then back up toward the body. Movement of the arms through the water when the hands are positioned with palms facing back and at a slight tilt toward the feet results in lift propulsion as well.

To experience lift propulsion, try the following exercise.

Activity 1

1. Stand in chest-deep water.

2. With your palms open and facing downward with a slight tilt, make sculling movements with your arms. (See **Chapter 5** for more information on proper sculling technique.)

3. Continue to scull and lift your feet off the bottom.

Swimming Efficiency

Isaac Newton's two other laws of motion are the law of inertia and the law of acceleration. These are also important for swimming efficiency. Experimenting with these laws can help demonstrate how each law works and how they interact as the body moves through water.

Law of Inertia

The *law of inertia* states three things. An external force is needed to get a body at rest to begin movement. An external force is needed to stop a moving body. An external force is needed to change the direction of a moving body. The three parts of this law affect swimming in the following ways:

1. An external force is needed to get a body at rest to begin movement. Swimmers need more energy to start a stroke than they do to maintain a stroke. This is why it is more efficient for swimmers to keep moving forward rather than starting and stopping repeatedly. Strokes, like front crawl and back crawl, are most efficient because they involve continuous motion. However, it is impossible to keep moving the arms as fast as possible for an extended period. Inertia allows a swimmer who is underway to rest and still keep moving forward during the glide portion of other strokes, like breaststroke and elementary backstroke. However, if the glide is too long, a swimmer could slow down too much, requiring more work to start the next stroke. Swimmers must find a balance between continuous arm movements and glides to manage their energy.

2. An external force is needed to stop a moving body. The water is an external force that can stop a moving body. Swimmers need less force to keep moving when they are in the streamlined position than they do in other positions that create more drag.

3. An external force is needed to change the direction of a moving body. Inertia keeps swimmers moving in the same direction. To change the direction of travel, swimmers must apply force to change the direction of their bodies. As speed increases, more and more force is needed to change direction. Incorrect body position and/or improper stroke mechanics can act as an external force on a moving body, causing the body to change direction unnecessarily. This is one of the reasons why beginning swimmers often have difficulty swimming in a straight line and sometimes fail to reach their desired direction.

Law of Acceleration

The *law of acceleration* states that the change in speed of an object depends on the amount of force applied to it and the direction of that force. This law relates to swimming in two ways. First, the more force swimmers apply when pushing water back, the faster they will swim. Second, concentrating all propulsive force in one single direction and maintaining direction make swimming more efficient. Incorrect body position and/or improper stroke mechanics can direct propulsion away from a swimmer's intended direction. If forces are applied away from a swimmer's intended direction, the body will be pushed off course and additional forces are necessary to readjust body motion and get back on track.

The following activities help illustrate this law.

Activity 1

1. Forcefully push off the pool wall and move into a streamlined position. Do not kick or stroke with the arms, but allow the body to slow to a stop.

2. Forcefully push off the pool wall and move into a streamlined position. Start swimming the front crawl as fast as possible.

Forcefully pushing off the wall causes rapid acceleration from a stationary position to a full glide speed. Without any kicking or arm action, the glide slows to a stop because of drag resistance. In the second step, when the front crawl is added and maximum speed is reached, the additional acceleration produced by the arms and legs is counterbalanced by the deceleration caused by drag resistance. The net effect is no acceleration. This is why in the second step the swimmer is able to move through the water with constant speed.

Activity 2

1. Swim the elementary backstroke one length of the pool as quickly as possible.

2. Return using only one arm for each stroke (alternate arms, keeping the opposite arm at the side).

In the first step, the swimmer is likely able to stay in a straight line and move rather quickly. In the second step, the swimmer is likely moving in a zigzag pattern. As a result, the swimmer must spend a good deal of effort on adjusting the direction of motion rather than accelerating forward.

Law of Levers

Applying the law of levers has helped researchers analyze strokes to find the best limb positions and motions for effective swimming. A *lever* consists of a pivot point and one or two rigid parts called arms. A common example of a lever is a seesaw. The pivot point is in the center, and the arms extend on each side. The weights of two children riding the seesaw are the forces acting on the lever. The law of levers states that the product of the force and force arm is equal to the product of the resistance and resistance arms.

The law of levers includes these four components:

- Force applied (the weight of the first child)

- Resistance encountered (the weight of the second child)

- Force arm (the distance between the first child and the pivot point)

- Resistance arm (the distance between the second child and the pivot point)

The law of levers suggests that to be most effective, forces of propulsion should be applied close to the body. This is why arm strokes are more efficient and provide better propulsion when the hands and wrists stay close to the body as opposed to going out to the sides or down deep in the water. During the front crawl, the arm acts as a lever with the shoulder as the pivot point. The shoulder muscles are the applied force and the length of bone between the shoulder and muscle attachment is the force arm. Encountered resistance is water resistance against the arm. The resistance arm is the distance from the shoulder point to the middle of the forearm. In the front crawl, bending the elbow during the pull shortens the resistance arm, reducing the force needed to

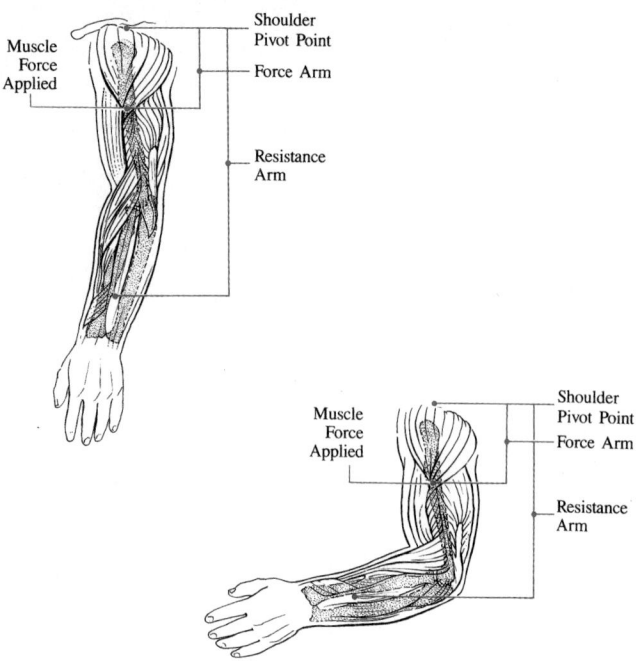

Fig. 4-12

Fig. 4-13

propel the swimmer forward (**Fig. 4-12**). (Bending the elbow during the arm stroke involves more muscles, which maximizes the swimmer's strength.) Practically speaking, the bend of the elbow used during the pull effectively brings the hand close to the chest. Without the bend, the elbow would be straighter, and the hand would go deep in the water, resulting in less efficient application of propulsion.

Effective arm strokes used in the back crawl, breaststroke and butterfly also keep the hands from going too deep or wide. Similarly, the kicks for each stroke should be kept close to the centerline of the body, rather than going out too wide. The kicks should also be horizontal to the body, rather than going too deep in the water. The law of levers also explains why bending the arms while treading water provides more upward force than straight arms (**Fig. 4-13**).

Try this exercise to better understand the law of levers.

Activity 1

1. In shallow water near the side of the pool, place your hands on the edge of the pool deck.
2. With your arms straight, try to lift out of the water without pushing off from the bottom of the pool.
3. Do the exercise again. But this time, bend your arms at the elbows to try to lift out of the water. This shortening of the resistance arm should make it easier to lift your body from the water.

Applying the law of levers has helped swimming researchers analyze all types of strokes to find the best limb positions and motions for each. These results are included in the description of swimming strokes in **Chapter 6.**

CHAPTER 5
Basic Aquatic Skills

By learning basic aquatic skills, people gain the skills necessary to float and move around in the water as well as the ability to safely enter and adjust to the water. In an emergency, these skills can save a life! Basic aquatic skills are also the building blocks for learning strokes that are more advanced. Mastering safety skills, like floating, changing directions and breath control, is necessary before learning advanced strokes, such as the front crawl or the breaststroke.

Starting with basic skills for entering the water, this chapter outlines the aquatic skills necessary to remain safe and feel comfortable and confident in the water. All the steps involved in each of these skills are clearly laid out and important survival and safety skills are also identified.

Basic Skills

Physical and Mental Adjustment

Anyone entering the water needs to take time to get used to the water both physically and mentally. Most aquatic environments are much cooler than bath water. Even relatively warm pool water (83° to 86° F) may feel cool and cause breathing to quicken. In water up to the neck, the temperature and added pressure of the water around the chest may even make breathing seem strenuous. When breathing speeds up, it becomes hard to relax. Rapid breathing may also increase anxiety in fearful or novice swimmers, making it even more difficult to adjust to the water.

Physical adjustments to the water involve gradually getting used to the water temperature and the effects of buoyancy. Mental adjustments involve taking efforts to remain relaxed and control breathing. Once a swimmer becomes comfortable in the water, these effects may no longer be noticeable.

Adjusting to the Water Temperature

Getting wet gradually will help the body get used to the cooler water temperature (**Fig. 5-1**). Accomplish this by—

- Entering on the steps, ramp or slope until thigh-deep and scooping water onto the arms, chest, neck and face.

Fig. 5-1

- Sitting on the edge of the pool and scooping water onto the body.

Relaxation

Many inexperienced swimmers feel afraid around the water and are often apprehensive about entering it. Relaxation is the key to mentally adjusting to an aquatic environment, and learning to control breathing helps people relax. Cold or nervous swimmers should practice breath control before entering the water.

Swimmers can practice breath control by—

- Breathing in and out slowly and deeply while sitting on the edge of the pool.
- Taking a deep breath, holding it for a couple of seconds then slowly exhaling.

Bobbing and Breath Control

Coordinated breath control is necessary to swim well. Holding the breath for a long time is not necessary, but it is important to be able to breathe in and out rhythmically and steadily while swimming. To practice breath control while in the water, try bobbing (**Fig. 5-2**).

Fig. 5-2

To bob–

1. Hold onto the overflow trough or the pool wall in chest-deep water.

2. Take a breath.

3. Bend the knees and fully submerge the head, then straighten the legs and resurface.

4. While coming back up, gently exhale through the mouth and nose.

5. Inhale when the mouth rises above the surface of the water.

6. Repeat this movement until comfortable.

7. Move to chin-deep water and practice bobbing away from the wall.

Entering the Water

There are several ways to enter the water. Some ways are safer than others are. The best method to use will depend on the body of water and the surroundings, the size and ability of the swimmer and the purpose for getting into the water. Beginning swimmers should only enter the water feetfirst. In most pools and some other swim areas, this can be done by sitting down, rolling on to the front and sliding into the water or by using a ladder, ramp or stairs (**Fig. 5-3**). Swimmers with certain types of disabilities may use a ramp, hoist or lift to enter a pool. At designated ocean beaches, swimmers should enter the water from shore and shuffle their feet to stir up marine life resting on the bottom to avoid stepping on anything that could cause harm as they make their way toward deeper water.

Staying Afloat

A big part of staying safe in the water is feeling confident. Confidence helps prevent panic and allows for clear thinking. Being able to float is a tremendous confidence builder. The ability to stay on the surface is also an important safety skill that is especially important for the beginner or nonswimmer. Anyone involved in an aquatic emergency can use any of the following floating techniques to stay on the surface until help arrives or to rest when tired.

Even though floating is an easy way for many people to stay near the surface, not everyone floats easily and no one naturally floats in the same position in the water. A number of factors and hydrodynamic principles affect how or if a person floats. Understanding and applying these principles makes learning to float easier. Floating also is made easier by physically and mentally adjusting to the water before entering and keeping the body relaxed. (See **Chapter 4** for more information on the hydrodynamic principles related to floating.)

Fig. 5-3

Back Float

The back, or supine, float is especially useful for survival. One of the main benefits of the back float is that the mouth stays above water throughout.

Learn to float on the back by letting the body rise to its natural floating position. Do not push off the bottom but let the feet move to the floating position that is comfortable–horizontal, diagonal or nearly vertical, (**Fig. 5-4, A–C**). Try to keep the lungs full of air because it will create extra buoyancy and make floating on the back easier.

To float on the back–

1. In chest-deep water, submerge to the neck.
2. Hold the arms overhead and slightly out to the side.
3. Lay the head back until the ears are in the water.
4. Arch the body gently at the hips, pushing the chest and stomach toward the surface.
5. Keep the legs relaxed, knees slightly bent and feet beneath the surface.
6. Breathe in and out through the mouth every few seconds.

Swimmers whose natural floating position is diagonal or nearly vertical may need to change position slightly. For these swimmers, floating in a more horizontal position may be possible by keeping the arms in the water and moving them above the head, flexing the wrists so the hands (or fingers) are out of the water and bending the knees. Swimmers having trouble floating motionlessly can use sculling or finning motions to help stay near the surface with little effort.

To recover to a standing position–

1. Take a breath, tuck the chin toward the chest and bring the knees forward by bending at the hips.
2. Sweep the arms back, down then forward in a circular motion to bring the body back to vertical, exhale and then stand up (**Fig. 5-5**).

This motion is like pulling up a chair to sit in.

Floating on the Front

There are several ways to float on the front. Like floating on the back, floating on the front is an important survival skill. Both the survival float and survival swimming involve floating on the front.

Fig. 5-4, A

Fig. 5-4, B

Fig. 5-4, C

Fig. 5-5

Jellyfish Float

The jellyfish float helps demonstrate buoyancy (**Fig. 5-6**).

1. In chest-deep water, submerge to the neck.
2. Take a deep breath and hold it.
3. Bend forward at the waist and put the head face down in the water.
4. Flex the knees slightly to raise the feet off the bottom.
5. Let the arms and legs hang naturally from the body.
6. Continue holding the breath and relax as much as possible.
7. Allow the back to rise to the surface of the water.
8. To recover, drop the feet, exhale slowly and stand up.

Tuck Float

The tuck, or turtle, float is similar to the jellyfish float. Sinking a few inches is possible before getting into the final position. If any sinking takes place, the shoulders will eventually rise slowly toward the surface until they are just above or below the surface of the water.

Use the tuck float to check buoyancy (**Fig. 5-7**).

1. In chest-deep water, submerge to the neck.
2. Take a deep breath and hold it.
3. Bend forward at the waist and put the head face down in the water with the chin on the chest.
4. Flex the hips and bring the knees to the chest.
5. Hold on to the legs at mid-calf.
6. Continue holding the breath and relax as much as possible.
7. Allow the body to rise to the surface.
8. To recover, let go of the legs, exhale slowly and stand up.

Front Float

The front, or prone, float helps beginning swimmers become more comfortable in a horizontal position. It is easier to learn this skill in water that is shallow enough to reach the bottom surface with the hands. However, it may be difficult for some swimmers to keep their toes off the bottom in this situation because the water is not deep enough for the body to rotate into its natural (diagonal or nearly vertical) floating position.

Fig. 5-6

Fig. 5-7

Learn the front float in shallow water.

1. Start by lying face down with the hands on the bottom surface.
2. Take a breath then put the face in the water until the ears are covered.
3. Slowly lift the hands off the bottom.
4. Relax and extend the arms in the water above the head.
5. Gently blow out some air through the nose to keep the nose from filling with water.
6. If the toes are still on the bottom, relax the legs and gently push up off the bottom to get the toes to rise.
7. To recover, exhale slowly, lift the head and press down with the arms, pull the knees under the body toward the chest and place the feet on the bottom then stand up.

Learn the front float in chest-deep water (**Fig. 5-8**).

1. Start by submerging to the neck in chest-deep water with the arms extended and the palms facing down.
2. Take a breath then lean forward and put the face in the water until the ears are covered.
3. Gently push off the bottom and let the feet and legs float to the surface.
4. Relax and extend the arms in the water above the head.
5. To keep the nose from filling with water, gently blow out some air through the nose.
6. If the toes are still on the bottom, relax the legs and gently push up off the bottom to get the toes to rise.

Fig. 5-8

7. To recover, exhale slowly, lift the head, press down with the arms, pull the knees under the body toward the chest and place the feet on the bottom to stand up.

Basic Movement in the Water

Basic movement in the water includes gliding, finning, sculling and treading water. Learning the skills gives swimmers the ability to move efficiently through the water. Finning and sculling are the basic skills necessary for creating movement or staying in position. Swimmers who are able to tread water can remain in place with their head above water. Gliding, finning, sculling and treading water are essential survival skills. Swimmers can use these skills to move through the water with direction and reach safety in an emergency.

Front Glide

Gliding involves moving through the water in a streamlined position. The position places the body in a narrow shape, which reduces form drag. To attain a streamlined position, swimmers extend the arms overhead, press them against the ears, and clasp the hands, then extend the legs and point the toes.

1. Begin in the front float position and push off the side or bottom with the feet to move forward in a streamlined position (front glide) (**Fig. 5-9**).
2. Glide until the momentum slows to swimming speed and then start swimming.

Back Glide

1. Begin in the back float position and push off the side or bottom with the feet to move forward in a streamlined position (**Fig. 5-10**).
2. Glide until the momentum slows to swimming speed and then start swimming.

Finning

Finning is a way to move through the water using a pushing motion with the arms. This technique can also be used to help stay at the surface of the water while floating on the back.

1. Move into a back float position with the head back and arms at the side. The hands are relaxed under the surface of the water with the palms facing the bottom of the pool.

Fig. 5-9

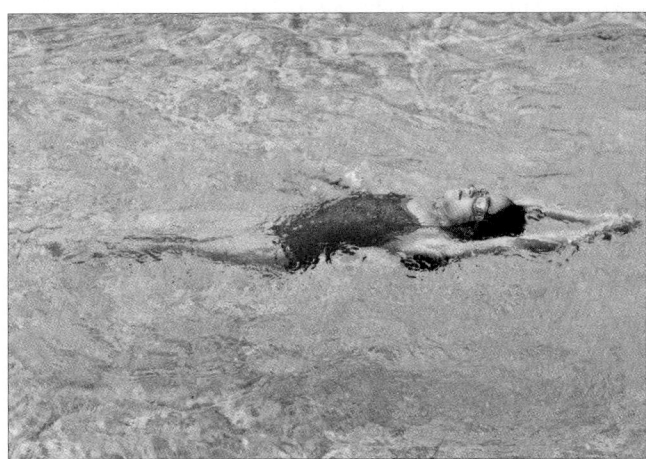

Fig. 5-10

2. Bend the elbows and slowly move the hands out from the side.
3. Flex the wrists and push the water with the palms toward the feet in a short stroke. Arm movements may be simultaneous or slightly alternating.

Sculling

Sculling refers to movements of the arms and hands that manipulate the flow of water. These movements create a force perpendicular to the direction of motion resulting in lift. The lift generated through sculling allows a person to move forward, backward or remain in place while floating or treading water. Sculling is an important skill for water survival. This technique can help a swimmer keep the mouth above water while resting or moving toward safety. Sculling is also a fundamental skill used in synchronized swimming.

To practice the sculling motion–

1. Hold the hands just below the surface while standing in waist-deep water.
2. Keep the palms flat, facing downward, and rapidly move them side to side to create whirlpools. While holding the elbows about a tennis ball's distance from the ribs, move the forearms out and then back in. Keep your upper arms still while the lower arms and hands maintain consistent water pressure.

During the sculling motion, the elbows gradually straighten as the arms move away from the body and then bend as they come back in. The forearm, wrist and hand must remain firm and work as a single unit. The entire movement resembles

pushing little piles of sand away from and back toward the body. Changing the pitch of the hands, moving the fingertips either up or down, helps achieve the desired direction of travel.

Standard Scull

The standard scull provides additional support while on the back using only minimal movement (**Fig. 5-11**).

To get into the sculling position on the back–

1. Move into a back float, lean the head back and place the arms at the side. Keep the hands flat and the fingers and wrists firm.

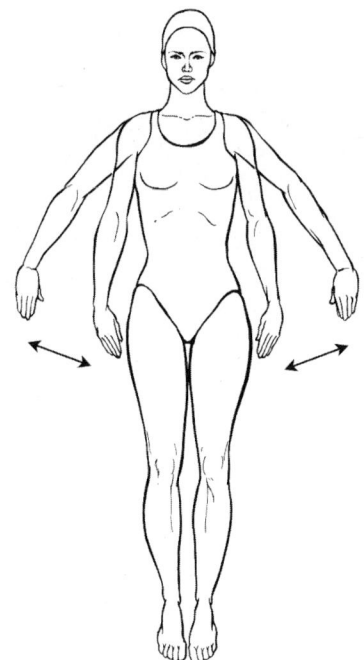

Fig. 5-11

The canoe scull is used to maintain a stationary position or move the swimmer forward. To perform the canoe scull, the swimmer begins in a streamlined position on the front. The swimmer presses down gently with the chest and presses up on the heels. These actions keep the heels, buttocks and head at the surface of the water. The face may be in or out of the water. While keeping the upper arms firm, the swimmer rotates the forearms so that the palms remain flat and facing downward, then presses the forearms away from the body. As the arms become nearly straight, the swimmer brings the forearms back toward the body, keeping the elbows wide. The hands always maintain pressure against the water. The hands should remain flat with all the fingers "glued" together.

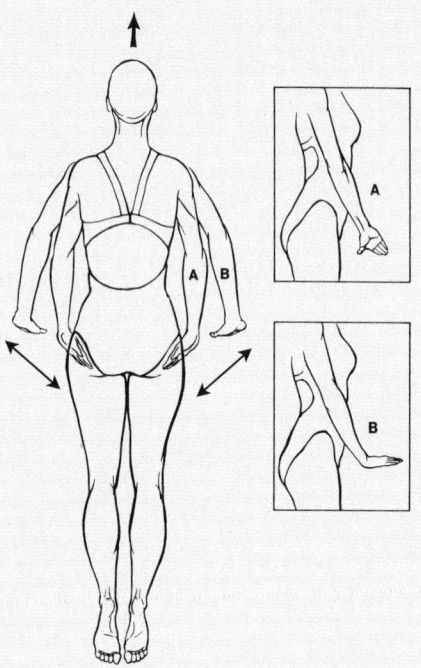

The movement of the arms and wrists should resemble that of moving a small pile of pebbles back and forth without loosing any material.

The torpedo scull is used to move a swimmer in a footfirst position. In a torpedo scull, the swimmer is in a streamlined position on the back and the face, hips, thighs and feet are at the surface. The arms are above the head. The hands are hyperextended at the wrists so that the palms are facing away from the body. When moving the forearm in the out-and-in motion, the heels of the hands should press away from each other on the way out and come to meet each other on the way in.

The support scull allows the swimmer to lift the legs out of the water and stay in a stationary, inverted position. It is an extremely important scull in synchronized swimming. Once in the inverted position, the swimmer brings the forearms and hands to waist level and perpendicular to the body. The hands should be flat and the palms facing the bottom of the pool. The motion is similar to that of the other sculls with constant water pressure from the palms of the hands through the forearms. Due to the inverted position, there will be more pressure on the forearms than in the other sculls. The elbows should remain about a tennis ball's width away from the side of the body and the range of motion in the forearm should remain wide, but never coming in so far as to have the fingertips touch. The wider the range of motion in the forearms, the more stable the scull. This same technique can be used to move the body footfirst while in a front floating position with the hands in the same position, palms facing toward the face.

2. Press the shoulders down and back so that the hips are at the surface. Bend the arms at the elbows so that the hands are beside the hips, keeping the point of the elbow away from the body.

3. Keep the palms flat, facing downward, while moving the forearms away from the body keeping the elbows wide.

4. Bend the elbows and move the arms back to the body so the hands are about 2 inches next to and slightly below the hips.

5. Continuously repeat Steps 3 and 4.

From this position, the headfirst and footfirst sculls are all possible.

Headfirst Scull

The headfirst scull can be used with the back float. The motion is similar to the standard scull, but the fingers are lifted towards the surface so the palms are flat and facing toward the feet. The force of the water is directed toward the feet, which moves the whole body in a headfirst direction. To perform a headfirst scull, make a continuous out-and-in sculling motion. During the sculling motion, keep the upper arms still and elbows wide while keeping the forearms slightly lower than the hips. Keep the toes, hips and head at the surface of the water.

Footfirst Scull

The footfirst scull also can be used with the back float. To perform a footfirst scull, start in the sculling position on the back, then flex the wrists so that the fingers point downward and the palms face toward the head. Make the continuous out-and-in sculling motion. During the sculling motion, keep the upper arms still and elbows wide while keeping the forearms slightly lower than the hips. Keep the toes, hips and head at the surface of the water.

Treading Water

Treading water is an important personal safety skill that allows swimmers to remain upright in deep water with the head out of the water. Treading water typically involves a scissors, breaststroke or rotary kick along with sculling or finning movements of the hands and arms. The combination of these movements allows swimmers to remain in place with the head above water. However, treading water is a versatile technique. With practice, people can tread water using only the arms or the legs. Whichever movements are used, treading water should be done using just enough movement to keep the body vertical.

To tread water with the scissors or breaststroke kick—

1. Stay nearly vertical, with the upper body bent slightly forward at the waist and the legs separated (**Fig. 5-12, A**).

2. Make continuous sculling movements with the hands a few inches below the surface in front of the body, with the palms facing downward and elbows bent. Make sculling movements with a much wider reach than used to hold position during a back float.

3. Kick with just enough thrust to keep the head above water (**Fig. 5-12, B**).

The rotary, or "eggbeater," kick is another effective kick for treading water. Because it has

Fig. 5-12, A

Fig. 5-12, B

Fig. 5-13, A

Fig. 5-13, B

no resting phase, this kick provides continuous support. This strong kick is also used in water polo, synchronized swimming and lifeguarding.

To tread water with the rotary kick—

1. Stay nearly vertical, with the upper body bent slightly forward at the waist, making the same sculling movements with the arms.

2. Keep the back straight and the hips flexed so that the thighs are comfortably forward (**Fig. 5-13, A**).

3. Pull up the lower legs so that they are at an angle of nearly 90 degrees to the thighs and the knees are slightly wider than hip-width apart.

4. Rotate the lower legs at the knees, one leg at a time, making large circular movements with the foot and lower leg. One leg moves clockwise and the other counterclockwise.

5. As each foot moves sideways and forward, extend it sharply outward (**Fig. 5-13, B**). The power of the kick comes from lift forces created by the inward sweeping action of the foot.

6. As one leg kicks, the other leg recovers to kick immediately after the first leg kick. Kick just hard enough to keep the head out of the water (**Fig. 5-14**).

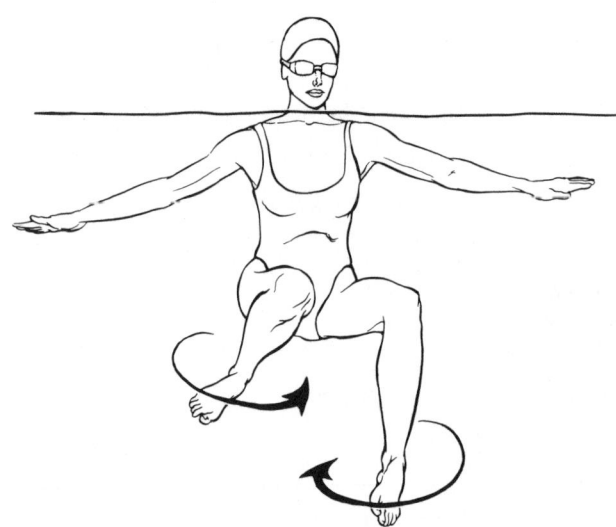

Fig. 5-14

Changing Directions, Turning Over and Starting

All beginning swimmers need to know how to change directions, turn over and how to start and resume swimming from a vertical position. All of these techniques help beginning swimmers learn new strokes and become more mobile in the water. While some of these skills might seem self-explanatory, they require practice and knowledge to master.

Changing Directions

The ability to change directions while swimming on the front or the back is an important safety skill because it allows swimmers to avoid unsafe situations.

When swimming on the front—

1. Reach an arm in the desired direction.
2. Look toward the desired direction and pull slightly wider with the opposite arm during the arm stroke.

When swimming on the back—

1. Tilt the head in the desired direction.
2. Make a stronger stroke with the opposite arm.

Turning Over

While swimming on the back keeps the mouth out of the water at all times, it is easier to see while swimming on the front. The ability to turn over is an important safety skill because it allows swimmers to switch between these two positions. It is also helpful to know how to turn over to change strokes or rest in a floating position. When turning over, the momentum from the stroke will help complete the turn.

To turn over while swimming on front—

1. Exhale slowly into the water.
2. Lower one shoulder and turn the head in the opposite direction.

○ To turn over counterclockwise, lower the left shoulder and turn the head to the right.

○ To turn over clockwise, lower the right shoulder and turn the head to the left.

3. Breathe normally and rest by floating on the back or continue swimming on the back.

To turn over while swimming on the back—

1. Take a breath.
2. Lower one shoulder and turn the head in the same direction.
3. Keep the arms underwater while turning, and reach across the body in the direction of the turn until positioned on the front.

Moving from a Vertical to a Horizontal Position

To move from a vertical to a horizontal position on the front—

1. Take a breath.
2. Lean forward and put the face in the water until the ears are covered.
3. Extend the arms in front and toward the intended direction.
4. Push off the bottom or kick the legs to help move into a horizontal position, then begin swimming.

To move from a vertical to a horizontal position on the back—

1. Move the arms overhead and slightly out to the side.
2. Lay the head back until the ears are in the water.
3. Arch the body gently at the hips, pushing the chest and stomach toward the surface.
4. Push off the bottom or kick the legs to help move into a horizontal position, then begin swimming.

Fig. 5-15, A

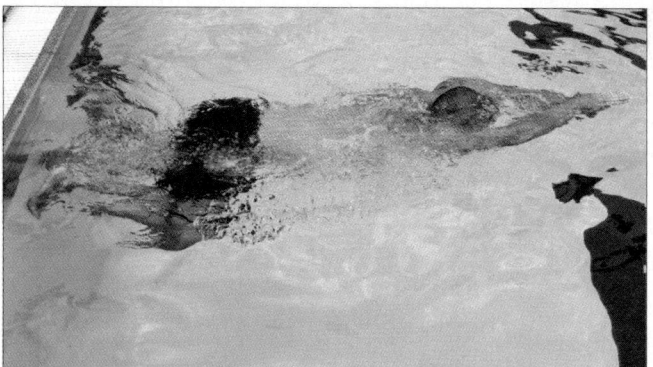

Fig. 5-15, B

Starting on the Front from the Pool Wall

To start face-down from the pool wall–

1. Grasp the overflow trough or the pool wall with one hand. Extend the other arm in front and toward the intended direction (**Fig. 5-15, A**).

2. Rotate the body and lean forward slightly so that the left shoulder and arm are under the surface, if holding on with the right hand. The right shoulder and arm are under the surface, if holding on with the left hand.

3. Place the feet against the pool wall and hold them hip-width apart. One foot will be higher, depending on which hand is holding onto the wall.

4. Take a breath and put the face in the water.

5. Let go of the wall, rotate the body into a face-down position. Extend the arms into a streamlined position (**Fig. 5-15, B**).

6. Push off the wall with both feet. Keep the legs together and the toes pointed. Glide until the momentum slows to swimming speed and then start swimming.

Starting on the Back from the Pool Wall

To start face-up from the pool wall–

1. Hold onto the overflow trough or the pool wall with both hands about shoulder-width apart.

2. Tuck the body and place the feet against the pool wall, just under the surface of the water and hold them hip-width apart. The knees should be inside the arms (**Fig. 5-16, A**).

3. Bend the arms slightly and put the chin on the chest and pull the body closer to the wall.

4. Take a breath then lean the head back into the water and arch the back slightly.

5. Let go of the wall, bring the hands close to the body and push off the wall while arching the back slightly.

   ○ Move into a streamlined position with arms over the head and glide to start the back crawl (**Fig. 5-16, B**). (See **Chapter 6** for details on the back crawl.)

   ○ Glide with the arms at the side to start the elementary backstroke. (See **Chapter 6** for details on the elementary backstroke.)

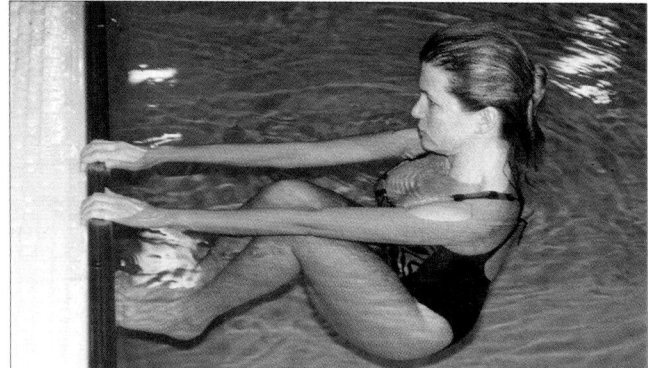

Fig. 5-16, A

Fig. 5-16, B

Starting on the Side

Use this start to begin swimming on the side from the pool wall.

1. Grasp the overflow trough or the pool wall with one hand.

2. Extend the other arm in front of the body and toward the intended direction but do not rotate the body.

3. Push off with both feet and place the hand used to hold the pool wall against the thigh.

4. Glide until the speed slows and then start the sidestroke. (See **Chapter 6** for details on the sidestroke.)

Underwater Skills

Surface Diving

Surface diving is a technique used to go under the water when swimming on the surface. It is the quickest and most effective way to go underwater. This skill can be used to retrieve objects from the bottom or in certain activities, such as skin diving.

There are two ways to perform a surface dive: feetfirst and headfirst. Additionally, in a headfirst surface dive, the body can either be in a tuck (curled) or pike (bent at the hips) position. The key to an effective surface dive is to raise part of the body above the surface so that the weight out of the water forces the body downward.

To avoid hitting an object when descending or coming back up, always keep the eyes open and arms above the head during a surface dive.

Exhaling through the nose while descending prevents water from entering the nose no matter which type of surface dive is used. Anyone who experiences ear pain, uncomfortable pressure during the descent or when swimming underwater should pinch the nostrils and gently attempt to blow air out through the nose. If this does not relieve the discomfort, swim to shallower water or to the surface to prevent damage to the ears.

Feetfirst Surface Dive

A feetfirst surface dive is the only safe way to go down into murky water or water of unknown depth.

1. Start by treading water and maintaining a vertical position.

2. Press down forcefully with both hands at the same time and bring them to the sides of the thighs while simultaneously performing a strong scissors or breaststroke kick. These movements help you rise in the water for a better descent (**Fig. 5-17, A**).

3. Take a breath at the top of this rise.

4. Keep the body vertical and in a streamlined position as you start moving downward.

5. Turn the palms outward then sweep the hands upward for more downward propulsion. This sweeping action should occur completely underwater (**Fig. 5-17, B**). More hand sweeps may be necessary to reach the desired depth.

6. Once downward motion slows down, tuck the body and roll into a horizontal position.

7. Extend the arms and legs and swim underwater.

Fig. 5-17, A

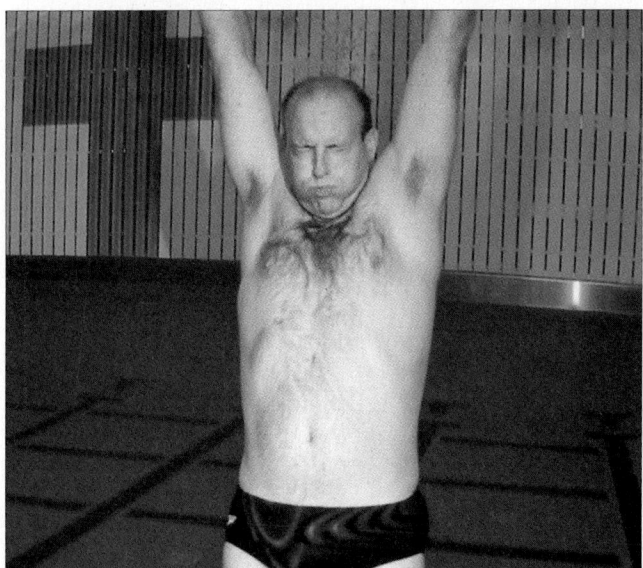

Fig. 5-17, B

Fig. 5-18, A

Fig. 5-18, B

Tuck Surface Dive

The tuck surface dive is a headfirst surface dive. If depth of the water is unknown or it is less than 8 feet, keep one arm extended over the head when moving toward the bottom.

1. Use a swimming stroke or glide to gain forward momentum.
2. Take a breath, sweep the arms backward to the thighs then turn the palms downward.
3. Tuck the chin to the chest, bend the body at a right angle at the hips and draw the legs into a tuck position.
4. Roll forward until almost upside down (**Fig. 5-18, A**).
5. Extend the legs upward quickly while pressing the arms and hands forward with the palms facing the bottom (**Fig. 5-18, B**).

6. Use a simultaneous breaststroke arm pull (see **Chapter 6**) for greater depth after the initial descent slows down.

Pike Surface Dive

The pike surface dive is similar to the tuck surface dive except that the legs are kept straight and the pike position is used. If depth of the water is unknown or it is less than 8 feet, keep one arm extended over the head when moving toward the bottom.

1. Use a swimming stroke or glide to gain forward momentum.
2. Take a breath, sweep the arms backward to the thighs and turn the palms downward.
3. Tuck the chin to the chest and flex at the hip sharply while the arms reach forward and downward toward the bottom (**Fig. 5-19, A**).

Fig. 5-19, A

Fig. 5-19, B

4. Lift the legs upward, straight and together, putting the body into a fully extended, streamlined and nearly vertical position (**Fig. 5-19, B**).

5. Allow the weight of the legs and forward momentum to cause descent.

Swimming Underwater
Safety Precautions

Swimming underwater is a way to recover lost objects, avoid surface hazards and explore the underwater world. This skill is easy to learn, but safety precautions must be followed to prevent injury. Keep at least one hand extended in front when descending and ascending and always swim with the eyes open (goggles should not be worn). Swimmers with contact lenses should remove them before opening the eyes underwater. These precautions help avoid obstructions and provide information about your surroundings. Never hyperventilate before swimming underwater. Hyperventilation is always dangerous but it is especially dangerous in an aquatic environment. Underwater activities that involve breath-holding should never be competitive or repetitive. Prolonged breath-holding while

WATER ORIENTATION AND LEARN-TO-SWIM EQUIPMENT

A swimsuit is not the only item people may need when they participate in water orientation and learn-to-swim programs. Learning to swim and getting used to the water also involves other devices that may ease beginners' fears, increase their comfort and help them become proficient in the water.

Here are some types of learn-to-swim equipment:

- Floating barbells and noodles are good for practicing swimming skills and fun for children. They are very popular in Learn-to-Swim classes with young children.

- Pool toys that float, such as rubber ducks or toy boats, can be used to help children adjust to the water and help make spending time in the water more enjoyable.

- Dive rings and other pool toys that sink can help children practice submerging or underwater swimming.

- Kickboards help support the upper body and make it easier to breathe while practicing kicking. People can use kickboards when learning to swim or learning to swim new strokes. More advanced swimmers use kickboards to improve their kicking efficiency as well.

- Pull buoys are commonly used in the upper levels of Learn-to-Swim. Participants hold the pull buoy between the thighs, knees or ankles to provide buoyancy so they can concentrate on their arm strokes.

- Life jackets have limited usefulness as teaching aids because their bulk reduces effectiveness in performing skills. Life jackets also can promote poor body position. However, anyone who spends time in, on or around the water needs to know how to enter the water and swim while wearing this important lifesaving device. The Red Cross strongly advocates that everyone, including parents, know how to choose, use, wear and swim in a properly fitted U.S. Coast Guard-approved life jacket.

With the exception of the life jacket, equipment used during water orientation and Learn-to-Swim programs is not personal flotation devices designed for safety. But they are useful tools that can help build the confidence of new swimmers as they learn new water skills.

Fig. 5-20

swimming underwater can cause even an accomplished swimmer to blackout underwater and possibly drown.

Underwater Strokes

Many different types of strokes and modified strokes are used to swim underwater. Although there is no one stroke that works best for all people in all situations, a modified breaststroke is probably the most commonly used stroke.

The breaststroke can be modified for underwater swimming in several ways, including–

- Using a breaststroke arm pull with a scissors or dolphin kick (**Fig. 5-20**).

- Extending the arm pull all the way back to the thighs. Another method is to use the arm pull and kick together followed by a glide with the arms at the sides. These methods help make the stroke longer and stronger when used underwater.

- Shortening the arm pull or not using it at all, if visibility is poor.

- Keeping the arms stretched out in front of the body to feel for obstacles.

To change direction or depth while swimming underwater, turn the head in the desired direction and reach the arms in that same direction then pull them back. Flexing or extending the hips also helps direct the body up or down.

CHAPTER 6
Stroke Mechanics

In the past, swimmers and their coaches used trial-and-error methods to improve their performances. Now, swimmers and coaches apply hydrodynamics to improve strokes. The science of stroke mechanics has led to new and more efficient ways to move through the water. Although new developments still occur, recent focus has been on improving the basic swimming strokes.

This chapter provides a detailed description of six basic strokes: front crawl, back crawl, breaststroke, butterfly, elementary backstroke and sidestroke. This chapter also briefly describes less commonly used strokes, including the trudgen, trudgen crawl, double trudgen, overarm sidestroke and inverted breaststroke. Each stroke is broken down into components that are simple enough for beginners to use in evaluating their own progress and provide enough detail to benefit experienced swimmers.

Basic Stroke Elements

One of the best ways to improve swimming is by focusing on how to propel the body through the water with little wasted effort. Whether swimming for recreation or competition, moving easily and efficiently through the water is the goal. In an aquatic emergency, efficiency helps people swim longer and farther. However, there is not one "perfect" way to swim. A number of factors, such as size, strength, body composition and flexibility, affect how each individual performs a stroke. This chapter focuses on the basic elements of each stroke, which swimmers can adjust to fit their individual characteristics. The better swimmers understand the components of the strokes, the better swimmers they will be.

Throughout this chapter, each stroke is explained in a clear, consistent approach that illustrates the following movements, aspects and phases of the stroke:

- Hydrodynamic principles involved in the stroke
- Body position, balance and motion
- Arm stroke
- Kick
- Breathing and timing

Front Crawl (Freestyle)

The front crawl, sometimes called freestyle, is the fastest stroke (**Fig. 6-1**). It is also one of the most popular strokes. When most people think swimming, the first stroke they think of is the front

Fig. 6-1

EVOLUTION OF THE FRONT CRAWL

John Trudgen developed a hand-over-hand stroke that became known as the trudgen. He copied the stroke from South American Indians and introduced it in England in 1873. Each arm recovered out of the water as the body rolled from side to side. The swimmer did a scissors kick with every two arm strokes. This stroke was the forerunner of the front crawl. The inefficiency of the trudgen kick led Australian Richard Cavill to try new methods of kicking. He used a stroke that he observed natives of the Solomon Islands using, which combined

an up-and-down kick with an alternating overarm stroke. He used the new stroke in 1902 at the International Championships to set a new world record (100 yards in 58.4 seconds). The stroke he used became known as the "Australian crawl."

The Australian men's swimming team introduced a front crawl stroke that took advantage of body roll at the 1956 Olympic Games in Melbourne. This roll increased speed through the water and soon became common.

crawl. Likewise, most people who start learning to swim expect to learn it first—and fast! Like all strokes, the front crawl has three characteristics:

- The goal is efficiency of motion.
- The stroke depends on principles of hydrodynamics.
- Stroke components, such as body position, arm and leg action, breathing and timing, are critical for success.

Hydrodynamic Principles

Almost all the hydrodynamic principles discussed in **Chapter 4** are involved in the front crawl. Body position is the foundation for the stroke. The position of the head and the kick determine body position in the water. The front crawl, like other strokes, is a "feel stroke" in that the more the swimmer "feels" the arms and legs pushing the water backward, the better he or she swims forward. The focus of stroke mechanics is on sweeping arm motions that drive forward upon entry and then apply force backward during the underwater arm motion.

It is also important to keep the body aligned in this stroke. Good body alignment makes these strokes more efficient. Any sideways movement away from the body increases the resistance of the water against the body. Holding the head too high has a similar effect. In either case, a swimmer expends excess energy to make up for poor body position rather than using it to propel forward.

Body Position, Balance and Motion

The body position of the front crawl is prone (face-down), horizontal and streamlined. Effective body position begins with the head. Swimmers should get into a face-down position and submerge the head to the ears. They should look down toward the bottom of the pool with the head in a relaxed position just as when standing up straight. The back of the neck remains flat and the water line is at the middle of the top of the head (**Fig. 6-2**). The head should not be pushed forward.

Head movement also is critical—where the head goes, the body follows. Any unnecessary movement requires extra energy to move forward. If the head moves from side-to-side, the body will move side-to-side. If the head bobs up and down, the hips will do the same. Keeping the head facing down and relaxed helps keep the hips and legs at the surface and allows for efficient swimming.

Fig. 6-2

Body roll is necessary to support the propulsion generated by the arms and legs. Body roll is a rotating movement around the midline of the body, an imaginary line from head to feet that divides the body equally into left and right parts.

During body roll, the whole body rotates as a unit, not just the shoulders, to each side about 30 degrees from the surface of the water (**Fig. 6-3**). At the point of maximum rotation, the shoulder stays next to the cheek and the body remains facing more toward the bottom than to the side. If the shoulder rotates below the cheek and in front of the chin, the arm stroke will be less effective. Likewise, if the hips rotate too far, the kick is likely to pause and falter.

Body roll is very important to several aspects of the front crawl. First, it allows for a dynamic reach

Fig. 6-3

forward with the arms upon entry. When the arm drives forward during the entry, body roll helps maintain the body's forward movement. Second, body roll improves arm propulsion. For example, a person standing on the ground and pulling a rope with outstretched arms generates more force by rotating the hips. The same is true during the arm stroke. A swimmer can generate more force with each arm if the body rolls during each arm stroke. Body roll also allows for a relaxed arm recovery with a bent elbow.

The legs also affect body position. Poor body position can cause a poor kick, and a poor kick can cause poor body position. In an effective kick, the heels just break the surface of the water and the legs roll with the rest of the body.

Arm Stroke

Power Phase

The power phase of the arm stroke consists of the catch, mid-pull and finish. The power phase begins by placing the hand into the water in front of the shoulder.

- Slide the fingers into the water first with the palm pitched slightly outward.
- Keep the elbow partly flexed so that the point of entry is about three-fourths as far as the arm could reach if straight.
- Allow the hand to enter the water smoothly, keeping the elbow higher than the rest of the arm. The elbow enters the water last (**Fig. 6-4**).

Think of this part of the stroke as the forearm going through a hole that the hand makes in the water's surface. The hands should be relaxed with the fingertips straight. The catch is where

Fig. 6-4

the power starts. This part of the arm stroke is called the catch because it feels like grabbing a semi-solid mass of water (**Fig. 6-5, A**). Extend the arm forward in front of the shoulder. Bend the elbow so that the palm and forearm face toward the feet and press backward, fingertips pointing down (**Fig. 6-5, B**). Allow the elbow and hand to move naturally, just outside the shoulders, as the arm travels backward. The elbow remains higher than the hand throughout the pull.

The body starts to rotate along the midline as soon as the catch position is established. When the hand is pitched effectively and the body is allowed to roll, the catch seems to lead the body forward automatically. There will be tension in the wrist and pressure on the palm and forearm.

During the mid-pull, continue pressing the palm and forearm directly backward. The hand follows a path straight backward that traces the side of the body. Keep the elbow slightly wider than the hand so the elbow can remain bent and the palm and forearm facing back.

During the catch and mid-pull, push the water backward and propel the body forward using the entire arm. As the arm moves water backward, the body rotates so that the opposite hip moves toward the bottom surface. The hand never crosses the midline of the body.

In the finish of the stroke, the hand remains facing back for as long as possible and then moves upward as the arm extends (**Fig. 6-5, C and D**). Extend the wrist (bend it back) to keep the palm pressing toward the feet while the fingertips remain pointed toward the bottom until the arm is nearly extended. At the end of the stroke, the arm reaches full extension. Accelerate the hand from the catch to the finish so that it is moving fastest at the end of the stroke. Completing the body rotation along the midline allows the arm to exit the water without obstruction.

Recovery

The recovery is not propulsive; it is simply a movement that puts the hand back in position for the next power phase. The most important point of the recovery is to keep the arm, hands and fingers relaxed. While the arm recovers to the starting position, the muscles can rest. If the arm, hand and fingers cannot relax, they will tire more quickly and the recovery will be stiff and mechanical.

Fig. 6-5, A

Fig. 6-5, B

Fig. 6-5, C

Fig. 6-5, D

Make a smooth transition from the finish of the power phase to the beginning of the recovery. Lift the elbow so that it is the first part of the arm to exit out of the water. As you lift the elbow, keep the arm relaxed with the forearm hanging down (**Fig. 6-6, A**). The elbow should be the highest part of the arm throughout the recovery, but not so high as to create stress on the shoulder. Swing the arm around the side of the body in a relaxed motion, keeping the hand wider than the elbow. As the hand passes the shoulder, let it lead the rest of the arm until it enters the water (**Fig. 6-6, B**). Allow the body to rotate throughout the recovery motion.

Fig. 6-6, A

Fig. 6-6, B

Fig. 6-7, A

Fig. 6-7, B

For many recreational swimmers, the arms are always in opposition. That is, one is back, the other forward. For competitive swimmers, however, the recovering arm can almost catch up with the pulling arm.

Kick

More propulsion is generated from the arms than from the kick (called a flutter kick), but the kick is still an important part of this stroke. In fact, proper stroke mechanics would be impossible without a good kick.

The flutter kick is most effective when the feet stay relaxed and "floppy." This is why good ankle position is essential in this kick. If the ankles remain loose and relaxed, the kick will still be moderately effective even if other aspects of the kick need work.

The kicking motion begins with the hips. The thigh starts to move downward even while the calf and foot are still moving upward. This motion continues through the whole leg and the feet follow through. For most of the downbeat (the downward motion of the leg), the knee remains slightly flexed (**Fig. 6-7, A**). The propulsion occurs when the leg straightens. Snapping the foot downward (as though kicking a ball) completes the motion (**Fig. 6-7, B**).

The upbeat begins by raising the leg straight toward the surface with little or no bend in the knee, until the heel just breaks the surface. Make sure to extend the leg completely before moving

the thigh upward during the upbeat. The leg stays straight in the upbeat. The size of the flutter kick— the distance the leg moves up and down—will vary with body type and flexibility.

The kicking action continues throughout the rotation of the body. Swimmers can use different cadences or "beats" for their kick. The cadence is the number of kicks in an arm cycle. An arm cycle is the time it takes for one hand to enter the water and begin the pull until it returns to that position. Cadences are typically either a 2-beat kick or a 6-beat kick. Each of these cadences is used at different times and at different speeds. Most swimmers use a 6-beat kick for shorter distances, a 2-beat kick for longer distances.

Breathing and Timing

Swimmers may either breathe during each arm cycle (e.g., each time their right arm recovers) or every 1½ arm cycles (alternating the side on which they breathe). Both methods are acceptable, although most people learn this stroke by breathing every cycle. Breathing on alternating sides helps promote a balanced technique between the right and left arm strokes. Whichever technique is used, swimmers should coordinate breathing so that there is no pause in the stroke to take a breath. It is not necessary to inhale a large amount of air with each breath because the next opportunity to take a breath is coming soon.

The position and motion of the head are the keys to breathing and timing. Proper head motion for breathing lets the head remain low in the water, which helps maintain good body position. Start by turning the head toward the recovery arm as it exits the water. Look to the side, keeping the face horizontal and the water line at the top of the head. One ear stays in the water. The head turn should not make the body twist or rotate more to one side than the other. Inhale when body roll is at its maximum and the recovery elbow is high. In this way, you breathe in the trough made by the head as it moves through the water (**Fig. 6-8**). After inhaling, return the face to the water in a quick motion before the recovery arm reenters the water. Exhale slowly underwater through the mouth and nose between breaths.

Fig. 6-8

TRUDGEN, TRUDGEN CRAWL AND DOUBLE TRUDGEN

The trudgen family of strokes uses a shortened scissors kick by itself or combined with a flutter kick along with the breathing and arm pull of the front crawl. In this scissors kick, the knees do not recover as far as in the sidestroke. An alternative is a wider flutter kick, which also produces a greater body roll. The table below presents the details of the three strokes.

	Trudgen	Trudgen Crawl	Double Trudgen
Body Position	Prone; accentuated roll to breathing side	Same as trudgen	Prone; greater body roll away from the breathing side to accommodate second kick
Kick	Scissors kick during final phase of arm stroke on breathing side; legs trail between kicks	Same as trudgen, with the addition of two or three flutter kicks between scissors kicks	Two scissors kicks for each arm cycle
Arm Stroke	Similar to front crawl (more body roll to breathing side)	Same as trudgen	Catch-up stroke: Each arm does a complete stroke and recovery before opposite arm strokes
Breathing and Timing	Leg on breathing side kicks as arm on breathing side finishes power phase; inhalation at start of arm recovery	Same as trudgen	Same as trudgen; may breathe to alternate sides

Back Crawl (Backstroke)

Introduced in 1902, the back crawl developed from the inverted breaststroke and the trudgen. The back crawl is one of the four competitive strokes and it is the fastest stroke on the back (**Fig. 6-9**). For this reason, it is often called the backstroke. The back crawl is popular in recreational swimming, primarily for exercise.

Hydrodynamic Principles

The back crawl is similar to the front crawl. In the back crawl, both the arms and legs provide propulsive forces. The focus of stroke mechanics is on making the most of propulsive movements while maintaining efficient body position. Good body alignment is also important for an efficient stroke. As in the front crawl, any side-to-side movement of the body increases the resistance of the water against the body as does holding the head too high.

Body Position, Balance and Motion

The body position of this stroke is face-up (supine), streamlined and horizontal. As in the front crawl, body rotation along the midline is important. The body should only rotate to each side about 30 degrees from the surface of the water. This allows the arms to achieve the strongest catch position at the optimal depth.

Throughout the stroke, the head remains still and aligned with the spine. Because the face is out of the water, it is not necessary to roll the head to breathe. For most swimmers, the water line runs from the middle of the top of the head to the tip of the chin, with the ears underwater. The most efficient head position is tilted very slightly toward the feet. The back is slightly rounded so that the legs are horizontal and the upper body is relaxed, but sitting up a small amount. The hips and legs are just below the surface of the water. During the kick, the feet churn the surface of the water.

Arm Stroke

The arms move continuously in constant opposition to each other, one arm recovers while the other arm pulls (**Fig. 6-10**). Except for differences of speed between the power phase and the recovery, each arm is always opposite the other arm.

Fig. 6-9

EVOLUTION OF THE BACKSTROKE

Before 1900, swimming on the back was not used in competition. Because the breaststroke was still the stroke of choice, the recreational backstroke was done like an upside-down breaststroke. As the front crawl became popular, swimmers tried the alternating overarm style on the back. Combined with a flutter kick, this created a fast and efficient way to swim on the back. In 1912, the backstroke became a competitive event. The continued effort to gain greater speed, along with studying and experimenting with the stroke, led to the back crawl as we know it today.

Fig. 6-10

Power Phase

With the arm straight, one hand enters the water above the head, just outside the shoulder, little finger first. The palm faces out and the wrist is bent slightly (**Fig. 6-11, A**). The hands should be relaxed with the fingers straight. The body should stay streamlined and the head steady throughout the stroke.

The propulsive action starts with the catch (**Fig. 6-11, B**). The entry hand slices downward 8 to 12 inches and at an angle slightly outward to the catch position. The best catch position is similar to front crawl, in that the palm and forearm face toward the feet to push water backward most efficiently. After the arm enters the water, bend the elbow so that the fingertips are pointing away from the body to the side of the pool. The arm stays to the side of the body and the hand and forearm are horizontal once the catch position is achieved. Be careful not to let the arm bend behind the back. This is a weak position that can make the shoulder vulnerable to injury.

After the catch, keep the palm and forearm facing toward the feet while pushing water back (**Fig. 6-11, C**). The hand follows a straight path toward the feet while the fingertips continue pointing to the side. Try to minimize the up-and-down movement of the arm to achieve the optimal pull.

For the finish of the power phase, the hand speeds up as it follows through towards the feet, with the wrist extended and the palm pitched slightly downward. The arm is straight and the hand is below the thigh. It is important to maintain pressure on the water through the finish. A strong finish helps the body rotate. The power phase ends with the arm straight and the hand below the hips (**Fig. 6-11, D**).

Fig. 6-11, A

Fig. 6-11, B

Fig. 6-11, C

Fig. 6-11, D

Fig. 6-12, A

Fig. 6-12, B

Fig. 6-12, C

Recovery

Start the recovery by lifting the arm from the water, hand first with the palm facing inward (**Fig. 6-12, A**). Relax the wrist so that the thumb leaves the water first. This arm position allows the large muscles on the back of the upper arm to relax. In the recovery, the arm moves almost perpendicular to the water (**Fig. 6-12, B**). Body roll helps make this easier. Keep the arms to the side of the head. Keep the arm straight but relaxed in the recovery. Midway through the recovery, rotate the hand so that the little finger enters the water first (**Fig. 6-12, C**).

Kick

The back crawl kick is similar to the flutter kick used in the front crawl. The kicking motion is a continuous, up-and-down movement that begins in the hips. Most of the propulsive force comes from the upward kick. Start the upbeat by bending the knee and whipping the foot upward until the leg is straight and the toes reach the surface, like kicking a ball. Keep the leg nearly straight in the downbeat. At the end of the downward motion, bend the knee and start the upward kick. The thighs pass each other and the knees stay relaxed (**Fig. 6-13, A and B**). Throughout the kick, keep the ankles loose and floppy. The kick is very important for body position because it helps maintain stability as the body rolls.

The depth of the kick depends on the length of the legs, the hip and ankle flexibility and the pace of the stroke. A kick that is too deep will create greater form drag and cancel out any added propulsion. The back crawl kick is continuous. Although most swimmers use a 6-beat kick

Fig. 6-13, A

Fig. 6-13, B

for each full arm cycle, the beat depends on the individual.

Breathing and Timing

Use a regular breathing pattern during each stroke. Inhale when one arm recovers and exhale when the other arm recovers.

The timing of the body roll is crucial in back crawl. The body rolls toward the recovery arm just before that hand enters the water. Complete the body roll before reaching the catch position. Do not rotate in the middle of the power phase of the arm stroke.

Breaststroke

The breaststroke is the oldest known swimming stroke and for many centuries, people thought the breaststroke was the best stroke to teach beginners (**Fig. 6-14**). With slight variations, the head can be kept up throughout the stroke, which makes vision and breathing easy. By adding an extended glide, swimmers can rest briefly between strokes making this a good stroke to use for survival swimming. Very popular with recreational swimmers, the breaststroke is also the oldest known swimming stroke used in organized competition.

Hydrodynamic Principles

Body alignment is important for all strokes, although this is more difficult to achieve with strokes that involve alternating movements, like the front and back crawls. It is easier to keep the body aligned with strokes that utilize symmetrical movements (breaststroke, elementary backstroke and butterfly), because the propulsive forces involved are naturally balanced. These forces are balanced because the arm and leg actions on both sides of the body are performed together, thus counteracting the forces that would push the body out of line.

Because of the glide involved, the law of inertia is an important part of this stroke. If the swimmer glides for too long, it will require more energy to resume stroking. If the swimmer begins stroking too soon, the propulsion of the previous arm and leg action will be reduced.

To achieve optimal efficiency, swimmers must find a balance between the propulsive forces involved in the arm and leg actions and the effect they have on the glide.

Body Position, Balance and Motion

The body position in this stroke is face-down and streamlined during the glide. In the glide,

Fig. 6-14

Fig. 6-15, A

Fig. 6-15, B

Fig. 6-15, C

extend the arms to the front with the palms face-down and below the surface. The head position is between the arms and just below the surface. The back stays straight and the body is nearly horizontal. The arms and legs move in the same motion, at the same time on each side of the body.

Arm Stroke

Power Phase

Throughout the power phase, the elbows are higher than the hands and lower than the shoulders. Elbow position is important for good propulsion. The hands should be relaxed with the fingers straight. Start the catch in the glide position, turning the palms outward about 45 degrees to the surface of the water (**Fig. 6-15, A**). With the arms slightly bent, press the palms outward until the hands are spread wider than the shoulders. Imagine a clock with the head at 12:00 and the feet at 6:00; the hands should be at about the 11:00 and 1:00 positions.

During the mid-pull, bend the elbows and sweep the hands downward and inward (**Fig. 6-15, B**). Keep the elbows near the surface. Allow the hands to pass under the elbows with the forearms in a nearly vertical position. Sweep the hands inward and upward until the hands are in front of the chest. The hands should be pitched slightly upward and almost touching each other (**Fig. 6-15, C**). Continue to bend the elbows more while squeezing them to the side of the body.

Recovery

The arm recovery is a continuous motion from the end of the power phase. After sweeping the hands together in front of the chest, squeeze the elbows close together and push forward with the elbows so that the hands start moving forward, rounding out the power phase. Angle the palms slightly upward. Continue to extend the arms forward while rotating the wrists until the palms are facing

Fig. 6-16, A

Fig. 6-16, B

Fig. 6-16, C

Fig. 6-16, D

down and below the surface at full extension in the glide position.

Kick

The breaststroke kick starts from the glide position. Recover by bringing the heels toward the buttocks as much as possible without upsetting body position and allowing the knees to drop toward the bottom of the pool (**Fig. 6-16, A**). As the legs recover, gradually separate the knees and heels until the knees are about hip-width apart and the feet are outside the knees. Keep the heels just under the surface. At the end of the recovery, flex the ankles and rotate the feet so that the toes point outward (**Fig. 6-16, B**). With a continuous pushing action, forcefully press the feet and knees backward until the legs are extended, toes pointed and the feet and ankles touch, and then hold the legs in a straight line (**Fig. 6-16, C and D**).

The pressing action generates backward thrust. Propulsion results from the reactive pressure of the water against the insides of the feet and lower legs.

Breathing and Timing

As the arms and hands start to pull backward, the head and upper body lift naturally for a breath. As the arms recover, lean forward with the upper body and head to drive forward into the water.

Fig. 6-17, A

Fig. 6-17, B

Fig. 6-17, C

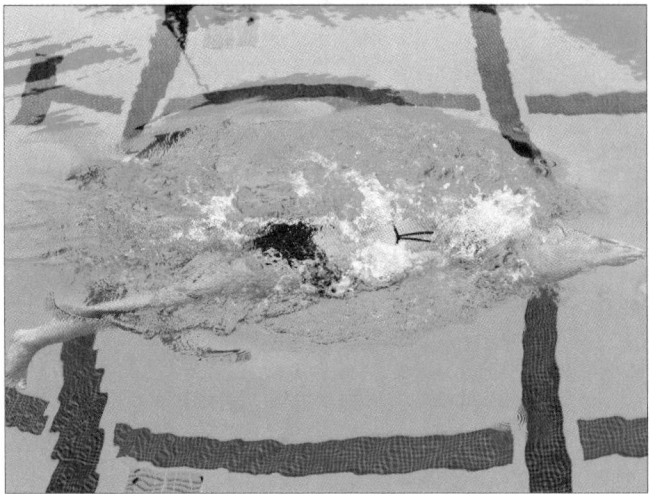

Fig. 6-17, D

Exhale in a slow, steady manner until just before the next breath. Breathe during each arm stroke. In competition, glide only briefly and start the next stroke before losing forward momentum.

Remember the timing of this stroke with the phrase, "Pull and breathe, kick and glide." From the glide position, start the power phase with the arms (**Fig. 6-17, A**). Near the end of the arm pull, take a breath and start to bend the legs to prepare for the kick (**Fig. 6-17, B**). Without pause, start to recover the arms and drive forward with the upper body. Start the power phase of the kick by pressing backward with the feet as soon as the arms reach full extension, just before the head lowers into a position between the arms (**Fig. 6-17, C**). The upper body and arms will be in the glide position just before the kick ends (**Fig. 6-17, D**).

Butterfly

Many people think of the butterfly as a difficult stroke that is useful only for competition. As a result, many swimmers, even those who are good at other strokes, do not try to learn it. However, even beginning swimmers can learn the butterfly by practicing timing and technique (**Fig. 6-18**). The key to this stroke is to stay relaxed and use the whole body in a flowing forward motion. The time and effort spent learning this stroke is well spent— swimming the butterfly offers a rewarding feeling of power and grace.

Hydrodynamic Principles

The power of each stroke maintains body speed throughout all phases of the stroke. To perform the butterfly effectively, the movements of the torso, hips and legs must be in harmony with each

Fig. 6-18

other while also working with the arms to achieve forward progress. If the swimmer does not use this combined movement well, the stroke becomes awkward or does not work at all.

Body Position, Balance and Motion

The body position of the butterfly is face-down. In this position, the upper body drives off the hips to surge the body forward. The leg and body motions of the butterfly create the feeling of the whole body surging forward. The legs stabilize the hips so that the upper body and arms can do their job in the stroke. The kick, breath and pull are very closely related. For this reason, the full explanation of body motion is described during

the breathing and timing section, after the pull and kick have already been described.

Arm Stroke
Power Phase

The power phase of the butterfly arm stroke consists of the catch, mid-pull and finish. The arms pull simultaneously with the objective of pushing water backward. Because the arms are moving together, the catch starts wider than in the front crawl. The hands come closer together as the arm stroke progresses (**Fig. 6-19**).

EVOLUTION OF THE BUTTERFLY

The simultaneous overarm recovery out of the water and first form of the dolphin kick were developed at the University of Iowa during the 1930s. University of Iowa swimmer Jack Sieg swam 100 yards using these initial forms of what is now known as the butterfly in 1:00.2. However, the butterfly breaststroke, as it was called, was declared a violation of competitive rules. In the 1950s, the butterfly stroke with the dolphin kick was finally legalized and has been a mainstay of competitive swimming ever since.

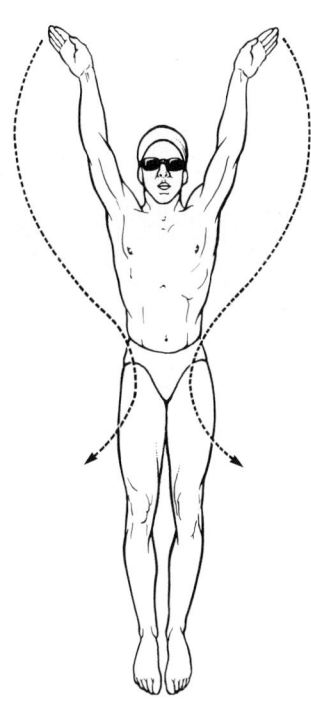

Fig. 6-19

Fig. 6-20, A

Fig. 6-20, B

Fig. 6-20, C

Fig. 6-20, D

Fig. 6-20, E

The catch starts with the arms extended in front of the shoulders (**Fig. 6-20, A**). The elbows begin to bend so that the palms and forearms start facing the feet. The elbows must remain high and fingertips pointing down and slightly

outward. To do that, the elbow and hand must move wider than the shoulder, with the hands making a circular path (**Fig. 6-20, B**). The hands should be relaxed with the fingers straight. Flex the wrists so as to not let the palms face outward too much. The wide catch helps lift the body and prepare the upper body for the breath and the next stroke. The catch ends with the elbows to the side of the shoulders and slightly in front of the body. At this point, the hands are directly below the elbows with the fingers pointing down.

The next part of the arm stroke is the mid-pull. In the mid-pull, continue pressing backward with the palms and forearms. The hands move from the wide position at the end of the catch to a point at the waist that is just inside the width of the body (**Fig. 6-20, C**). Achieve this by facing the palms and forearms directly backward. The arms extend toward the feet throughout the mid-pull and the hands come closer to the body as a result. As the hands sweep together, keep the elbows higher than the hands.

The last part of the power phase is the finish (**Fig. 6-20, D**). During the finish, continue pressing the hands back past the hips (**Fig. 6-20, E**). Sweep the hands outward into the recovery. As in the front crawl, the arms accelerate throughout the arm stroke so that the arms are moving the fastest at the end of the stroke.

Recovery

The recovery takes more effort than in the front crawl, but relaxing the arms is still important. Unlike the front crawl, there is no body roll to help and the arms do not bend as much. To make the recovery easier, accelerate hard through the finish of the stroke and then lower the head as the arms recover.

The recovery starts as the hands finish their press toward the feet. Begin the recovery by sweeping the hands toward the side. During the sweep, the elbows bend slightly and come out of the water first (**Fig. 6-21, A**). Then swing the arms wide to the sides with little or no bend in the elbows, making sure to lead this motion with the hands (**Fig. 6-21, B**). Move the arms just above the surface to enter the water in front of the shoulders (**Fig. 6-21, C**). Keep the wrists relaxed and the thumbs down through the recovery.

The recovery ends when the hands enter the water. The hands enter the water with the thumbs facing down and the elbows remaining slightly flexed in front of or slightly outside of the shoulders. After the entry, extend the elbows to prepare for the next arm stroke and pitch the hands down and slightly outward for the catch.

Kick

The kick used in the butterfly is called the dolphin kick. The power of this kick comes

Fig. 6-21, A

Fig. 6-21, B

Fig. 6-21, C

from the same dynamics as the flutter kick. The leg action is the same as in the front and back crawl except that the legs stay together. The kicking motion begins in the upper abdominals, hips and thighs and makes the same whiplike motion as the front crawl. Most of the power comes from this quick extension of the legs. Bend the knees to start the downbeat. Extend the legs during the downbeat and keep them straight on the upbeat (**Fig. 6-22, A–C**). Keep the ankles relaxed during the upbeat. The heels should just break the surface at the end of the recovery.

Fig. 6-22, A

Although there appears to be a lot of up-and-down movement, the hips should only rise above and return just below the surface during this stroke. As explained in the next section, the most effective dolphin kick involves the whole body, not just the legs.

Breathing and Timing

The butterfly uses two kicks of equal size at specific moments in each arm stroke. The timing of these movements is critical. With good timing, this stroke is graceful. With poor timing, the stroke is awkward and very difficult.

Fig. 6-22, B

The timing of the butterfly depends on the relationship of the kicks to the entry and finish of the arm stroke. During the arm recovery, bend the knees to prepare for the first kick. As the hands enter the water, press downward with the chin and the chest and extend the legs for the downbeat of the first kick (**Fig. 6-23, A**). Because the upper body angles slightly downward at this point, it appears to bend or "pivot" at the waist. Throughout the catch and the mid-pull, the upper body rises toward the surface while the knees bend to prepare for the second kick (**Fig. 6-23, B**).

Fig. 6-22, C

The downbeat of the second kick starts during the mid-pull (**Fig. 6-23, C**). End the second kick just as the pull finishes and just prior to the hands exiting into the recovery. The upper body rises throughout the arm pull, reaching its highest point at the finish of the arm stroke and the end of the second kick. Exhale fully during the underwater pull as the body is rising up (**Fig. 6-23, D**).

Fig. 6-23, A

Fig. 6-23, B

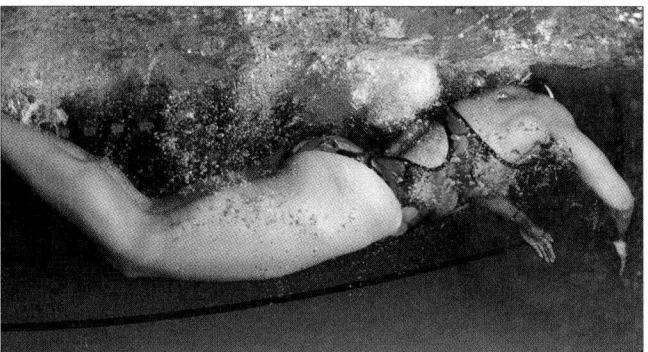

Fig. 6-23, C

Fig. 6-23, D

Fig. 6-23, E

Fig. 6-23, F

Inhale just as the arms begin the recovery. Be careful not to lift the head up too much otherwise the hips will sink. Thrust the chin forward (not upward) just as the face clears the water (**Fig. 6-23, E**). Some swimmers learn to breathe every two or more strokes to gain efficiency. Start the arm recovery by pressing down with the chin and chest to return the face underwater (**Fig. 6-23, F**).

Learn to use a pivoting movement around the hips. In the downbeat of the first kick, the hips go up and stabilize, while the upper body goes deeper. As the upper body comes up during the mid-pull phase, the hips drop and the legs recover. As the second kick finishes, the hips go up again while the upper body is at its high point along the

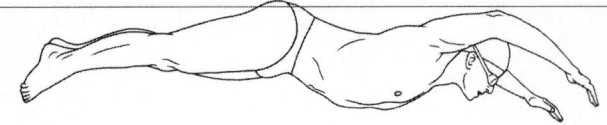

Fig. 6-24, A

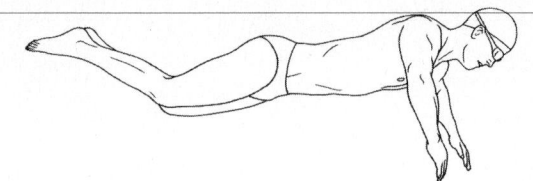

Fig. 6-24, B

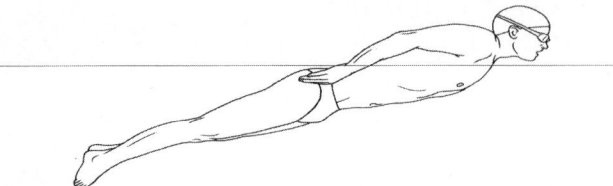

Fig. 6-24, C

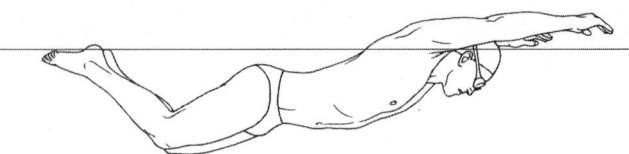

Fig. 6-24, D

surface of the water during the arm recovery (**Fig. 6-24, A–D**).

Elementary Backstroke

The elementary backstroke is used for recreation, survival swimming and exercising muscle groups not used in other strokes (**Fig. 6-25**). Breathing is easy because the face stays out of the water. Swimmers can use this stroke to rest while still making slow but effective progress through the water. Because the head stays above the water and this stroke is less strenuous than other strokes, the elementary backstroke is very

useful in some survival swimming situations. Some lifesaving techniques use the elementary backstroke kick.

Hydrodynamic Principles

The most obvious hydrodynamic principle involved in this stroke is the way the arms function as levers in the power phase. Because this stroke involves a glide, the law of inertia is also a large factor in this stroke. The muscles used to rotate the arm at the shoulder use action–reaction propulsion to overcome the resistance of the arms and hands and drive the body forward.

Fig. 6-25

Fig. 6-26

Fig. 6-27, A

Fig. 6-27, B

Fig. 6-27, C

The movement of the knees and the position of the ankles also create leverage that is used for forward propulsion.

Body Position, Balance and Motion

This stroke uses symmetrical and simultaneous movements of the arms and legs. In the glide, the body is in a horizontal, streamlined position on the back (**Fig. 6-26**). Most swimmers keep their head submerged only to the ears with the face out of the water at all times. The arms extend along the body with palms against the thighs, and the legs fully extended and together. The hips stay near the surface throughout the stroke.

Arm Stroke

Recovery

Move the arms continuously and smoothly from the start of the recovery to the completion of the power phase. Keep the arms and hands just below the surface throughout the stroke. From the glide position, recover the arms by bending the elbows so the hands (palms facing down or toward the body) slide along the sides to near the armpits (**Fig. 6-27, A**).

Power Phase

Point the fingers outward from the shoulders so that the palms face back toward the feet. Leading with the fingers, extend the arms out to the sides until the hands are no farther forward than the top of the head (**Fig. 6-27, B**). Imagine a clock with the head at 12:00 and the feet at 6:00; the hands should extend no farther than 2:00 and 10:00. Without pausing, simultaneously press the palms and the insides of both arms in a broad sweeping motion back toward the feet (**Fig. 6-27, C**). Keep the arms straight or slightly bent in the power phase. End this motion with the arms and hands in the glide position.

Kick

The kick for this stroke is similar to the kick used in the breaststroke. Both legs bend at the knee and make a circular kicking action. The pressing action of this kick starts slowly and speeds up to completion. The kicking action is continuous and smooth, without a pause between the recovery and the power phase.

To start, the legs are together and extended with the toes pointed during the glide (**Fig. 6-28, A**). From this position, recover the legs by bending and slightly separating the knees then dropping the heels downward to a point under and outside the knees (**Fig. 6-28, B**). The knees are spread hip-width or slightly wider. This position varies slightly among swimmers. Keep the thighs in line with the hips—the hips should stay near the surface. Do not drop the hips when dropping the heels.

The recovery uses an easy, rhythmical motion, with the back, hips and thighs kept nearly straight. At the end of the recovery, the knees rotate inward slightly while the ankles flex and the feet turn outward. Finish by pressing the feet backward with a slightly rounded motion (**Fig. 6-28, C**), ending with the legs in the glide position. As the feet press backward, they move into a pointed position. The feet should be close together and may touch at the end of this motion. The legs remain underwater throughout the entire kick.

Breathing and Timing

Breathe during each arm stroke. Because the face is always out of the water, breathing is very easy. Inhale as the arms recover up the sides and exhale as the arms press backward during the power phase. Remember to relax and to exhale slowly throughout the arm action.

The arms start their recovery just ahead of the legs. Because they are stronger and travel a shorter distance, the legs finish their thrust at the same time as the arms (**Fig. 6-29, A–D**). After this combined

Fig. 6-28, A

Fig. 6-28, B

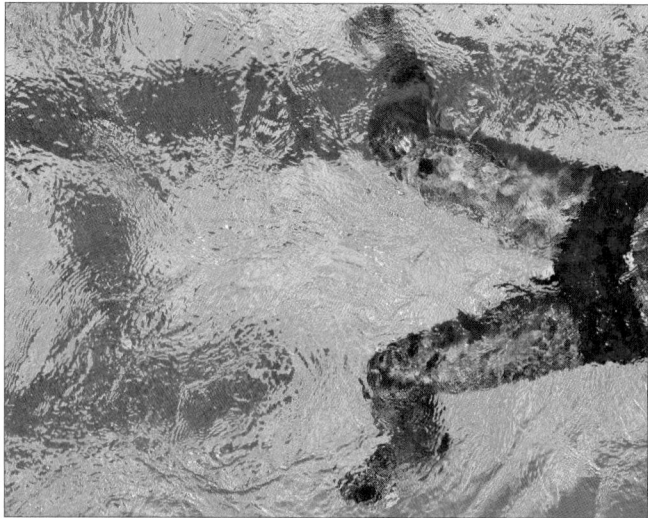

Fig. 6-28, C

propulsion, glide with the body streamlined. To minimize the drag of the arm and leg recovery, glide until most of the forward momentum is lost.

Fig. 6-29, A

Fig. 6-29, B

Fig. 6-29, C

Fig. 6-29, D

Sidestroke

The sidestroke is used for both recreational swimming and lifesaving (**Fig. 6-30**). The body position of the sidestroke reduces frontal resistance and lets the face and one ear stay out of the water. Propulsion comes mainly from the kick.

The arms provide some propulsion and stabilize the body in the side-lying position. Because the sidestroke is a resting stroke, it requires less energy and a swimmer can use it for long distances without tiring. These features make the sidestroke a good stroke to use in some survival swimming situations.

Fig. 6-30

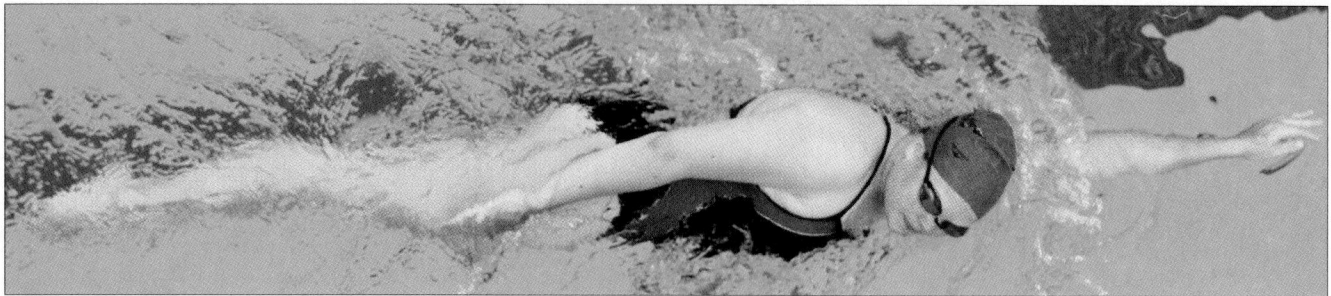
Fig. 6-31

Hydrodynamic Principles

The sidestroke evolved from the breaststroke to reduce form drag. Form drag is one of the most important primary hydrodynamic principles at work in this stroke. Offering a smaller shape while moving through the water, with part of the head and one shoulder out of the water, reduces the water resistance to forward movement.

Body Position, Balance and Motion

The body is nearly horizontal and on the side during the glide. The head, back and legs stay in a straight line and the legs are together and fully extended (**Fig. 6-31**). The leading arm (or bottom arm) extends in front of the body, parallel to and 6 to 8 inches below the surface. The palm of the leading arm faces down and in

INVERTED BREASTSTROKE

The inverted breaststroke, which evolved from the breaststroke and elementary backstroke, is a relaxed style of swimming on the back, especially for those with good buoyancy. It has the following characteristics:

- The glide position is streamlined, horizontal and on the back, with arms extended beyond the head and legs straight.
- The kick is the same as in the elementary backstroke.

The arms, with elbows slightly bent, press outward and back toward the feet until the palms are along the thighs. Without pause, the arms recover along the body to the armpits, where the palms turn up as the hands pass over the shoulders. Fingers first, the hands slide under the ears and extend to the glide position.

The swimmer inhales during arm recovery and exhales during the power phase. The legs recover as the hands move under the ears. The arms are two-thirds of the way through the recovery when the propulsive phase of the kick starts, and they reach the thighs just before the kick is finished.

Fig. 6-32, A

Fig. 6-32, B

Fig. 6-32, C

line with the body. Fully extend the trailing arm (or top arm) toward the feet, keeping the hand above the thigh. The lower ear rests in the water close to the shoulder. The face is just high enough to allow the mouth and nose to remain above the water for easy breathing. In general, keep the face looking across the surface of the water, but occasionally glance to the front to maintain direction. Keep the head and back aligned throughout the stroke.

Arm Stroke

Leading Arm

The power phase of the leading arm begins in the glide position and uses a shallow pull. Begin the power phase by rotating the leading arm slightly to position the palm down and angled slightly outward in the direction that you are facing. This is the catch position. From the catch position, bend the elbow and sweep the hand downward slightly and then back toward the feet, until the hand almost reaches the upper chest (**Fig. 6-32, A**). Without pausing, recover the leading arm by rotating the shoulder and dropping the elbow. Pass the hand under the ear until the fingers point forward (**Fig. 6-32, B**). Thrust the leading arm forward, rotating it so the palm is down for the glide position (**Fig. 6-32, C**).

Trailing Arm

During the power phase of the leading arm, recover the trailing arm by drawing the forearm along the body until the hand is nearly in front of the shoulder of the leading arm (see **Fig. 6-32, A**). Keep the palm down and angled slightly backward. This position will create the necessary lift to help keep the face above water during the pull. Start the power phase by sweeping the trailing hand downward slightly and then back toward the body and into the glide position (see **Fig. 6-32, B and C**). Start this phase with the wrist flexed but finish with it extended, so the palm is always facing toward the feet.

Kick

The sidestroke uses the scissors kick. This kick and the inverted scissors kick are both used for

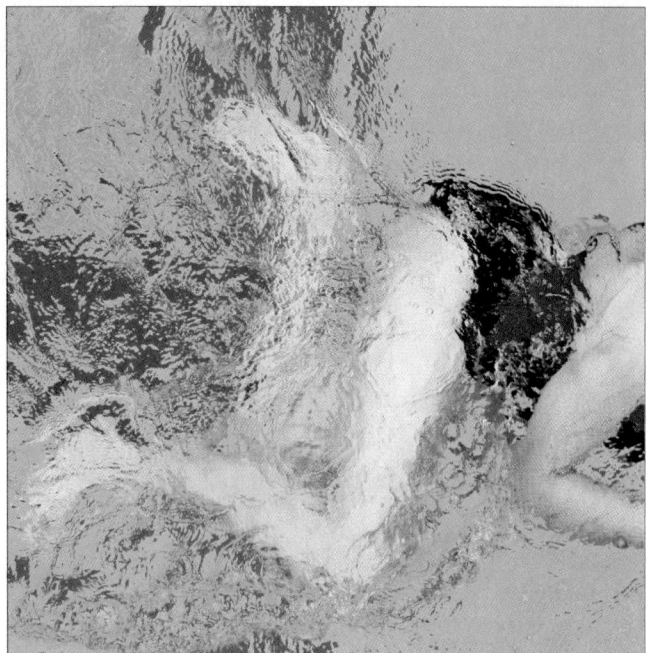

Fig. 6-33, A

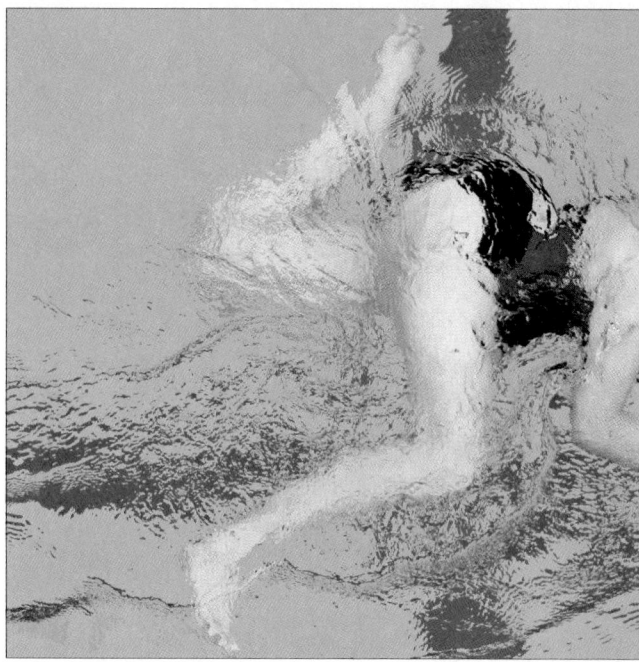

Fig. 6-33, B

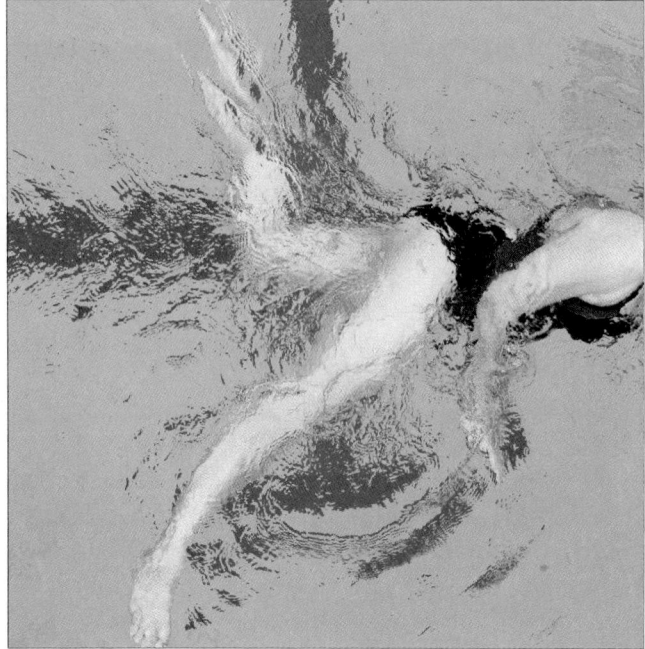

Fig. 6-33, C

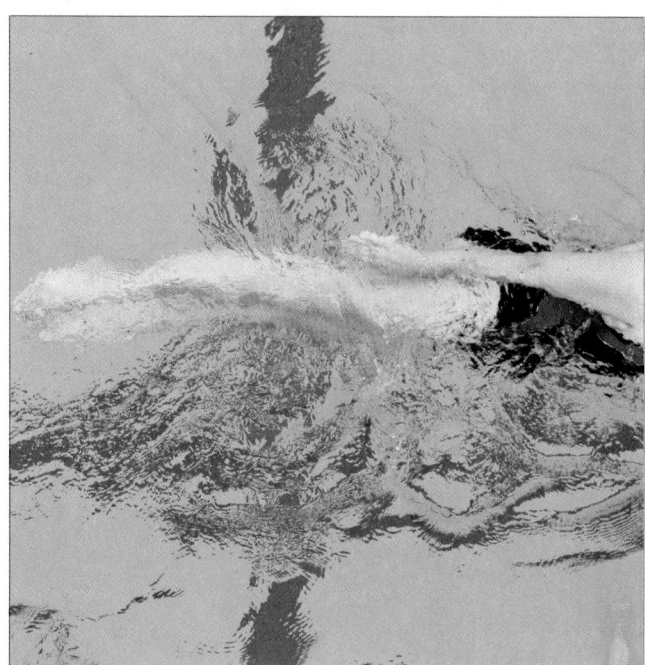

Fig. 6-33, D

lifesaving carries, treading water, underwater swimming and the trudgen strokes. A good scissors kick provides enough propulsion for a short rest between strokes. Move the legs smoothly on a path that is nearly parallel to the surface of the water. Avoid rolling the hips forward and backward during the recovery or the kick. Unlike the flutter kick, in the scissors kick the legs rest during the glide. From the glide position, recover the legs by flexing the hips and

knees and drawing the heels slowly toward the buttocks. Keep the knees close together during this movement (**Fig. 6-33, A**).

At the end of the recovery (**Fig. 6-33, B**), flex the top ankle and point the toes of the lower foot to prepare for the kick. Move the legs into their catch positions, top leg toward the front of the body, bottom leg toward the back. When extended, the top leg should be nearly straight

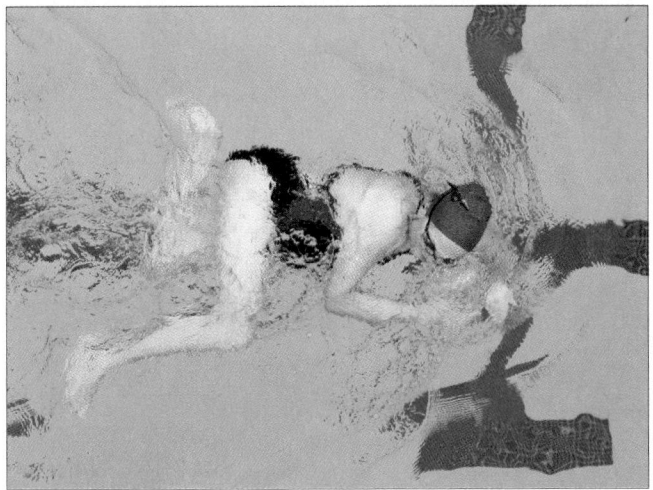

Fig. 6-34, A

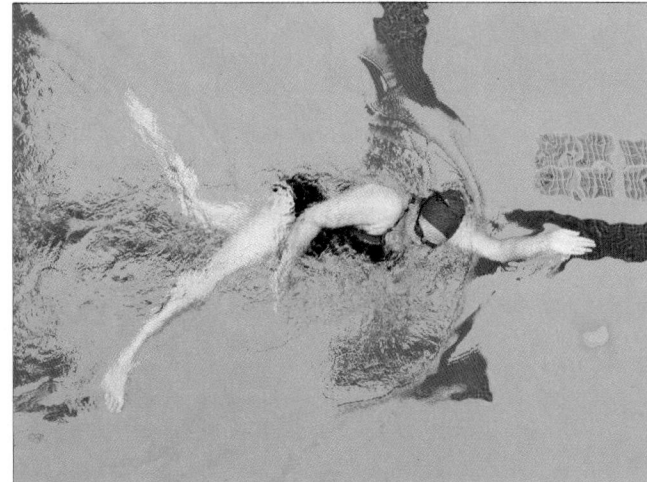

Fig. 6-34, B

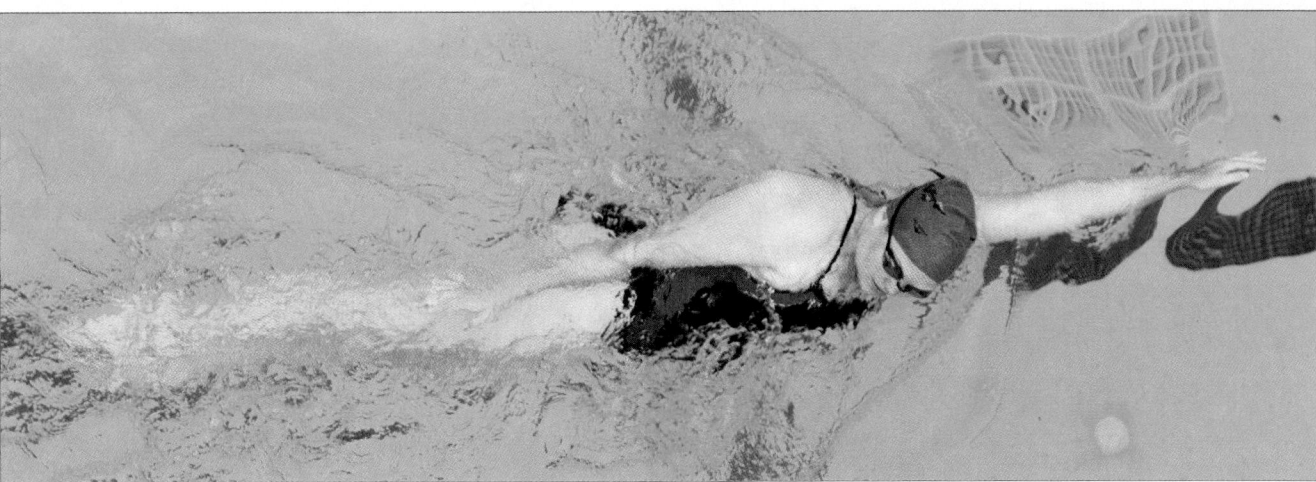

Fig. 6-34, C

(**Fig. 6-33, C**). Without pausing, press the top leg backward while keeping it straight. At the same time, extend the bottom leg in a motion similar to kicking a ball until both legs are fully extended and together in the glide position (**Fig. 6-33, D**). Push the water with the bottom of the top foot and the top of the bottom foot. While moving the top foot backward, transition the ankle from a flexed position into a toes-pointed position. This allows the sole of the foot to press against the water with the greatest pressure. Do not let the feet pass each other at the end of the kick. Keep the toes pointed during the glide to reduce drag.

The inverted scissors kick is identical to the scissors kick, except that it reverses the top and bottom leg actions. The top leg (with toes pointed) moves toward the rear of the body, and the bottom leg (with ankle flexed) moves toward the front of the body.

Breathing and Timing

Breathe with each stroke. Inhale while the trailing arm recovers and exhale during the power phase of the trailing arm.

From the glide position, start the stroke with the sweep of the leading arm. Recover the trailing arm and the legs, then kick and stroke with the trailing arm as the leading arm recovers (**Fig. 6-34, A and B**). By the completion of the kick and the stroke of the trailing arm, the arms and legs should be fully extended (**Fig. 6-34, C**). Glide until the speed slows. Remember not to glide too long, because it takes more energy to start and stop than to keep moving.

OVERARM SIDESTROKE

This stroke, which evolved from the sidestroke in 1871, differs from the sidestroke in that the trailing arm recovers out of the water. This reduces the drag of the water on the swimmer. Leisure swimmers often use this stroke. It has the following characteristics:

- Body position, kick, leading arm action and breathing are the same as the sidestroke.

- The trailing arm recovers out of the water with a "high" elbow, and the hand enters just in front of the face, similar to the front crawl.

- The trailing hand enters the water as the leading arm finishes its power phase and the legs recover.

- As the trailing hand starts its power phase, the legs extend and the leading arm recovers.

CHAPTER 7
Starts and Turns

Simple starts are used to enter the water and basic turns are used to turn around in a pool. More advanced starts and turns are used to swim laps efficiently and in competitive swimming. Swimmers working out often use fast, smooth flip turns to change directions at each end of the pool. With a little practice, most people can learn these skills, which also helps improve swimming efficiency.

Starting with safety considerations and readiness, this chapter outlines the steps and skills involved in performing different types of starts and turns, including the progression for a headfirst entry; shallow-angle dive; grab, track and backstroke starts; front crawl, sidestroke and back crawl open turns; front and backstroke flip turns; and breaststroke and butterfly turns.

Safety Considerations for Diving and Headfirst Entries

Some of the skills outlined in this chapter involve headfirst entry into the water. Whenever a person enters the water in this position there is some degree of risk. However, with proper training and an awareness of the necessary safety considerations, diving and headfirst entries can be done in a safe manner.

The following guidelines are recommended for diving and headfirst entries:

- Follow safety rules at all times—never make exceptions.
- Be sure the water is at least 9 feet deep and ensure that the water is free from obstructions.
- Never dive or enter the water headfirst into an aboveground pool, the shallow end of any inground pool or at a beach.
- Never dive or enter the water headfirst into cloudy or murky water.
- Check the shape of the pool bottom to be sure it is safe for diving or headfirst entry.
- Pools at homes, motels and hotels might not have a safe envelope for diving or headfirst entry. (See **Chapter 2** for more information on diving safety for home pools.)
- When performing a headfirst entry from a deck, the area of entry should be free of obstructions (such as lane lines, kickboards and other pool users) for at least 4 feet on both sides and a clear, safe distance in front.

"No Diving" Signs

Because most head, neck and back injuries occur in shallow water and to people visiting an area for the first time, it is very important to warn everyone of shallow water. Placement of warning signs in key locations may help prevent injuries. Suggested locations are the deck near the edge of the pool and walls or fences by shallow water. Signs should be visible to anyone entering the pool or approaching shallow water.

Many kinds of warnings signs can be used, such as the following:

- "No Diving" painted on the deck in contrasting colors (**Fig. 7-1**)

Fig. 7-1

- Tiled lettering embedded into the deck in contrasting colors (**Fig. 7-2**)
- Universal "No Diving" tiles embedded into the deck
- "No Diving" signs mounted on the walls, fences or stands (**Figs. 7-3**)

Starting Blocks

Pools designed for competitive swimming are equipped with starting blocks, which can be permanent or removable. Competitive swimmers are trained to perform racing starts from blocks. People without training who dive from blocks are at risk. An entry into the water that is too shallow could lead to injury. Use of starting blocks

Fig. 7-2

Fig. 7-3

Fig. 7-4

should be restricted to supervised competitive swimming. At all other times, "No Diving" signs should be posted on each block, the blocks removed or access prevented. Starting blocks at the shallow end of a pool may be a hazard.

Headfirst Entries

Readiness

Physical Readiness

All advanced starts begin with a headfirst entry. Some basic swimming skills are necessary to do a headfirst entry. For example, the swimmer must be able to return to the surface of the water, change directions and swim back to the side of the pool.

Strength may also be a consideration. Swimmers entering the water headfirst must be able to keep the arms overhead when the body passes through the surface of the water. Swimmers can determine if they have the strength to do this by pushing forcefully off the side of the pool in a streamlined position and gliding (**Fig. 7-4**). Swimmers who cannot keep their arms aligned during the glide, probably do not have the strength to perform this skill. These swimmers should postpone learning this skill until upper body strength increases.

Psychological Readiness

People who are about to enter the water headfirst for the first time may feel fear or apprehension. Although caution should be exercised when entering the water in a headfirst position, headfirst entries should be attempted with confidence. The following progressions can help swimmers that are learning how to enter the water headfirst manage their fears and achieve success at each level. Taking the time to master the skills involved in each step will make learning headfirst entries easier and more fun. The following are the most common fears of people learning to enter the water headfirst.

Fear of Depth

Some beginners may be afraid that they will not be able to swim back to the surface. While attempting a headfirst entry, these beginners might lift the head in an effort to stay near the surface, resulting in a belly flop. Swimmers who are not comfortable in deep water should work on improving their comfort level in deep water before learning headfirst entries. Surface diving and underwater swimming can increase comfort in deep water. Practicing these skills may help some swimmers gain the necessary confidence to begin learning headfirst entry skills.

Fear of Injury

Fear of injury causes some to avoid headfirst entries entirely. Although minor pain can result from a poor landing, with proper safety precautions, headfirst entries can be practiced and learned with very little chance of injury. Some people may feel fear because they saw someone injured in a dive or may have become hurt attempting to enter the water headfirst in the past. Again, learning these skills in a safe, step-by-step manner prevents the risk of injury and helps overcome this fear.

Fear of Height

Fear of heights is quite common. Nearly everyone has a height at which they begin feeling afraid. Viewed from the pool deck, even the relatively short distance to the surface of the water can cause anxiety for some. These people may avoid headfirst entries altogether because the height seems too great. By starting with headfirst entries that take place as close to the surface of the water as possible, the progressions used in this chapter will help beginners overcome such fears.

Nervous or hesitant learners should not proceed to the next step. Those learning how to perform a headfirst entry should continue practicing each step until they feel confident to proceed to the next step. A swimmer who is so afraid that he or she cannot concentrate on the skill is at a greater risk for injury while attempting the skill.

Components of a Headfirst Entry

Although this skill is referred to as a "headfirst" entry, the fingertips actually enter the water first. Headfirst entries always take place with the arms extended above the head so that the fingertips enter first followed by the hands, arms, head and then the rest of the body. A simple headfirst entry has three parts: the stationary starting position; the moment of propulsion, called the takeoff; and the entry into the water. For most swimmers, the starting position takes place on the side of the pool. For competitive swimmers, the starting position usually takes place on starting blocks. The takeoff for a headfirst entry is a slight push with the feet. A good entry involves entering the water at a low angle and keeping the body aligned as it enters the water. The way the body moves through the water after entry is also important. After the body enters the water it should angle slightly upward in order to return to the surface so that stroking can begin.

To enter into the water at the desired point of entry, focus on a target (either an imaginary point on the surface or a real or imagined target on the bottom of the pool) until the hands enter the water. It is important to maintain concentration during any headfirst entry. Focusing attention on a target is a good way to stay focused when learning this skill.

Proper body alignment is crucial for a safe entry. Head position is very important because it affects the position of the body in general. Moving the head may cause the body to arch or bend. The beginner who lifts the head too quickly may end up doing a painful belly flop.

Muscle control also is important for proper body alignment and the body tension needed for a safe, effective entry. Try to stay in a streamlined position in flight (the passage of the body through the air) (**Fig. 7-5, A**). This helps maintain control and makes entries graceful. Good alignment when entering the water reduces drag and the risk of straining muscles or joints.

One of the main goals of the headfirst entry is to be able to start swimming after entering the water, whether it is for recreation, fitness or competition. Swimmers need to be able to steer back to the surface after entering the water (**Fig. 7-5, B and C**).

Body Alignment Skills

Body alignment skills are useful for practicing arm and head position in preparation for a headfirst entry.

Torpedoing

1. Push forcefully from the wall into a glide position in chest-deep water. Keep the eyes open.

2. Maintain straight body alignment: arms straight and overhead, arms covering the ears, thumbs together or interlocked, body tense from arms to feet, toes pointed, legs together.

3. Hold the position until momentum is lost.

Fig. 7-5, A

Fig. 7-5, B

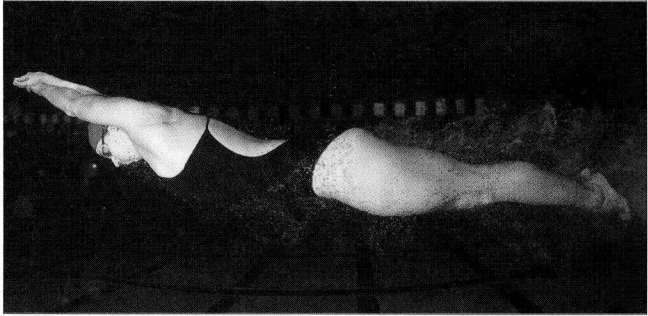

Fig. 7-5, C

Porpoising

1. Push forcefully from the wall into a glide position in chest-deep water. Keep the eyes open.

2. Maintain straight body alignment for a few seconds: arms straight and overhead and covering the ears, thumbs together or interlocked, body tense from arms to feet, toes pointed, legs together.

3. Keep the head cradled between the extended arms. Angle the head and arms down to submerge slightly toward the bottom, position the head and arms straight ahead to move parallel to the surface and angle them up to glide to the surface.

   - As a variation, jump forward and slightly upward from a standing position before angling the head and arms to submerge.

   - Change body angle in descent and ascent by raising and lowering the head and arms as a single unit.

   - At all times, cradle the head between the arms, which should be extended in the direction of the motion.

Progression for a Headfirst Entry

Swimmers who go through the progression of steps for learning a headfirst entry gain self-confidence and a feeling of success. Each swimmer should move through them at his or her own pace. Some steps require plenty of practice, others may not. Some people may be able to move more quickly through them than others. This progression may also be used later to learn to enter the water from starting blocks. In this situation, the hands will break the water at roughly a 45-degree angle, and the head, torso and legs will slide into the water following a safe path. This angle of entry allows swimmers to be parallel to the surface of the water after entry and in a position to steer up and start stroking (**Fig. 7-6**).

Fig. 7-6

Fig. 7-7

Fig. 7-8

Sitting Position

1. Sit on the pool edge with the feet on the edge of the gutter or against the side of the pool.

2. Extend the arms over the head.

3. Focus on a target on the surface that will allow for roughly a 45-degree entry into the water (**Fig. 7-7**).

4. Lean forward, try to touch the water and push with the legs.

5. Straighten the body and extend both legs upon entering the water.

6. Angle the hands toward the surface of the water to steer the body up.

Kneeling Position

1. Kneel on the pool deck with one leg while gripping the pool edge with the toes of the other foot. The foot of the kneeling leg should be in a position to help push from the deck.

2. Extend the arms above the head.

3. Focus on a target that will allow for roughly a 45-degree entry into the water (**Fig. 7-8**).

4. Lean forward, try to touch the water and push with the legs.

5. Straighten the body and extend both legs upon entering the water.

6. Angle the hands toward the surface of the water to steer the body up.

Compact Position

This entry is quite similar to the kneeling position.

1. Put one foot forward and one back, with the toes of the leading foot gripping the edge of the pool.

2. Starting from the kneeling position, lift up so that both knees are flexed and off the deck in order to remain close to the water.

3. Extend the arms above the head.

4. Focus on a target that will allow for roughly a 45-degree entry into the water (**Fig. 7-9**).

5. Bend forward and try to touch the surface of the water with the hands.

6. Push off toward the water. Bring the legs together upon entering the water.

Fig. 7-9

Fig. 7-10

7. Angle the hands toward the surface of the water to steer the body up.

Stride Position

After several successful headfirst entries from the compact position, the next step is to enter from the stride position.

1. Stand upright with one leg forward and one leg back, with the toes of the leading foot gripping the edge of the pool.

2. Extend the arms above the head.

3. Focus on a target that will allow for roughly a 45-degree entry into the water. Bend the legs only slightly while also bending at the waist toward the water (**Fig. 7-10**).

4. Try to touch the surface of the water, and lift the back leg until it is in line with the torso. The forward leg should stay as straight as

possible. Upon entering the water, bring the legs together.

5. Angle the hands toward the surface of the water to steer the body up.

Shallow-Angle Dive

The shallow-angle dive is a low-projecting headfirst entry with a streamlined body position. This skill is done by entering the water with great forward momentum at an angle that allows the swimmer to remain near the surface of the water. It is used to enter the water to travel away from the side of the pool and begin swimming and for racing starts in competition. Like all headfirst entries, this entry should only be performed in clear water of known depth. Misjudging the depth or angle of the entry could lead to hitting the bottom and injuring the head, neck or back, risking paralysis or death.

Fig. 7-11, A

Fig. 7-11, B

Fig. 7-11, C

1. Start on the edge of the pool with the feet about shoulder-width apart and the toes gripping the edge of the pool (**Fig. 7-11, A**).

2. Flex the hips and knees and bend forward until the upper back is nearly parallel to the pool deck.

3. Focus on a target. To gain momentum for the dive, swing the arms backward and upward, letting the heels rise and the body start to move forward.

4. When the arms reach the farthest point backward, immediately swing them forward. Extend the hips, knees, ankles and toes one after another forcibly to drive forward in a line of flight over and nearly parallel to the surface of the water (**Fig. 7-11, B**).

5. Keep the body stretched and the hands interlocked and out in front.

6. During the flight, drop the head slightly between the outstretched arms, which should be angled downward slightly (**Fig. 7-11, C**).

7. Make the entry at an angle no greater than 45-degrees to the surface of the water. Once under water, steer upward toward the surface with the hands and head.

8. Keep the body fully extended and streamlined while gliding underwater. Before losing too much speed, start the leg kick to rise to the surface and start swimming.

Proficiency at this entry leads naturally into competitive racing starts. Training and supervision are necessary when learning or practicing competitive racing starts. Without training and supervision, the following problems could result:

- Using the starting blocks improperly creates a risk of injuries to the head, neck and back.

- Using a starting block that is not anchored securely can lead to injury.

Grab Start

The grab start is the simplest start for all competitive strokes performed on the front. Before attempting the grab start, a swimmer must

Fig. 7-12, A

Fig. 7-12, B

Fig. 7-12, C

Fig. 7-12, D

Fig. 7-12, E

Fig. 7-12, F

be able to safely perform a shallow-angle dive from the deck.

1. To position for the start, curl the toes around the starting block with the feet about shoulder-width apart.

2. On the command, "Take your mark," grasp the front edge of the starting block. Put the hands either inside or outside the feet, whichever feels more comfortable. Look straight down and bend the knees slightly (**Fig. 7-12, A**).

3. On the starting signal, pull against the starting block and bend the knees further, so the body starts moving forward. Look toward the desired point of entry, release the block and quickly extend the arms forward to the entry point to lead the body's flight.

4. As the hands let go of the block, bend the knees further and then push off by driving the feet against the block and forcefully extending the hips, knees and ankles (**Fig. 7-12, B**).

5. As the feet leave the block, focus on the target and aim the arms and hands at the entry point (**Fig. 7-12, C**).

6. Just before hitting the water, lock the head between the arms and enter smoothly, as if going through a hole in the water (**Fig. 7-12, D and E**).

7. Once in the water, angle the hands up toward the surface. Glide in a streamlined position, hands out in front (**Fig. 7-12, F**).

8. Before losing speed, start the flutter or dolphin kick, followed by the first arm pull. (In the breaststroke, kicking does not start until after the underwater pull.)

Fig. 7-13, A

Fig. 7-13, B

Fig. 7-13, C

Fig. 7-13, D

Fig. 7-13, E

Fig. 7-13, F

Track Start

Many swimmers think the track start is the fastest start for all competitive strokes performed on the front. In the track start, the feet are staggered on the block. The push of the rear leg enables the body to move forward very quickly. Before attempting the track start, a swimmer must be able to safely perform a shallow-angle dive from the deck.

1. To position for the start, stand with one foot forward and one foot back. Curl the toes of the leading foot around the starting block.

2. On the command, "Take your mark," grasp the front edge of the starting block. Look straight down and bend the knees slightly (**Fig. 7-13, A**).

3. On the starting signal, pull against the starting block, push with the rear leg and bend the knees

forward, so the body starts moving forward. Look toward the entry point, release the block and quickly extend the arms forward to the entry point to lead the body's flight.

4. As the hands let go of the block, bend the knees further and then push off by driving the feet against the block and forcefully extending the hips, knees and ankles (**Fig. 7-13, B**).

5. As the feet leave the block, focus on the target and aim the arms and hands at the entry point (**Fig. 7-13, C**).

6. Just before hitting the water, lock the head between the arms and enter smoothly, as if going through a hole in the water (**Fig. 7-13, D and E**).

7. Once in the water, angle the hands toward the surface. Glide in a streamlined position, hands out in front.

Fig. 7-14, A

Fig. 7-14, B

Fig. 7-14, C

Fig. 7-14, D

Fig. 7-14, E

Fig. 7-14, F

8. Before losing speed, start the kick followed by the first arm pull (**Fig. 7-13, F**). (In the breaststroke, kicking does not start until after the underwater pull.)

Backstroke Start

1. To get in position for the backstroke start, grasp the starting block with both hands and put the feet parallel on the wall. (USA Swimming, National Collegiate Athletic Association [NCAA] and Federation Internationale de Natation Amateur [FINA] rules do not allow the toes to curl over the lip of the gutter.) Move the feet a comfortable distance apart. It is acceptable to stagger the feet, placing one foot slightly higher than the other, to help maintain a stable position on the wall.

2. On the command, "Take your mark," bend the arms and legs to pull the body up slightly and closer to the wall. Keep the back straight (**Fig. 7-14, A**).

3. On the starting signal, throw the head back and push the arms away from the block and over the head (**Fig. 7-14, B**). Push forcefully with the legs while arching the back and driving the body, hands first, up and out over the water (**Fig. 7-14, C**).

4. Tip the head back and get into a streamlined position. The whole body should enter smoothly through a single point in the water (**Fig. 7-14, D and E**).

5. Once in the water, adjust the angle of the hands for a streamlined glide (**Fig. 7-14, F**).

Fig. 7-15, A

Fig. 7-15, B

6. Before losing speed, begin either a flutter or a dolphin kick and use the first arm pull to come to the surface and begin swimming.

Many swimmers prefer to do several quick dolphin kicks after the start and after each turn instead of the flutter kick. Swimmers with a strong dolphin kick may wish to try this. Current rules for competitive backstroke start state that a swimmer's head must break the surface of the water within 15 meters after a start or turn (**Fig. 7-15, A and B**).

Turns

Swimming for fitness usually takes place in pools, so being able to turn effectively and efficiently at the wall is important. In the following sections, simple open turns, as well as more advanced, competitive turns are described.

Training and supervision are necessary when learning or practicing turns. Without training and supervision, the following problems could result:

- Misjudging the distance from the wall during a turn can cause injury by swimming into the wall or hitting the head.

- The heels could hit the wall during a flip turn.

- Pushing off at a steep angle is especially dangerous in shallow water.

Front Crawl (Freestyle) Open Turn

1. When approaching the wall, extend the leading arm until the hand touches the wall (**Fig. 7-16, A**).

2. Bend the elbow of the leading arm and drop the shoulder slightly while rotating the body to move the body toward the wall.

3. Tuck the body at the hips and knees; turn and spin away from the leading arm; swing the feet against the wall, one foot above the other (if the right hand is leading, the right foot will be on top); and extend the other arm toward the opposite end of the pool (**Fig. 7-16, B**).

Fig. 7-16, A

Fig. 7-16, B

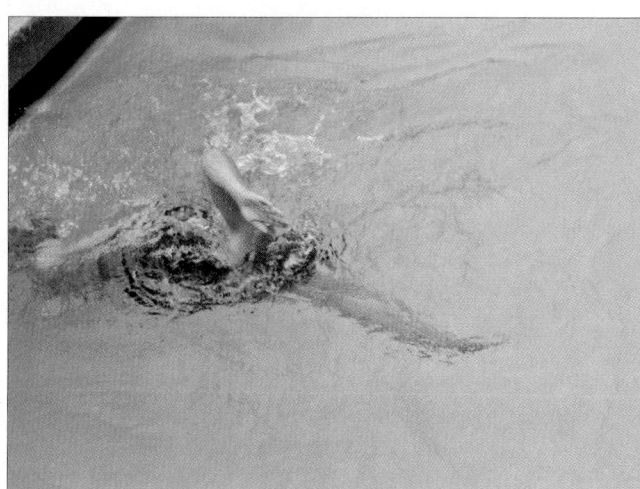

Fig. 7-16, C

4. During the spin, lift the face out of the water and take a breath.

5. Return the face to the water as the leading arm recovers over the surface (**Fig. 7-16, C**).

6. Extend both arms in front as the legs push off the wall. Keep the body in a streamlined position on one side.

7. Rotate in the glide until face-down.

8. Before losing momentum, start flutter kicking to rise to the surface and resume the arm stroke.

Sidestroke Open Turn

For a sidestroke open turn, vary the front crawl open turn slightly.

1. Approach with the arm extended and touch the wall with the leading arm.

2. Bend the elbow, drop the opposite shoulder and rotate the back toward the wall.

3. Tuck the body, and swing the legs underneath the body to place them on the wall. Feet should be planted sideways with the foot on the lead arm side of the body placed above the foot on the trailing arm side of the body.

4. Take a breath and extend the trailing arm while pushing off the wall. During this step, the trailing arm now becomes the new leading arm. The leading arm used during the approach stays by the side and becomes the new trailing arm.

5. Once in the glide position, stay on the side and resume swimming.

Back Crawl (Backstroke) Open Turn

This open turn is used for recreational swimming. When swimming back crawl, gauge the approach to the wall using a marker, such as the backstroke flags, the color change of the lane lines or a glance backward, to determine that you are approaching the wall.

Fig. 7-17, A

Fig. 7-17, B

Fig. 7-17, C

Fig. 7-17, D

Fig. 7-17, E

1. At one stroke short of touching the wall, start to rotate to the front by turning the head and looking toward the pulling arm (**Fig. 7-17, A and B**).

2. Continue the arm pull (underwater) as you complete the rotation onto the side. Extend the arm until it touches the wall (**Fig. 7-17, C**).

3. Bend the elbow of the leading arm and drop the shoulder slightly while rotating the body to move the body toward the wall.

4. Tuck the body at the hips and knees; turn and spin away from the leading hand; swing the feet against the wall, one foot above the other (if the right hand is the leading hand, the right foot will be on top); and extend the other arm toward the opposite end of the pool.

5. During the spin, lift the face out of the water and take a breath (**Fig. 7-17, D**).

6. Return the face to the water as the leading hand recovers over the surface.

7. Keep the body in a streamlined position on the back (**Fig. 7-17, E**).

8. Before losing momentum, start kicking to rise to the surface and resume the arm stroke.

Fig. 7-18, A

Fig. 7-18, B

Fig. 7-18, C

Fig. 7-18, D

Fig. 7-18, E

Fig. 7-18, F

Front Flip Turn

The flip turn is a fast and efficient turn for the front crawl (freestyle). Watch the bottom markings to help judge the distance from the wall.

1. When one stroke length away from the wall ($3\frac{1}{2}$ to 4 feet), keep the trailing arm at the side while taking the last stroke with the leading arm (**Fig. 7-18, A**). Both hands will end up at the thighs.

2. Perform a half-somersault by tucking the chin to the chest and bending at the waist while simultaneously using a single dolphin kick to push the hips forward and upward (**Fig. 7-18, B**). Turn the palms down and push the hands toward the head to help the legs flip over the water.

3. During the somersault, bend the legs to prepare to hit the wall. The hands will have reached the ears, which helps complete the forward flip (**Fig. 7-18, C**).

4. Plant the feet on the wall with the toes pointed up or slightly to the side and the knees bent (**Fig. 7-18, D**).

5. Extend the arms into a streamlined position above the head. Push off while facing up or facing diagonally to the side; then rotate into a face-down position during the glide (**Fig. 7-18, E**). The initial speed when pushing off will be faster than the swimming speed.

6. Before losing speed, start a steady kick and resume the arm stroke (**Fig. 7-18, F**).

Fig. 7-19, A

Fig. 7-19, B

Fig. 7-19, C

Fig. 7-19, D

Fig. 7-19, E

Fig. 7-19, F

Some swimmers prefer to rotate into a side-lying position as they plant their feet on the wall, but the push-off on the back is generally considered the faster method of turning.

Breaststroke Turn

1. Time the last stroke to allow the body to be fully stretched upon reaching the wall (**Fig. 7-19, A**).

2. Place both hands on the wall at the same time then dip the shoulder on the side of the body that the turn will occur. (In this example, the left shoulder dips because the turn is to the left. To turn to the right, simply reverse these directions.) Tuck the hips and legs in tight so that they are directly underneath the body as they continue to move toward the wall (**Fig. 7-19, B**).

3. As the hands touch the wall, turn the head to the left shoulder. Bend the left elbow and move the left arm backward, keeping it as close as possible to the body.

4. When the legs pass under the body, move the right arm over the head, keeping it close to the

Fig. 7-19, G

Fig. 7-19, H

Fig. 7-19, I

head. Plant both feet on the wall with toes pointing toward the side and the knees bent (**Fig. 7-19, C**).

5. Take a deep breath before the head submerges. Extend the arms into a streamlined position while pushing off with the body somewhat on its side (**Fig. 7-19, D**).

6. Rotate into a face-down position while gliding below the surface (**Fig. 7-19, E**).

7. Before losing speed, take a complete underwater breaststroke pull to the thighs, glide again and then kick upward as the hands recover close to

the body (**Fig. 7-19, F–I**). Return to the surface to resume stroking.

The underwater pull for the breaststroke turn differs from the pull used in the stroke because the arm pull extends all the way to the thighs. During the underwater pull, the hands follow a path that resembles the outline of a light bulb. The hands recover close to the body. This is called a pullout. In competition, one pullout is allowed at the beginning of each length, and then the head must surface.

Butterfly Turn

The turn for the butterfly is the same as the breaststroke turn through step 5. The difference between the turns is that the pushing off the wall in the butterfly turn is followed by dolphin kick and the arm stroke.

1. Time the last stroke to allow the body to be fully stretched upon reaching the wall (See **Fig. 7-19, A**).

2. Place both hands on the wall at the same time then dip the shoulder in the direction of the turn. (In this example, the left shoulder dips because the turn is to the left. To turn to the right, simply reverse these directions.) Tuck the hips and legs in tight as they continue to move toward the wall (See **Fig. 7-19, B**).

3. As the hands touch the wall, turn the head toward the left shoulder. Bend the left elbow and move the left arm backward as close as possible to the body.

4. When the legs pass under the body, move the right arm over the head, keeping it close to the head. Plant both feet on the wall with toes pointing toward the side and the knees bent (See **Fig. 7-19, C**).

5. Take a deep breath before the head submerges. Extend the arms into a streamlined position with the body somewhat on its side while pushing off the wall (See **Fig. 7-19, D**).

6. Rotate into a face-down position while gliding a short distance then dolphin kick to the surface and start stroking.

Backstroke Flip Turn

Rules for the competitive backstroke turn require the swimmer to touch the wall with any part of the body. During the turn, the shoulders may turn past vertical as long as the motion is part of a continuous turning action. Returning to a position on the back before the feet leave the wall is required.

Fig. 7-20, A

Fig. 7-20, B

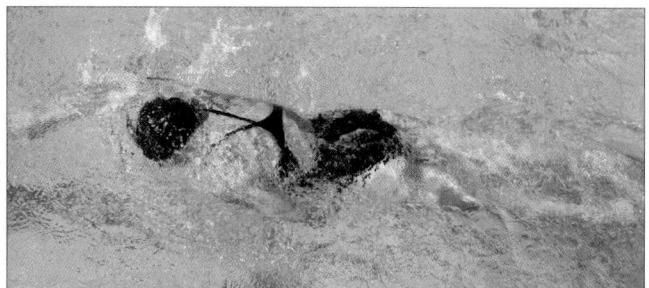

Fig. 7-20, C

Fig. 7-20, D

Fig. 7-20, E

Fig. 7-20, F

1. After passing the backstroke flags, accelerate toward the wall (**Fig. 7-20, A**).

2. Start the flip one stroke from the wall by turning the head and looking toward the pulling arm as it does during the catch (**Fig. 7-20, B**).

3. While pulling, rotate onto the stomach, drive the head downward and stop the pulling hand at the hips (**Fig. 7-20, C**). At the same time, the other arm recovers across the body, enters the water in the same position as in the front crawl and pulls to the hips.

4. Drive the head down and start somersaulting while tucking the knees tightly to the chest (**Fig. 7-20, D**). During the somersault, turn both

palms down and push the hands toward the head to complete the flip. Keep the legs tucked until the feet contact the wall, toes pointed upward (**Fig. 7-20, E**).

5. While still on the back, push straight off forcefully and go into a streamlined position while leaving the wall (**Fig. 7-20, F**).

6. Before losing speed, kick to rise to the surface and resume the arm stroke.

The motion in the turn must be continuous. Any hesitation, dolphin kicks or extra strokes after turning onto the stomach may lead to disqualification in a competition.

CHAPTER 8
Diving

Jumping into the water from a diving board is great fun, but under the wrong circumstances, diving can be dangerous. Knowing how to recognize a safe place for diving, using safe equipment and applying a heavy dose of common sense are the keys to preventing injury. Before using a diving board, it is important to have instruction from a competent instructor or coach—all diving should be carefully supervised.

Building upon the water entry skills learned in the previous chapter, this chapter explains the principles of safe diving and focuses on the progressions for learning how to dive from poolside and from a diving board. These progressions should help reduce any fears or doubts about diving and help make learning how to dive fun and safe.

Principles of Diving Safety

Records maintained by USA Diving, the national governing body of competitive diving, show that competitive diving has been and continues to be a safe activity. This safety record is mostly a result of careful training and supervision. It is also a result of the construction and maintenance of safe swimming pools and diving boards that meet approved minimum standards, as well as safe locations of diving boards and diving towers.

Although diving is a safe activity under adequate supervision in designated diving areas using the proper equipment, a head, neck or back injury can happen if safe diving principles are not followed—even in the deep end of a pool. Diving-related injuries have occurred from collisions with other pool users, from the dives themselves or from falls from diving boards, jumpboards, 3-meter stands and from poolside. Whether learning how to dive for fun or competition, everyone should learn from a qualified instructor how to dive and adhere to the principles of safe diving.

The following guidelines are recommended for safe diving:

- Follow safety rules at all times—never make exceptions.
- Learn how to dive safely from a qualified instructor. A self-taught diver is much more likely to be injured.
- In a headfirst dive, extend the arms with elbows locked alongside the head. Hold the hands together with the palms facing toward the water. Keeping the arms, wrists and fingers in line with the head helps control the angle of entry. This reduces the impact of the water on the top of the head and helps protect from injury. A diver's body should be tensed and straight from the hands to the pointed toes (**Fig. 8-1**).
- Do not wear earplugs; pressure changes make them dangerous.
- Dive only in designated diving areas. Be sure of water depth and that the water is free from obstructions. Never dive into cloudy or murky water.
- Be aware—the presence of a diving board does not necessarily mean it is safe for diving. For dives

Fig. 8-1

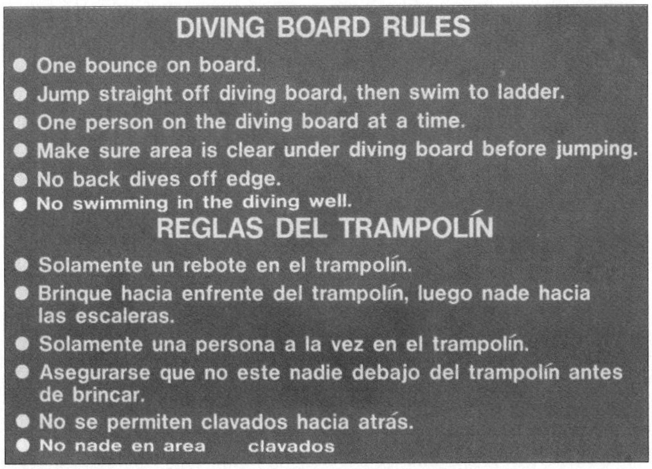

Fig. 8-2

from a 1-meter diving board, there should be 10 feet of clearance to the side of the pool. Many pools at homes, motels and hotels might not have a safe diving envelope. (See **Chapter 2** for more information on diving safety for home pools.)

- Dive only off the end of a diving board. Diving off the side of a diving board might result in striking the side of the pool or entering water that is too shallow.

- Do not bounce more than once on the end of a diving board, unless supervised by a coach. Bouncing more than once might result in missing the edge or slipping off the diving board.

- Do not run on a diving board or attempt to dive a long way forward through the air. The water might be too shallow at the point of entry.

- Check that the springboard diving equipment meets the same standards set for competition.

- Do not dive from a height greater than 1 meter unless trained to do so.

- Swim away from the diving board after entering the water. Do not be a hazard for the next diver.

- Never use drugs or alcohol when diving.

Pools with Diving Facilities

Pool operators must ensure that their pools meet minimum standards for safe diving. Public and private facilities with 1-meter or 3-meter diving boards and/or towers suitable for competition must meet stringent pool design standards. The National Collegiate Athletic Association (NCAA), Fédération Internationale de Natation Amateur

(FINA), USA Diving and other organizations that sponsor diving competition set such standards.

All swimming pools with diving boards and towers should display their diving rules near the diving board or tower (**Fig. 8-2**). These rules should be strictly enforced. Such rules may include the following:

- Use the ladder to climb onto the diving board or tower. Climbing in any other way is prohibited.

- Only one bounce on the end of the diving board, unless supervised by a coach.

- Only one person on the diving board at a time.

- No other swimmers in the diving area when the diving board or tower is in use.

- Only dive or jump straight out from the end of the diving board or tower.

- Look before diving or jumping to make sure no one is in the diving area.

- Swim to the closest ladder or wall immediately after diving or jumping.

- The hands must enter the water first when performing a headfirst dive.

- The tower can be used only with supervision from a qualified instructor or coach.

- Learn or practice twisting, somersaulting and inward and reverse dives only under the close supervision of a qualified instructor or coach.

Underwater Hazards

Underwater Ledges

Some swimming pools have underwater ledges (sometimes called safety ledges) that may present a diving hazard (**Fig. 8-3**). If the ledge is hard to

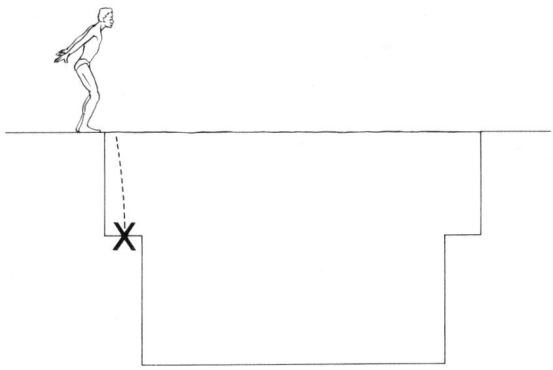

Fig. 8-3

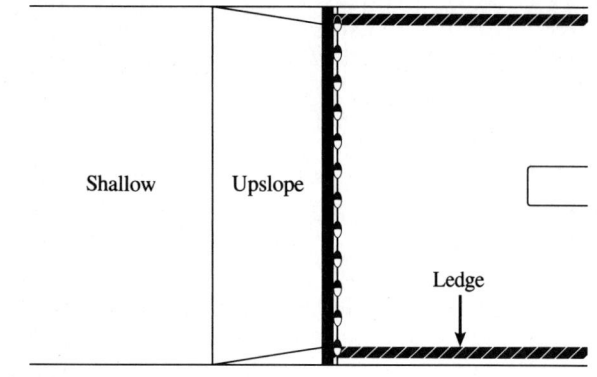

Fig. 8-4

see, it is possible to dive into what seems to be deep water, hit the ledge and injure the head, neck or back. To reduce this risk, diving facilities should use color-contrasting tile or paint to clearly mark both the horizontal and vertical borders of the ledge (**Fig. 8-4**).

Overflow Troughs (Gutters)

Be very careful when practicing dives from poolsides with overflow troughs, or gutters. Not only can the gutter be slippery when wet, but it can also create a hazard if the diver does not dive far enough away from the edge.

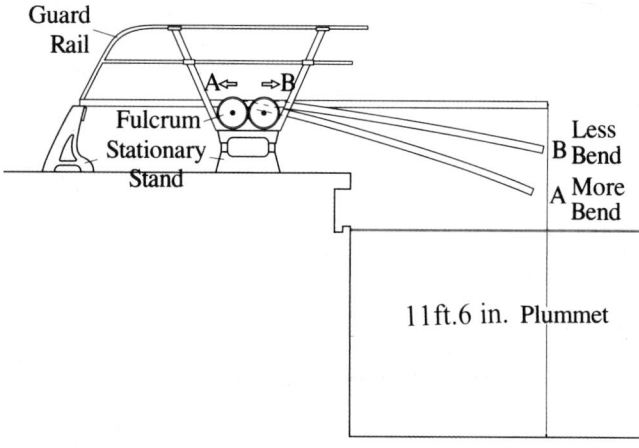

Fig. 8-5

Diving Equipment

Diving equipment varies greatly among facilities. Years ago, a diving board was just a long wooden plank crudely attached to a stand. It angled upward, making the diver's approach uphill. The stiffness and angle of the board limited the dives that could be done and sometimes made dives from the board unsafe. Today, diving equipment utilizes a wide range of sophisticated materials resulting in much safer diving equipment and consistent performance.

Some diving boards have a wooden core surrounded by a fiberglass outer surface, with a top made of nonslip material. The stand for this kind of diving board generally secures the back end of the board and has a stationary fulcrum (a pivot near the center of a diving board that lets the board bend and spring) (**Fig. 8-5**). Diving facilities not built to minimum standards may have different board lengths, fulcrum placement, height of the board over the water and board resiliency. These inconsistencies could be dangerous, because a diver cannot tell if the equipment is reliable. Advanced dives should only be learned on equipment that meets the standards for competitive diving.

Equipment for competitive diving has evolved into an advanced system of diving board, movable fulcrum and stationary stand. Diving boards used for competition are made of aluminum and coated with a nonslip surface. They are 1 meter or 3 meters in height over the water.

The quality of the stand is important. The stand for a diving board is comprised of a solid base and a movable fulcrum. The movable fulcrum allows adjustments according to strength, weight and timing. Diving performance depends on proper adjustment of the fulcrum for each individual diver's ability. The diving board should stay level when the fulcrum is moved. A level board helps divers reach the proper distance from the board in flight and entry. A guardrail on each side of the board helps prevent a fall onto the deck. The surface of steps or stairs should be made of

VISUAL AND KINESTHETIC AWARENESS

Visual and kinesthetic awareness are very important in learning diving skills. Visual awareness is the ability to keep the eyes focused on a reference point to determine and control the body's position in space, such as during flight from a diving board. Kinesthetic awareness is the ability to perceive what the body or parts of the body are doing at any given moment, such as being aware of the position of the arms and legs during rotation. Divers use both visual and kinesthetic awareness when performing both simple and complex dives. These skills help them maintain awareness of their body position in relation to the water, achieve good body alignment for entry and maintain muscular control.

Diving Readiness

The previous chapter identified readiness factors, such as strength, muscular control and common fears, which can determine whether a person is ready to learn headfirst entries. These same factors may apply as swimmers learn the basic dive from the pool deck. Entries for springboard dives are even more perpendicular to the surface of the water and result from a more powerful downward thrust achieved during the takeoff than when basic dives are performed from the deck.

The American Red Cross recommends that people first learn to perform headfirst entries at a shallow angle of entry (i.e., enter the water at a slight angle), swim parallel to the surface, steer back to the surface and then begin stroking. After swimmers are skilled in a shallow-angle headfirst entry for swimming, also known as the

nonslip material and give easy access to the diving board from the deck.

Some diving facilities have diving platforms (stationary structures for diving), which are constructed in various ways. A properly constructed platform includes a solid foundation and a nonslip surface. Well-equipped diving facilities may have 1-meter and 3-meter springboards as well as 5-meter, 7½-meter and 10-meter platforms (**Fig. 8-6**). Use diving platforms only under the direct supervision of a qualified diving coach or instructor.

The depth of the water for springboard diving is an important safety factor. Facilities should adhere to standards set by governing bodies, such as NCAA, FINA and USA Diving, before permitting any diving.

Fig. 8-6

Fig. 8-7

Fig. 8-8

shallow-angle dive (**Fig. 8-7**), they may move on to a basic dive and then to diving from a board (**Fig. 8-8**).

While the progressions for learning the basic dive are quite similar to the progressions for learning the shallow-angle dive, it is important to recognize the differences. The primary differences are in the angles of takeoff and entry, as well as the resulting underwater swimming path. The following progressions can help minimize fears and maximize success at each level. A diver who takes the time to master the skills of each step before moving to the next will enjoy the learning experience more and feel more ready to try the skills at the next level.

Beginning Diving

Components of a Basic Dive

A basic dive has four parts: the stationary starting position; the moment of propulsion, called the takeoff; the flight or trajectory; and the entry into the water. A diver can begin a basic dive from different starting positions that are discussed later in this chapter. The takeoff for a basic dive is quite easy, usually a slight push with one or both feet. A good entry involves entering the water at an appropriate angle while keeping the body aligned. Any well-executed dive requires concentration.

To maintain concentration and dive into the water at a correct point of entry, divers should focus on a target (either an imaginary point on the surface or a real or imagined target on the bottom of the pool) until the hands enter the water. The diver may close the eyes at that point and open them again after entering the water. Focusing on a target helps divers enter the water at the right place and at an appropriate angle, avoiding a belly flop.

Keeping the body aligned in an extended position is crucial for a safe and graceful dive. Keeping the head aligned between the upper arms is also very important because it can affect the position of the rest of the body. Moving the head back or up may cause the body to arch, while tucking in the chin too much may cause the body to bend at the waist. Lifting the head too far or too quickly can result in a painful belly flop for many beginners.

Fig. 8-9

Muscular control is important for proper body alignment and the body tension needed for a safe, effective dive. To maintain control and make the dive more graceful, divers should try to stay in a streamlined position in flight (i.e., during the passage of the body through the air) (**Fig. 8-9**). Proper alignment when entering the water reduces both drag and the risk of straining muscles or joints.

Physical Principles Involved

Form drag is an important principle in diving. Try to keep form drag to a minimum during the entry. Lifting the head before and during a headfirst entry, for example, increases form drag. Not keeping other body parts aligned (e.g., bending the body at the hips or knees) can also cause a part of the body to be stung by the impact with the water. A body that is not in alignment causes a big splash and results in an unattractive dive.

Other physical principles are at work in any dive. One of these principles is the law of action and reaction. When the feet push down and back against the deck with sufficient force during the takeoff (the action), the body is propelled upward and outward through the air (the reaction).

The law of inertia is also at work. Once in the air, the only external force acting on the diver is the diver's weight (gravity force). Because it acts downward, it slows, stops and reverses the upward momentum the diver generated during the takeoff and the diver then falls back toward the water after reaching the highest point of the dive.

As a diver submerges, the same force still tends to increase the diver's downward momentum. However, this force is largely counteracted by the buoyant force that acts upward. As a result, the diver's descent underwater slows and then stops, and the diver begins to rise slowly to the surface once the diver's specific gravity is less than that of water. If the diver's specific gravity is greater than that of water, as is the case for some individuals, the buoyant force will be less than the diver's weight and the diver will continue toward the bottom. In any case, it is necessary for the diver to assist the buoyant force and swim upward toward the surface.

Position for Headfirst Entry from a Diving Board

Body position for a diving board entry is even more important than from the deck because of the height and speed with which the body makes contact with the water surface. The diver must maintain a streamlined body alignment and sufficient muscular tension, as well as enter the water as close to vertical as possible. Practice proper body alignment in a standing position before trying headfirst dives from the diving board in the following way:

1. Hand position: Place the palm of one hand on top of the back of the other and grip the bottom hand with the fingers of the top hand. Interlock the thumbs. Hyperextend both wrists so the palm of the bottom hand hits flat on the surface.

Fig. 8-10, A

Fig. 8-10, B

This helps protect the head, neck and back and helps reduce splash upon entry (**Fig. 8-10, A**).

2. Arm position: Raise the arms overhead with hands in line with the shoulders and hips. Lock the elbows. Press the upper arms tightly against the ears and head.

3. Head position: Keep the head erect and tilted back very slightly to maintain alignment between the arms and with the torso. Tilting the head back or forward too far may reduce the streamlined body alignment, produce too much or too little muscular tension and possibly cause neck or spinal injury.

4. Upper body position: Lift the ribs up and align the back in a straight line (**Fig. 8-10, B**).

5. Hip position: Tilt the top of the pelvis (hips) backward to help reduce excess curvature or

sway in the lower back. Such sway creates tension in the lower back and spine and could lead to injury.

6. Leg and foot positions: Keep the legs straight at the hips and knees, and the toes pointed.

Progression for a Basic Dive from Poolside

Performing the steps for learning a basic dive from poolside will boost self-confidence and give a feeling of success. Divers should move through the progressions at their own pace, achieving competency in each level before moving on and not skipping any levels. Some steps might need more practice than others. Some divers with good coordination and kinesthetic awareness may be able to move more quickly through the steps than those with less coordination or kinesthetic awareness.

Fig. 8-11, A

Fig. 8-11, B

Surface Dive

1. Push off the wall into a glide to gain forward momentum.

2. Take a breath then tuck the chin while sweeping the arms back toward the thighs and flex at the hips sharply (pike position). Once the hands reach the thighs, slide the arms above the head and reach forward and downward toward the bottom, stretching the arms over the head (**Fig. 8-11, A**).

3. Lift the legs upward, keeping the knees straight and together so that the weight of the legs helps the downward descent (**Fig. 8-11, B**).

Kneeling Position from Poolside

1. Kneel on one knee on the pool edge. The leg in front should be bent with the toes of the forward foot gripping the pool edge. The other leg should be bent at the knee and the foot bent at the ankle in a position for the toes to help push from the deck.

2. Extend the arms over head with the upper arms pressing together against the ears (**Fig. 8-12**).

3. Focus on a target on the surface of the water about 2 feet from poolside.

4. Lean forward, keeping the chin tucked against the chest, try to touch the water with your hands and, when starting to lose balance, push with the legs. The objective is to dive downward, not outward.

5. On entering the water, straighten the body at the hips and extend both legs.

Divers should practice diving from a kneeling position until they are able to do it comfortably and enter the water smoothly each time.

Forward Dive Fall-In from Poolside

1. Stand with feet together or up to shoulder-width apart with the toes of both feet on the edge of the deck.

2. Bend at the waist so the upper body is at about a 45- to 90-degree angle to the legs (pike position) and focus on a target on the surface of the water about 2 feet from poolside.

Fig. 8-12

SPARGING SYSTEMS

Although diving is a noncontact sport, divers do collide with the water without any protective padding. Surprising as this may sound, if divers land horizontally on the water from a height of 10 meters, the force of the impact is measured in thousands of pounds. Such an impact can be quite painful and can cause severe injury, including ruptured organs and detached retinas.

The air sparging system, or "bubble machine," was invented to reduce the pain and risk of injury when divers learn new dives. Located on the pool bottom, the air sparger shoots air at high velocity into the pool, creating a uniform mixture of air and water in the area where divers enter the pool. The bubbles form a "mound" of water above the normal surface level of the water to cushion divers' entries. This protection allows divers to concentrate on the techniques of the dives rather than on the landing. It is especially useful for beginning divers who can build their skills and confidence in a more relaxed fashion and reduce their risk of injury.

Sparging systems can reduce the force of impact on the water by as much as 80 percent. This means that landing flat from 10 meters on bubbles would have almost the same impact as landing flat from 2 meters on "solid" water. Coaches control the system with a handheld remote that starts and stops the instant air release. They can start the system before divers leave the tower or board and stop it as soon as divers enter the water.

Although the sparging machine can reduce the force of impact, proper alignment is still important. When divers' bodies are not "tight" on entry, the force of impact can knock the wind out of them and even cause severe tissue injury.

Sparging machines are not a substitute for proper skills and should not be used as a crutch. But they can help divers gain the confidence and skill they need to perform dives into "solid" water.

Aside from reducing the risk of injuries to competitive divers, sparging systems also are used in many other ways. Surf-simulation (wave pools), treadmill swimming and whitewater canoeing are just a few examples of different uses for sparging systems. When safety precautions are properly taken, bubble machines can provide hours of recreational activity for people of all ages.

3. Tuck the chin to the chest and extend the arms overhead with the upper arms pressing together against the ears (**Fig. 8-13**).

4. Rise up onto the balls of the feet and fall forward toward the water, keeping the knees straight.

5. Fall forward, lift the hips and extend the legs upward so they are in line with the torso.

Depending on level of flexibility, divers may start with the feet closer together than shoulder-width.

Fig. 8-13

Standing Dive from Poolside

1. Stand with feet together or up to shoulder-width apart with toes gripping the edge of the deck.
2. Extend the arms over head with the upper arms pressing together against the ears.

3. Focus on a target on the surface of the water about 3 feet from poolside.
4. Bend at the knees and begin to angle the hands down toward the target.
5. Push off the deck, then lift the hips and extend the legs so they are in line with the torso, angle the hands down toward the target and keep the chin tucked toward the chest.

As divers gain confidence, they may move the feet closer together than shoulder-width.

Springboard Diving

Components of a Springboard Dive

A forward springboard dive adds several features to the elements of a basic dive from poolside. First, there is a moving start, involving a one- or two-part approach. Second, there is the interaction between the diver and the diving board, involving the downward press and the upward lift. The press is the diver's final downward push on the diving board assisted by the landing from the approach (**Fig. 8-14, A**). The lift is the force of the diving board pushing the diver into the air (**Fig. 8-14, B**). Third, there is the

Fig. 8-14, A

Fig. 8-14, B

Fig. 8-15, A

Fig. 8-15, B

Fig. 8-15, C

height component as the diving board is higher above the water than the pool deck. Additionally, the diver can execute a dive from a springboard in many different ways. The propulsive lifting

action of the diving board provides time for a diver to add somersaults and twists to the dive. Finally, depending on the type of dive, the entry is either feetfirst or headfirst.

There are several parts to the interaction between the diver and the diving board. The first is establishing the rhythm of the board with the approach, press and lift. The strength/power of the leg extension, the efficiency of the takeoff and the angle of the diver's body at the last instant of contact with the board determine the height and distance of the diver's flight.

Diving from a diving board requires more awareness than diving from a deck due to the bounce of the board, as well as the diver's movement during the takeoff. Before starting on a diving board, the diver must be able to do a standing dive from poolside with confidence. It is important for divers to master the progression of skills learned so far to develop greater ability, confidence and skill.

As mentioned earlier, springboard diving should only be taught and practiced under the supervision of a competent instructor or coach. The information that follows is for use in Red Cross Learn-to-Swim courses using a 1-meter diving board. Those interested in the sport of competitive diving should seek instruction from a competent and qualified diving instructor or coach.

The three basic positions for executing any dive are the tuck, pike and straight positions.

- In the tuck position, the body bends at the hips and knees so it forms a tight ball shape. Keep the body in a tight ball by grabbing both legs at the shins midway between the ankles and knees and pulling the knees close to the chest. Draw the heels up to the buttocks and point the toes (**Fig. 8-15, A**). Because of its compact position, it is easiest to do somersaults in the tuck position.

- In the pike position, the body bends only at the hips while the legs remain straight at the knees (**Fig. 8-15, B**). The arms and hands either reach toward the toes or grab both legs at the calves midway between the ankles and knees. The thighs are brought close to the chest.

- In the straight position, the torso of the body is straight or arched slightly backward with the legs together and straight at the hips and knees (**Fig. 8-15, C**).

In competitive diving, there is also a free position, which gives the diver an option to use any of the three basic positions, or combinations of the positions, when performing a twisting dive.

Physical Principles Involved

The height of a dive and its horizontal distance are the result of the diver's interaction with the springboard during the takeoff. During the takeoff, the diver gains energy from the board as it recoils. The diver's vertical velocity at the end of the takeoff determines how high the dive will go and how long the diver will be in the air while the horizontal velocity determines how far out the dive will go. Gravity, an external force acting downward, continuously reduces the diver's vertical velocity. As a result, the upward motion from the board becomes progressively slower until the diver reaches the peak of the flight and begins to fall back toward the water. The downward motion becomes progressively faster until contact is made with the water. Since there is no horizontal external force to change the diver's horizontal velocity during the flight, the diver will continue to move away from the board at a constant speed. The vertical and horizontal velocity along with gravity cause the diver's center of gravity (or mass center) to follow a parabolic (cone-shaped) path during the flight of the dive. Nothing the diver does while in the air can change this path.

Progression for a Basic Dive from the Diving Board

Learning a basic dive from a diving board should take place only after the diver learns how to dive from poolside. Learning to dive from the diving board begins with the kneeling dive. To practice the kneeling dive, move the fulcrum (if the diving board has one) all the way forward to make the diving board more stable. Once a diver is able to perform the kneeling dive, he or she should move on to the forward dive fall-in and standing dive from a diving board. When a diver is able

Fig. 8-16

to perform the kneeling dive, forward dive fall-in and then the standing dive confidently while using proper body alignment, he or she is ready to start learning springboard diving skills.

Kneeling Position from the Diving Board

Because the surface of the diving board may be rough and scrape the knee, consider putting a nonslip chamois or wet towel on the end of the board when using the kneeling position.

1. Kneel on one knee on the diving board. The leg in front should be bent with the forward foot flat on the board. The other leg should be bent at the knee with the foot bent at the ankle in a position for the toes to help push from the board.
2. Extend the arms over head with the upper arms pressing together against the ears.
3. Focus on a target on the surface of the water about 3 feet from the tip of the diving board.
4. Roll forward by dropping the hands and head, try to touch the water and, when starting to lose balance, push with the feet and legs (**Fig. 8-16**).
5. Straighten the body, extend both legs and point the toes immediately upon leaving the board.

Divers should practice the kneeling dive from the board until they can enter the water in a streamlined body position creating a minimal

Fig. 8-17

splash before moving on to the next step in the progression.

Forward Dive Fall-In from the Diving Board

The forward dive fall-in provides an opportunity to work on a streamlined body alignment and appropriate muscular tension for the entry without being concerned with the takeoff or flight. Practice proper body position first on dry land, as described on pages 145–146. Because the springboard is 1 meter (more than 3 feet) above the water surface, the forward fall-in dive provides plenty of time for the body to rotate forward enough to produce a streamlined entry, even for most beginners.

1. Stand with the toes at the tip of the diving board.

2. Grab the hands over head with the upper arms pressing together against the ears.

3. Bend at the waist so the upper body is at a 90-degree angle to the legs and focus on a target on the surface of the water about 3 feet from the tip of the diving board (**Fig. 8-17**).

4. Rise up slightly onto the balls of the feet and fall forward toward the water, keeping focused on the target.

5. Squeeze the upper arms against the ears while falling toward the water. The head should remain aligned between the arms.

6. Extend the body to a streamlined position for the entry.

Fig. 8-18, A

Fig. 8-18, B

Divers should practice the forward dive fall-in from the board until they can enter the water in a streamlined body position creating a minimal splash before moving on to the next step in the progression—a standing dive from the diving board.

Standing Dive from the Diving Board

1. Stand with feet together with the toes of both feet on the tip of the diving board.

2. Extend the arms over head with the upper arms pressing together against the ears (**Fig. 8-18, A**).

3. Focus on a target on the surface of the water about 3 feet from the tip of the diving board.

4. Bend the knees slightly and begin to angle the hands down toward the target.

5. Push off the board, lift the hips and extend the legs so they are in line with the torso (**Fig. 8-18, B**). Enter the water in a streamlined body position.

Divers should practice the standing dive from the board until they can enter the water in a streamlined body position creating a minimal splash before moving on to the next step in the progression.

Takeoffs
Dry-Land Practice
Dry-Land One-Part Takeoff on the Deck

The standing takeoff uses coordination of both the arms and legs to gain greater height for the flight. Start by standing upright with arms at the sides. Then move the body up-down-up into a jump as follows:

1. Slowly raise the heels up as the arms lift overhead into a "Y" position (**Fig. 8-19, A**).

2. Circle the arms slowly back and down as the knees begin to bend.

3. With the feet flat on the ground, continue to bend the knees into a squat and swing the arms from behind the hips forward and upward, extending into a straight jump (**Fig. 8-19, B**).

Dry-Land Two-Part Takeoff on the Deck

The body moves up-down-up, jumps forward from two feet, lands on two feet, rebounds and simulates a straight jump into the water as follows:

1. Slowly raise the heels up as the arms lift overhead into a "Y" position.

Fig. 8-19, A

Fig. 8-19, B

Fig. 8-20, A

Fig. 8-20, B

Fig. 8-21, A

Fig. 8-21, B

2. Circle the arms slowly back and down as the knees begin to bend.

3. With the feet flat on the ground, continue to bend the knees into a squat and swing the arms from behind the hips forward and upward, extending into a straight jump that travels forward about 2 foot lengths (**Fig. 8-20, A**).

4. Jump again immediately after touching down, circling the arms back and down while jumping high and traveling forward (**Fig. 8-20, B**).

Poolside Practice
One-Part Takeoff from Poolside

1. Slowly raise the heels up as the arms lift overhead into a "Y" position.

2. Circle the arms slowly back and down as the knees begin to bend (**Fig. 8-21, A**).

3. With the feet flat on the ground, continue to bend the knees into a squat and swing the arms from behind the hips forward and upward, extending into a straight jump that lands feetfirst in the water (**Fig. 8-21, B**).

Diving Board Practice

Divers should always begin diving from the diving board with the fulcrum as far forward as possible for better stability. Once they become comfortable with the takeoff motion, they can adjust the fulcrum.

One-Part Takeoff from the Diving Board

Focusing on a point in the middle of the pool helps keep the head in the proper position.

1. Stand upright at the tip of the diving board with the toes at the edge.

2. Slowly raise the heels up as the arms lift overhead into a "Y" position.

3. Circle the arms slowly back and down as the knees begin to bend.

4. With the feet flat on the board, continue to bend the knees into a squat and swing the arms from behind the hips forward and upward, extending into a straight jump that lands feetfirst in the water (**Fig. 8-22, A and B**).

Fig. 8-22, A

Fig. 8-22, B

COMPONENTS OF A COMPETITIVE DIVE

Competitive dives have grown in variety and difficulty over the past several decades. Divers continue to prepare new combinations of skills to be used in competition. All dives, however, involve some combination of the following elements, although not all combinations are approved for competition—or are even possible.

Equipment: Dives may be made from a 1-meter or 3-meter springboard or from a platform that is 1, 3, 5, 7$\frac{1}{2}$ or 10 meters high.

Takeoff: A diver may leave the apparatus facing forward (e.g., using an approach and hurdle from a springboard or a standing jump from a platform) or facing backward (e.g., using a backward press).

Somersaults: Regardless of the takeoff direction, somersaults may be forward (with a rotation in the direction the diver is facing) or backward (with the opposite rotation).

Body position: The body may be in tuck, pike, straight or free positions.

Twists: A twist is a rotation along the midline of the body, which is held straight during the twist. Twisting may be combined with somersaults in some dives.

Entry: The water entry may be headfirst or feetfirst.

Depending on the combination of elements, each dive is assigned a degree of difficulty. Judges' evaluations are based on the approach, the height (whether the dive reaches an appropriate height), the execution and the entry (whether the diver creates a "ripped" entry or whether there is excessive splash). A diver's score in competition is based on both the degree of difficulty of the dive and the judges' scores.

Two-Part Takeoff from the Diving Board

As divers gain confidence, have them move to a starting point 2 foot lengths back from the tip of the board. Focusing on a point in the middle of the pool helps keep the head in the proper position.

1. Measure 2 foot lengths back from the tip of the board.

1. Slowly raise the heels up as the arms lift overhead into a "Y" position.

2. Circle the arms slowly back and down as the knees begin to bend.

3. With the feet flat on the board, continue to bend the knees into a squat and swing the arms from behind the hips forward and upward, extending into a straight jump that travels forward about 2 foot lengths (**Fig. 8-23**).

4. Jump again immediately after touching down, circling the arms back and down while jumping high and traveling forward into a straight jump that lands feetfirst in the water.

Tuck and Pike Positions
The Tuck Position

A simple dry-land exercise helps divers get used to the tuck position.

1. Sit or lie on the deck and pull the knees up to the chest.

2. Grab both legs at the shins midway between the ankles and knees, pulling the knees tight to the chest to form a tight ball shape.

Forward Jump, Tuck Position

The forward jump tuck lets the diver experience the feeling of the tuck position during flight. This skill also helps the diver maintain upright body position control. Start with a jump from poolside and progress to greater heights to become more comfortable. The gradual progression from poolside to greater heights also helps ensure success with a jump tuck from the 1-meter diving board.

Fig. 8-23

Fig. 8-24

One-Part Takeoff with Forward Jump Tuck from Poolside

After practicing the tuck position sitting or lying on the deck, try the jump tuck from poolside in the following way:

1. Stand with feet together on the edge of the deck.
2. Perform a one-part takeoff, jumping as high as possible and moving into a straight jump position.
3. While in flight, pull the knees up to the chest and grab them briefly (**Fig. 8-24**).
4. Kick the legs and straighten them toward the water. Enter feetfirst in a streamlined position.

One-Part Takeoff with Forward Jump Tuck from the Diving Board

The standing jump tuck from a diving board is done in the same manner as from poolside (**Fig. 8-25**). Practice this skill

Fig. 8-25

until comfortable and able to enter in a streamlined position with minimum splash before moving on.

Two-Part Takeoff with Forward Jump Tuck from Diving Board

The next step is to combine the two-part takeoff with a tuck jump and kick out into deep water. Although this gives greater height for doing the jump tuck, divers should perform the tuck on the ascent and stretch into a straight line as they pass the board on the descent. As divers gain confidence, have them move to a starting point 2 foot lengths back from the tip of the board.

Forward Dive, Tuck Position

One-Part Takeoff with Forward Dive Tuck from Poolside

Once proper entry technique and one-part takeoff with forward jump tuck positions have been mastered, divers should try a forward dive tuck from poolside into deep water. Begin the forward dive tuck by standing at the edge of the deck with arms overhead.

1. Focus on a target point at a 45-degree angle across the pool. This will help keep the head in the proper position at the start of the dive and help the body rotate forward for the headfirst entry.

2. Start by using the one-part takeoff. Just before the legs push against the deck to begin the dive, throw the arms overhead to propel the upper body, arms and head into a tuck position. The motion of the arms is similar to the one used to throw a ball overhead using two hands (**Fig. 8-26, A**).

3. Grab the middle of the shins for the tuck position with the thighs on the chest and the heels on the buttocks as the body rotates forward (**Fig. 8-26, B**).

4. Attempt to kick the legs out on the way up.

5. While coming out of the tuck, bend the elbows and move the hands up the midline and grab the hands overhead to prepare for entry. Swinging the arms straight out in front can cause the legs to go past vertical.

6. Align the body in a streamlined position and reach for the entry with the hands (**Fig. 8-26, C**).

Dropping the head too much before takeoff or pushing the hips over the head increases

Fig. 8-26, A

Fig. 8-26, B

Fig. 8-26, C

Fig. 8-27, A

Fig. 8-27, B

rotation. This rotation can be controlled in a number of ways. If it feels as if the dive is going past vertical, come out of the tuck position and reach for the entry. If it feels as if the dive is short of vertical, stay in the tuck position slightly longer. Practice will help the diver learn to rotate the right amount and when to come out of the tuck.

One-Part Takeoff with Forward Dive Tuck from the Diving Board

With toes on the tip of the board, repeat the forward dive tuck on the diving board using a one-part takeoff.

Two-Part Takeoff with Forward Dive Tuck from the Diving Board

Start 2 foot lengths back from the tip of the diving board. Perform the two-part takeoff and combine it with a forward dive tuck (**Fig. 8-27, A–C**).

Fig. 8-27, C

Fig. 8-28, A

Fig. 8-28, B

Forward Dive, Pike Position

To perform the forward dive in the pike position, allow the hips to rise up while reaching for the toes after the body has left the board (**Fig. 8-28, A–C**). Keep the legs straight at the knees and bend only at the hips. After touching the toes with the fingers, extend the arms in front, squeezing the ears between the arms, in preparation for the entry. Practice the forward dive pike using the following steps:

1. The pike position (on the deck)
2. One-part takeoff with forward jump pike from diving board
3. Two-part takeoff with forward jump pike from diving board
4. One-part takeoff with forward dive pike from diving board
5. Two-part takeoff with forward dive pike from diving board

Fig. 8-28, C

CHAPTER 9
Disabilities and Other Health Conditions

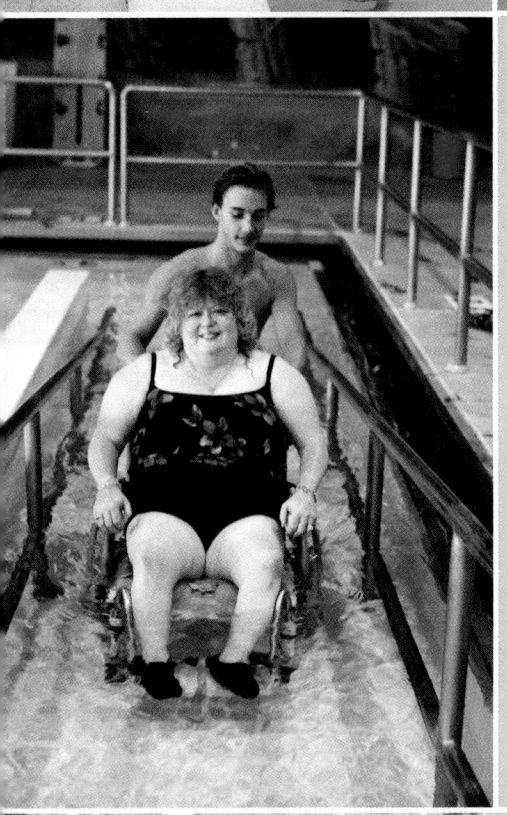

With the proper awareness, training and the right equipment, almost everyone can enjoy the health, fitness and recreational benefits of aquatics, including the approximately 50 million Americans who have disabilities or other activity-limiting health conditions, such as asthma or a heart ailment. Older adults and others, such as those who are obese or overweight, have a difficult time participating in various fitness activities as well. Yet none of these conditions should exclude a person from participation in aquatics.

This chapter provides an overview of certain disabilities and health conditions and explores the many advantages of aquatics for people with disabilities and other health conditions. It will also discuss specific facility accommodations, program choices and safety concerns that can better serve all swimmers.

Attitudes and Norms

According to the Americans with Disabilities Act (ADA), an individual with a disability is a person who has a physical or mental impairment that significantly limits one or more life activities. The ADA (Public Law [PL] 101–336) has helped to increase awareness that people with disabilities and other health conditions are entitled to the benefits of any type of program offered in our communities.

Disabilities are a normal part of human existence. Society has been enriched by the contributions of many individuals with disabilities, such as Harriet Tubman and Ludwig Van Beethoven. Given the opportunity, many individuals with a wide range of abilities can participate in and benefit from all types of activities, including aquatics.

The American Red Cross is supportive of people with disabilities and other health conditions who want to participate in its aquatic programs. All people are encouraged to join these programs based on their own performance standards. These programs do not seek to label the person or restrict participation but rather to meet everyone's individual needs and to focus on a person's ability, not his or her disability. The primary goal is to first try to include any person with a disability in a mainstream aquatics activity.

Just as with any exercise program, anyone interested in starting an aquatics program should first check with a health care provider to get approval to participate, especially those who have not exercised in a while. It is also important for anyone with specific concerns about limitations caused by a specific health condition to consult a health care provider before entering any aquatics program.

Disabilities and Aquatic Activities: Facts and Myths

The Individuals with Disabilities Education Act (IDEA) mandates free and appropriate education, including physical education, to all children with disabilities from birth through 21 years of age. A provision of this act is that children with disabilities be placed in the least restrictive environment (LRE) possible. This means, whenever possible and appropriate,

Fig. 9-1

individuals should be placed in the same setting as their peers.

These same principles apply to aquatic programs. Aquatic programs should make accommodations and modifications to help individuals with disabilities and other health conditions participate (**Fig. 9-1**). Accommodation means adjusting the way a program or class is run without changing the objectives in order to help an individual succeed. For example, an instructor may need to use visual cues in class or programs may need to create smaller classes or allow for more time. Modification means adjusting the way an individual participates in a class or program. By making accommodations for the individual and modifications to the learning environment, many people with disabilities can participate in most aquatic programs.

Benefits of Participation in Aquatics

There are many types of aquatic activities that offer opportunities for those with disabilities and other health conditions to fulfill their potential. Aquatic programs can help most individuals meet their desire for challenge, success, recognition, accomplishment and social activity. Swimming and aquatic exercise in particular have great rehabilitative value for individuals of all ages and health conditions. This chapter focuses on aquatic activities that are conducted in a pool or designated swimming area. However, the aquatics world is not limited to the pool or the beach. National organizations for many water sports also have addressed the needs of individuals with

WATER TEMPERATURES

When people begin swimming or any other aquatic activity their body temperatures increase. Because the whole body is immersed in it, the temperature of the water can dramatically affect the body's ability to cool down or maintain heat. This is why the temperature of pool water for most aquatic activities should be between 83 to 86 degrees Fahrenheit (28 to 30 degrees Celsius). Water in this temperature range allows the body to adjust naturally to physical demands of exercise without overheating or needing to conserve heat.

However, certain activities should take place in water temperatures slightly outside this range. Water temperature should be slightly cooler for vigorous activities, such as swim team practice, lap swimming or certain types of water aerobics. Aquatic programs for strength toning and other programs that involve slow controlled movements should take place in slightly warmer water.

Because the recommended water temperature for certain types of aqua therapy and rehabilitation is quite high when compared to other aquatic activities, many facilities have separate pool(s) for these types of programs.

Older adults, children and people with certain disabilities and health conditions can also benefit from slight adjustments to water temperature. For example, older adults involved in low-intensity exercise may feel more comfortable in warmer water. People with multiple sclerosis on the other hand, may enjoy slightly cooler water. It is important to remember that each person is unique. In most cases, swimmers should pay attention to their own bodies to determine the best water temperature. The table below shows some recommended water temperatures for different activities and groups of people.

Aquatic Exercise Association (AEA)—Recommended Water Temperatures

Activity/Population	Water Temperature
Swim team and lap swim	77°–82.4° F/25°–28° C
Resistance training	83°–86° F /28°–30° C
Therapy and rehabilitation	91°–95° F /33°–35° C
Multiple sclerosis	80°–84° F /26.5°–29° C
Pregnancy	83°–85° F /28°–29.4° C
Arthritis	84°–88° F /29°–31° C minimum range 86°–90° F /28°–32° C low-function range
Older adults, moderate to high intensity	83°–86° F /28°–30° C
Older adults, low intensity	86°–88° F /30°–31° C
Children, fitness	83°–86° F /28°–30° C
Children, swim lessons	84° F and up, depending on age, class length and activity
Obese	80°-86° F /26.5°-30° C

In addition to adequate water temperature, participants in most aquatic programs should be encouraged to begin movement as soon as they enter the pool and keep up some type of activity in order to maintain body heat. Many people can become cold quite quickly after a short pause in activity, even if the water is relatively warm. Participants who feel too warm can be encouraged to slow down their activity level to stay comfortable in the water.

disabilities. Canoeing, kayaking, rowing, sailing, scuba diving and waterskiing are open to a wide range of participants. A person who becomes comfortable in a pool setting can be encouraged to explore additional aquatic programs, making swimming a gateway into the larger world of aquatics. The personal rewards gained through participation in aquatics are endless, but for persons with disabilities they include physiological, psychological and social benefits.

Physiological Benefits

Swimming can enhance overall physical fitness. Swimming improves and maintains cardiovascular endurance (the ability of the heart and lungs to sustain vigorous activity), muscular strength, endurance and flexibility. It can also help with weight management.

Swimming also may help to improve motor function (the brain's ability to direct reflexive and voluntary movement activities). Motor function includes the following components:

- Speed–The ability to act or move with different velocities

- Agility–The ability to change direction during locomotion

- Perceptual motor function–The ability to integrate perception with action; to develop balance, control and visual and auditory discrimination; and to improve spatial orientation (the understanding of one's location in space and position with reference to other objects)

Although anyone who exercises regularly in the water may gain physiological benefits, these benefits may be particularly important to persons with disabilities and other health conditions. Because of its unique physical properties when compared with the land environment, water may be the only environment where people with certain physical limitations can move freely and improve their physical fitness (**Fig. 9-2**).

Psychological Benefits

For many people with disabilities, the water is a very special place. Because swimming gives many individuals with disabilities and other health conditions the chance to experience and be successful in a physical activity, it can be a tremendously positive psychological experience.

Fig. 9-2

The psychological benefits include–

- Experiencing success. The opportunity to do something well and to feel successful is central to happiness in life. Too often success is defined through major, hard-to-attain accomplishments, ignoring the smaller day-to-day victories that truly make us happy. Whether it is letting go of the side of the pool or swimming the entire length, swimmers have the opportunity to be successful every time they enter the water (**Fig. 9-3**).

- Enhancing self-confidence. Experiencing success can make people feel better about themselves. Swimmers can gain self-confidence by mastering basic aquatic skills, such as floating, swimming, entering the water or just getting wet. Other swimmers can develop greater self-confidence through increased fitness or physical ability. When others, especially peers, see a person as successful, self-confidence can also improve.

- Independent mobility. Many movements can be done in the water that are difficult or even

Fig. 9-3

impossible to do on land for some individuals with disabilities. Being able to move more freely in water can be a huge psychological boost, especially for those with few chances to move independently on their own.

- Having fun. Let's face it: swimming is a blast! Almost everyone enjoys swimming and people with disabilities and other health conditions are no exception. Jumping in and out, cooling off on a hot day or just playing around in the water with friends brings happiness to a great many (**Fig. 9-4**).

Social Benefits

Humans are social creatures and all of us need positive interactions with other human beings. Often times, individuals with disabilities and other health conditions do not participate or fail to succeed in certain programs and activities because low expectations are placed on them. As a result, society often denies the social benefits of full participation in mainstream activities to persons with disabilities. Organized aquatic activities are an excellent way to provide a positive social experience for all, offering a wide range of social benefits, including–

- Peer-group interaction. Activities in the water can provide opportunities for acceptance by peers and for learning acceptable social behavior, such as sharing and taking turns. Swimming in groups is also a way to make friends.

- Inclusion. Categories and labels for disabilities often focus on the impairment rather than the individual and can have the effect of discouraging individuals with disabilities and other health conditions from participating in certain activities. All people should have opportunities to function in the mainstream of society. Aquatic programs are no exception.

- Safety. Personal safety in, on or around the water improves as aquatic skills are gained. This benefit is a primary goal of the Red Cross Swimming and Water Safety program.

Needs of People with Disabilities

At the foundation of an inclusive aquatics program is the knowledge that all people differ in many ways, some of which may affect participation in aquatics. A basic understanding of how different types of impairment affect participation in

Fig. 9-4

aquatics is necessary to accommodate the diverse needs of all swimmers and make appropriate modifications. The following sections describe some categories of differences and techniques for including persons with these types of disabilities and other health conditions in aquatic programs.

Hearing Impairment

A person with a hearing impairment has some degree of hearing loss. People with mild to moderate hearing loss are referred to as "hard of hearing." People who are hard of hearing have some ability to hear and use it for communication purposes. People with total or near total hearing loss are referred to as "deaf," not to be confused with the uppercase "Deaf," which refers to a community of Deaf people who share the same language, such as American Sign Language (ASL). People who are deaf cannot rely on hearing for communication or processing auditory sensory information.

Some people are born deaf or hard of hearing while others develop hearing loss due to childhood disease, pregnancy-related illness, injury or advancing age. Hearing loss can also be brought on by certain medicines and long-term exposure to loud noise. Some people who are deaf or hard of hearing may also have impaired speech. Impaired speech does not indicate impairment in intelligence. A number of people who are deaf or hard of hearing also have trouble with balance and/or coordination, which can affect their adjustment to the water.

A person who is deaf or hard of hearing may receive only parts of a verbal message. In an aquatic environment, adjustments in communication techniques are often necessary to accommodate the needs of people who are deaf or hard of hearing. Visual communication, done through demonstration, gesture, speechreading and sign language, is often the most effective way to convey information (**Fig. 9-5**). A very small

Fig. 9-5

percentage of people who are deaf or hard of hearing use hearing aids, which makes the need for visual communication important because hearing aids cannot be worn in the water. As a result, people who are deaf or hard of hearing should wear goggles and keep their eyes open while swimming. Those who wear contact lenses should wear goggles or remove the lenses before opening their eyes under water.

The following tips can help instructors, lifeguards and aquatics staff better communicate with people who are deaf and hard of hearing:

- Use sign language, even if only a small amount is known.

- Reduce auditory distractions.

- Make sure the area is well lit.

- Look directly at the person when talking and maintain eye contact.

- Use facial expressions to help convey messages.

- Use body language or a gentle touch to get the person's attention.

- If possible, provide written information, charts or pictures.

- Speak slowly, naturally and clearly.

- Use interpreters when needed. If using an interpreter, address the person not the interpreter.

Vision Impairment

Vision impairment is a collective term used to refer to various degrees of vision loss, including low vision, legally blind and total blindness. Visual impairments may be congenital or caused by infection, injury or advancing age. They may also be caused by health conditions, such as diabetes or macular degeneration.

The specific parameters of low vision vary, but low vision generally refers to a person with a visual acuity of less than 20/70. A person with 20/70 visual acuity sees at 20 feet what a person with "normal" vision sees at 70 feet. A person with a visual acuity of less than 20/600 in the stronger eye using the best possible correction is legally blind. Total blindness refers to the inability to perceive shapes or light. Other individuals may have visual acuity that is in the "normal" range

but also have oversensitivity to light, which affects their ability to see in certain environments.

In an aquatic environment, people with vision impairments need to be able to listen to and hear others. Learning and using strokes that keep the ears out of the water allows swimmers with visual impairments to stay in communication with others and be aware of their environment. It is also often necessary to use touch and other audible signals, such as whistles to promote clear communication (**Fig. 9-6**).

Individuals with low vision should be encouraged to use as much functional vision as possible. They can wear prescription eyeglasses or use contact lenses while swimming to help utilize functional vision. Masks can also be fitted with prescription lenses. Swimmers electing to wear eyeglasses should wear an old pair because pool chemicals can corrode frames. An elastic strap or a swimming cap can be used to help keep the eyeglasses in place. Individuals with contact lenses should wear goggles or a mask and avoid diving and swimming under water. For safety reasons, diving must not be permitted when glasses are worn.

Some individuals who are blind or visually impaired may use a sighted guide. A sighted guide provides assistance by walking alongside a person

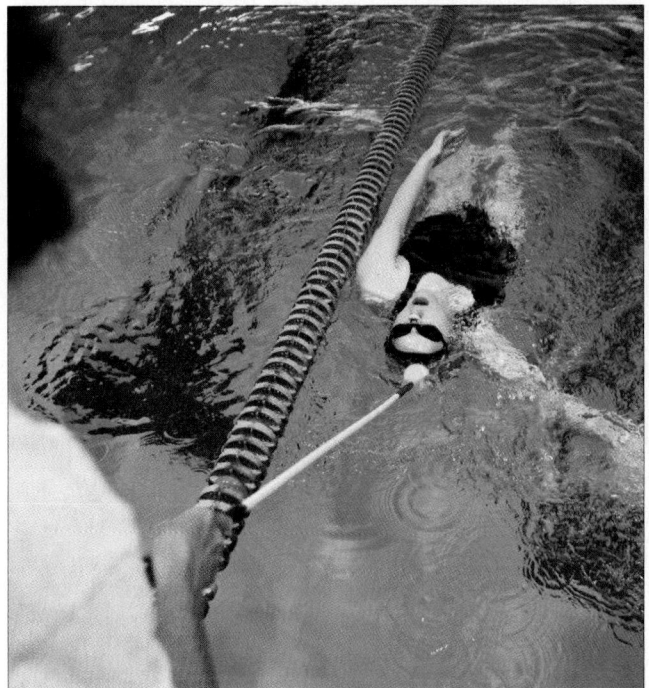

Fig. 9-6

who is blind or visually impaired. If you are asked or volunteer to perform this service, do not grab or hold onto the person. Instead, after determining whether a blind or visually impaired person needs assistance, offer your arm to the person and maintain contact until the final destination is reached or assistance is no longer necessary.

Developmental Disabilities

Developmental disabilities are a wide range of conditions affecting a person's intellectual, social and/or physical development. The term "developmental disabilities" specifically refers to conditions that appear before a person reaches the age of 21, resulting from trauma to the brain or nervous system that in some way affects its development.

Some developmental disabilities result from a genetic disorder, such as Down, Williams or Fragile X syndromes. Developmental disabilities can also be caused by childhood accidents, exposure to toxins and poisons and certain conditions that develop during pregnancy or in infants. Often times, the exact cause is unknown.

Individuals with developmental disabilities often have difficulties with language, social skills, mobility, learning and/or cognitive ability. Some types of conditions resulting from developmental disabilities include intellectual disability, epilepsy, autism and cerebral palsy.

Developmental delay is common in persons with developmental disabilities. In developmental delay, physical, social and cognitive development may take place at a slower rate. As a result, individuals with developmental disabilities may not reach certain developmental stages or milestones at the same time as other children their age. However, each person with developmental disabilities is unique and individual abilities vary greatly within this population. Many individuals with developmental disabilities are able to participate and benefit from inclusion in most aquatic programs.

Intellectual Disability

An intellectual disability is a condition that appears before the age of 18 that is characterized by below average intellectual function and limitations in the skills necessary for daily independent living. Many people with intellectual disabilities have additional conditions, such as a vision or hearing impairment. Approximately 1 percent of the total population lives with an intellectual disability.

Intellectual disabilities can be categorized into four main groups based on IQ: mild, moderate, severe and profound. People with a mild intellectual disability can develop the intellectual and communication skills necessary for independent living. People with a moderate intellectual disability have more difficulty developing the skills necessary for independent living and may or may not live on their own. Individuals with a severe to profound intellectual disability have very limited communication and self-care skills and usually need assistance for day-to-day living. Many individuals with a mild or moderate intellectual disability can participate in mainstream aquatic programs with little or no accommodation. Individuals with a severe-to-profound intellectual disability however, require specialized instruction.

Down Syndrome

Down Syndrome is a congenital disorder that usually causes delays in physical and cognitive development. People with Down Syndrome vary widely in cognitive abilities, behavior and physical development. Many people with Down Syndrome can benefit from aquatic exercise (**Fig. 9-7**).

Fig. 9-7

A small number of people with Down Syndrome may also have *atlantoaxial instability.* This is a weakness in the ligaments between the first two vertebrae. A swimmer with this condition must not dive, and a health care provider should be consulted about other possible limitations. The National Down Syndrome Congress recommends cervical x-rays to determine whether this condition exists.

Epilepsy

A person who has recurring seizures has a condition known as *epilepsy*, also known as seizure disorder. Seizures are the result of sudden, abnormal electrical activity in the brain lasting from 30 seconds to 2 minutes. While some seizures involve convulsions and loss of consciousness, there are many different types of seizures, some of which are mild. The great majority of seizures do not cause any harm. In children, epilepsy is often the result of a brain disorder, but epilepsy also occurs in adults often following a stroke, brain tumor or head injury.

Anyone with epilepsy is at a higher risk for drowning and must take care when near the water. No one should ever swim alone, but this is especially true for people with epilepsy. However, most people with epilepsy can join an aquatics program, as long as it is closely supervised. Anyone whose seizures are poorly controlled should consult with the appropriate medical professional before beginning an aquatics program. Additionally, anyone with poorly controlled seizures needs close supervision and should wear a U.S. Coast Guard-approved life jacket to help support the head in the event of a seizure. It may be appropriate to place these individuals in an adapted aquatics program staffed by specially trained personnel.

A seizure that occurs in the water is an emergency and should be treated as such. Anyone experiencing a seizure in the water needs help immediately. During a seizure, the person may go under water without warning or a calling for help. The person who is having a seizure or who has just had a seizure may not be breathing or may try to breathe while under water. Both conditions can cause life-threatening problems.

If someone has a seizure in the water, support the person to keep the head and face above the water so that he or she can breathe. Call the lifeguard for help and make sure that emergency medical services (EMS) personnel are called.

The following guidelines can help instructors, lifeguards and aquatic staff make their aquatic programs safer for individuals with epilepsy:

- Never let a person with epilepsy swim alone. When a person with epilepsy is in the water, make sure that someone is present at all times who knows what to do if the person has a seizure.
- Ensure that children (and in some cases adults) whose seizures are poorly controlled wear a Type 1 life jacket (supports the head and neck) when near water.
- Do not let a person with epilepsy get overtired or too cold while in the water.
- Remind individuals with epilepsy to take their seizure medication before swimming. Individuals with epilepsy should not swim if they have not taken their seizure medication.
- Provide a dry place to store seizure medications. Seizure medications should never get wet; several medications lose efficacy when exposed to the water.

Cerebral Palsy

Cerebral palsy is a group of disorders affecting balance and posture that develop in childhood. Cerebral palsy results from damage to the parts of the brain that are responsible for muscle control. This damage occurs before, during or shortly after birth often due to illness during pregnancy. A person with cerebral palsy might have any of these characteristics:

- Limited range of movement in affected joint areas
- Limited control over voluntary movement of affected limbs or joints
- Random or involuntary movements
- Absence of normal muscle tone or an overabundance of muscle tone
- Abnormal muscle reflex patterns
- Impaired speech
- Possible seizures

People with cerebral palsy have a difficult time controlling the movements of their bodies and many develop serious muscular damage due to spasticity or stiffness in the muscles later in life. The limitations caused by cerebral palsy range from mild to severe. One person with cerebral palsy may walk unassisted while another may lack the ability to control most body movements. Some children with cerebral palsy may also have intellectual disabilities, learning disabilities, epilepsy and/or hearing or vision impairment and some may not. Many individuals with cerebral palsy also have trouble speaking, but do not assume that a person with cerebral palsy also has a cognitive impairment because he or she has difficulty speaking.

Some people with cerebral palsy whose symptoms are mild can participate quite successfully in aquatic programs. Swimming is very good for increasing and maintaining range of motion in joints and muscle flexibility. The water also gives people with cerebral palsy a safe environment for physical activity. The increased buoyancy of water and the warmth of a heated pool also relieve body stiffness and stress. Specialized instruction may be needed for persons with cerebral palsy whose impairment is more severe (**Fig. 9-8**).

Autism

Autism, also called autistic spectrum disorders (ASD) is usually first diagnosed in early childhood. The exact cause of autism is unknown although the prevalence of autism is on the rise. According to the Centers for Disease Control and Prevention (CDC), one out of every 150

Fig. 9-8

Aquatic therapy is a type of physical therapy performed in water, usually a pool. Trained physical therapists or physical therapy assistants design aquatic therapy programs to help maintain or restore function in people of all ages who have acute or chronic impairments or disabilities. Aquatic therapy can be useful when treating people with many different medical problems, including—

- Pain.
- Weakness.
- Limited range of motion.
- Balance deficits.
- Heart disease.
- Obesity.
- Orthopedic injuries.
- Arthritis.
- Neurological disorders.

The water has several properties that make it a good environment for therapy. The buoyancy of water helps support people's weight while they exercise without placing stress on the joints. The resistance of the water can help people who need to strengthen their muscles. The hydrostatic pressure of the water helps reduce swelling and improve awareness of joint position. Aquatic therapy in warm water can help relax muscles and improve blood flow.

During aquatic therapy, people perform exercises and activities in the water, such as walking and jumping that may be difficult for them to do on dry land. The exercises can help them reach new functional goals and enhance their quality of life. For example, aquatic therapy can help maintain or improve—

- Balance and coordination.
- Agility.
- Endurance and aerobic capacity.
- Flexibility.
- Muscle strength and endurance.
- Body mechanics and posture.
- Gait.
- Self-esteem.

8-year-olds in the United States has autism. Autism frequently occurs with other health conditions such as seizures, attention deficit hyperactivity disorder (ADHD), sleep disorders, depression or a cognitive impairment. Individuals with autism may have difficulty with fine or gross motor skills and sensory perception.

Autism affects how a person communicates, interacts with others socially and participates in many activities. Communication impairments associated with autism often result in slower processing of information and delayed, atypical or non-existent speech. In social interactions, some individuals with autism may not make eye contact or be able to appreciate others' perspectives. These social impairments may lead people with autism to make statements or interact with others in ways outside of what is considered typical social behavior.

Many people with autism may engage in ritualized or repetitive behavior and may not adjust well to changes in routine or environment. Some people with autism react fearfully to new situations while others have very little fear, which may lead them into dangerous situations. In an aquatic environment, this means that some people with autism may need significantly more time to adjust to being around water, while others need vigilant supervision because they may be unable to fully appreciate the dangers associated with water.

It is important to recognize that autism is a spectrum of disorders. Sometimes the needs of those with higher functioning autism are overlooked because they do not possess the social and/or communication skills to express their needs, while people who are lower functioning (less able to participate in mainstream activities) may have many more apparent needs than higher functioning individuals. Each person with autism is unique and may have different needs for participation in aquatics.

The following tips can help instructors, lifeguards and aquatic staff better work with individuals with autism:

- Maintain routines.
- Give warnings of upcoming changes in activities or schedule.

- Use visuals to give directions, if possible, and try to pair with verbal instructions (**Fig. 9-9**).
- Verbal messages should be short and clear.
- Avoid using slang or jargon.
- Try simplifying messages if not first understood.
- Respect each individual's functional needs.
- Do not assume that an individual does not understand because of inappropriate behavior.
- Talk with parents to find out which techniques or types of cues work best for their child.
- Be aware that many individuals with ASD have sensory challenges that may make things, such as loud noises, physical contact and bright lights upsetting or confusing.

Learning Disability

A learning disability is not the same as an intellectual disability. Learning disabilities affect how a person understands, remembers and responds to new information. Most learning disabilities are not recognized until a child reaches school age.

Although some people with learning disabilities also have intellectual disabilities, many do not. People with learning disabilities may have difficulties staying focused, speaking, reading, writing or doing math. However, there are a number of adaptive strategies that people with learning disabilities can use to succeed while in a learning environment. In an aquatic environment, it is helpful to teach skills in small chunks that are repeated and reviewed frequently before moving on to the next skill.

Fig. 9-9

Attention Deficit Hyperactivity Disorder

Children or adults with an especially hard time paying attention or controlling their behavior may have ADHD, which is a condition diagnosed by health care providers who specialize in this disorder. Many people with ADHD also have a learning disability.

ADHD Facts:

- 8 to 10 percent of all children have ADHD.
- ADHD begins during preschool years.
- Boys are more likely to have ADHD than girls.
- Children with ADHD may need extra help learning to do things other children find easy.

ADHD is divided into three main categories: hyperactivity, inattention and impulsivity. Hyperactive behaviors include fidgeting, frequent moving around between locations or activities and difficulty staying still. Forgetfulness, difficulties paying close attention and difficulties with organizing tasks and activities are associated with inattention. Impulsivity behaviors include blurting out comments in inappropriate situations, interrupting others and difficulty taking turns. In an aquatic environment, it may be necessary to limit distractions and provide one-on-one instruction whenever possible for participants with ADHD.

Emotional Behavioral Disability

The term emotional behavioral disability refers to a range of conditions affecting how a person acts in social and other settings. Specific conditions include anxiety disorders, severe depression, bipolar disorder, conduct disorder and schizophrenia. People with emotional behavioral disabilities may not have the same level of emotional or social functioning as those in their peer group. Persons with emotional behavioral disabilities display serious and persistent age-inappropriate behaviors that result in social conflict, personal unhappiness and a lack of success in school and other settings.

There are two categories of emotional behavioral disorders: internalizing and externalizing. Externalizing behaviors include hyperactivity, defiance, hostility and cruelty. Males are more likely to be identified as exhibiting externalizing behaviors than females. Internalizing behaviors include social withdrawal, guilt and depression. Generally speaking, internalizing behaviors are focused more inward and externalizing behaviors are directed more toward others. In aquatic programs, rewarding positive behavior, ignoring disruptive behavior and consistently using appropriate consequences for negative behavior can help these individuals experience success.

Tactile Impairment

Tactile impairment is the partial or total loss of the sense of touch. Someone with a spinal injury might not feel anything in areas of the body below the injury. A person with spina bifida may also lack both sensation and motor function in the lower part of the body.

Lack of sensation should not keep anyone out of the water. Because people with tactile impairment would not feel scratches, abrasions, burns or the rubbing that causes blisters, they must take care to avoid scratching or scraping the skin in the pool. They must also take care to avoid temperature extremes, wear protective foot covering and check frequently for red skin (which may indicate a reaction to water pressure). Also, check the shower temperature when it is used before and after swimming.

Mobility Impairment

Mobility impairment refers to the large number of health conditions affecting a person's mobility. Some of the health conditions that cause mobility impairments include amputation, paralysis, cerebral palsy, stroke and spinal cord injury. There are varying degrees of limitation caused by mobility impairments. For example, one person who has a mobility impairment may not have the strength or control necessary to grasp or lift an object, while another person may not be able to use one or more of his or her extremities. The use of a wheelchair, crutches or a walker may be utilized to aid in mobility (**Fig. 9-10**).

Kinesthetic awareness is the conscious sense of where the body is, where its parts are positioned or how they are moving at any given moment. If this function is impaired, the person may not sense his or her body's position in relation to

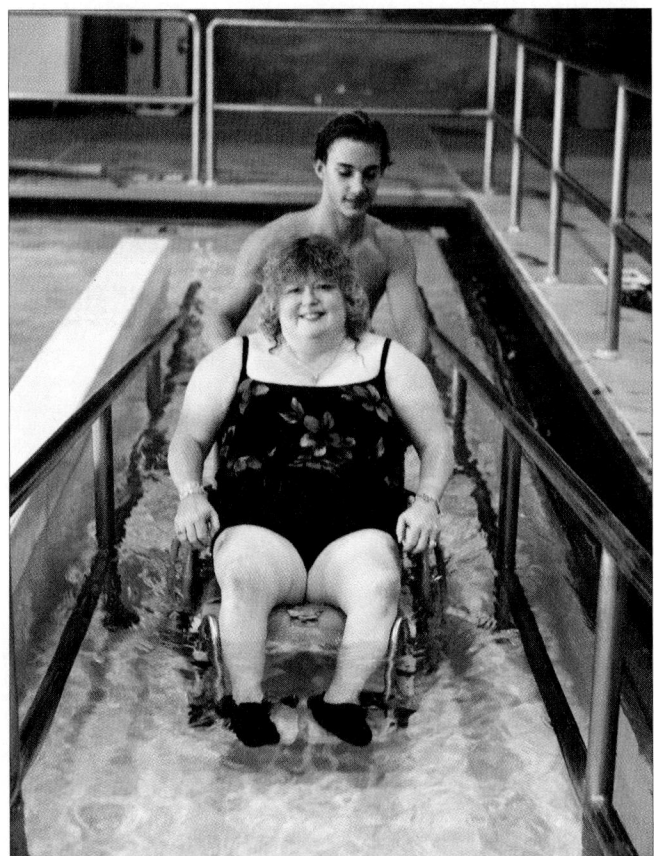

Fig. 9-10

space and other objects. There may be problems with balance in the water, swimming in a straight line and learning to float and recover.

Motor Function

Motor function refers to the brain's ability to direct both reflexive and voluntary movements. The brain and nervous system control the muscular and skeletal systems. Impairment in any of these systems can result in decreased physical capability. If the person cannot use a body part because of impaired or lost function, motor activity can be limited. Orthopedic impairments are disorders of bones, joints and tendons. Neurological impairments are disorders of the nervous system, including the spinal cord, nerves and brain. Such impairments may impede locomotor function and can be caused by trauma (such as amputation, spinal lesions, peripheral nerve injury, head injury or stroke), a congenital condition (such as spina bifida) or an infection (such as poliomyelitis or tuberculosis). Mobility impairment may also be caused by dislocated

hips, joint replacements and osteomyelitis (an inflammation of bone and bone marrow that is usually caused by bacterial infection).

Loss of Motor Function

Complete loss of use of a body part can result from congenital or traumatic amputation. People lacking the function of a body part can participate successfully in most aquatic programs. These individuals may need assistance in the locker room, moving to the pool and entering the water (**Fig. 9-11**).

Most people with amputations can participate successfully in regular swimming programs. While a prosthesis, such as an artificial limb, may be used for land activities, it cannot be worn in the water. As a result, entering and exiting the water may pose some difficulties. Also, a person who uses a prosthesis may need a larger locker or a nearby place to keep the prosthesis while swimming. A private dressing area is desirable.

Complete or partial loss of the use of a body part can also result from spinal cord injury, stroke or damage to nerves controlling those body parts. Whatever the cause, nerve impulses from the brain do not reach the muscles to move the body part. Paralysis (the loss of sensation, voluntary motion or both) or paresis (partial loss of sensation, voluntary motion or both) may affect the legs (as in paraplegia), one side of the body (as in hemiplegia) or both arms and legs (as in quadriplegia).

Fig. 9-11

Strokes happen when the flow of blood to the brain is cut off. A stroke can cause paralysis, usually on one side of the body. Some strokes result in weakness on one side of the body instead of paralysis. Other stroke conditions include a decreased sense of pain, touch or temperature; difficulty speaking, reading or writing; or *aphasia*–the absence or impairment of the ability to communicate through speech, writing or other nonverbal methods. Aqua therapy is often effective for people recovering from a stroke. The warm pool water and the buoyancy experienced in an aquatic environment can provide relaxation and improve flexibility, strength, range of motion and circulation.

Paralysis often results in other body complications. For example, some people with paralysis may lack bowel and bladder control and may wear a collection bag. Paralysis of multiple body parts may limit motor function severely and a specialized aquatics program may be needed until the person adjusts to and becomes mobile in the water. Special considerations for people with paralysis include–

- Offering programs conducted in uniform, warm temperatures. Avoid sudden temperature changes.
- Limiting weight-bearing activities, unless approved by a physician.
- Avoiding cuts or abrasions caused by scraping the hands and feet, especially if sensation is reduced.
- Preventing chilling and fatigue brought on by poor circulation.
- Emptying the collection bags of individuals with bowel or bladder control problems before swimming and ensuring the bags are secured to the body. If the person does not have a collection bag, a cloth diaper and tight-fitting rubber pants should be worn.

Impairment of Motor Function

Motor function can be temporarily impaired because of illness or trauma, such as from orthopedic surgery, a broken bone or muscle strains and sprains. It also may be a permanent but stable condition or a progressively degenerative condition, such as muscular dystrophy or amyotrophic lateral sclerosis (ALS), also called Lou Gehrig's disease.

Degenerative conditions may affect a person's participation in aquatics over time. Multiple sclerosis, ALS and various forms of muscular dystrophy lead to decreasing motor function, but many people can join an aquatics program in the early phases of these diseases. As the condition progresses, the following changes are likely:

- Decreased control over voluntary motor activity
- Weakened muscles
- Increased susceptibility to other illnesses
- Impaired balance
- Increased difficulty with locomotion
- Decreased thresholds for fatigue
- Impairment of other body functions
- Development of sensory symptoms, such as numbness, tingling and sensations of pain

For such people, aquatics can play an important part in rehabilitation. People who swam before the onset or progression of the disease can stay functional in the water long after motor function on land is severely impaired. Some help in the locker room and transfers to and from the pool may be all that is needed. Someone who joins a program after the disease is progressing or who is experiencing problems in breathing, maintaining head control, recovering balance or staying in a safe position in the water may need specialized instruction and assistance (**Fig. 9-12**).

Other Physical Conditions

Other physical conditions may require extra attention when the person joins an aquatic program. However, these conditions should not prevent the person from participating in aquatics. In fact, people who have any of the following conditions can benefit greatly from aquatic exercise.

Aging

With aging often comes an increase in chronic disease, especially cardiovascular disease. For many people however, much of the reduced function that occurs with aging is related to physical inactivity. Exercise is a key element for good health and independent living for senior citizens.

Fig. 9-12

Seniors who want to learn to swim or resume swimming again, but who have not gotten much exercise recently, should talk to a health care provider before starting any exercise program. They should also begin gradually. The primary goal is usually to reach and maintain a level of fitness, improve one's physical condition or delay the onset of chronic disease. Most aquatic programs for senior citizens are very similar to other programs. The water should be slightly warmer, at least 83° F (28° C), and the aquatic activity should be less intense than that for a younger group. For those with a chronic disease, the intensity may have to be reduced even more.

Arthritis

The major goal of an aquatic program for people with arthritis is to decrease pain and increase the range of motion in the affected joints. Aerobic exercise of moderate intensity can be effective at decreasing pain and increasing mobility and also improves cardiovascular endurance (**Fig. 9-13**). People with arthritis are generally more comfortable in warmer water (84° to 88° F or 29° to 31° C – minimum range, 86° to 90° F or 28° to 32° C – low functioning range), although water at the high end of this

range may be too warm for an aerobic workout. Aquatic activities should not worsen the pain. If pain results and does not subside within 2 hours after the workout, the person should shorten future workouts or modify the painful activity.

Asthma or Allergies

Someone with asthma or allergies can enjoy aquatics. Indeed, the breath control learned with aquatic skills often helps relieve the symptoms

Fig. 9-13

of asthma and allergies. Those who are allergic to pool chemicals should seek out a pool with a different chemical composition. A person using an asthma inhaler should keep the inhaler at poolside.

Cardiac and Blood Conditions

Aerobic exercise is therapeutic for people recovering from some cardiovascular or respiratory conditions. Walking and swimming are the most popular activities for cardiac rehabilitation, but aquatic exercise is also popular because it is easily tolerated, low impact and has a low risk of injury.

Cardiac patients should exercise at a lower intensity, depending on their physical abilities, but aquatic exercise is safe for most cardiac patients. An exception is the postoperative patient requiring continuous monitoring for variations in heart rate. Patients should follow guidelines set by their health care providers.

Persons with a blood disorder (such as sickle cell anemia) or a cardiac condition can join in aquatic activities that are paced to their level of endurance and involve minimal physical stress. Comfort is important for these individuals. If a person becomes cold or tired, experiences discomfort or otherwise becomes stressed, activity should be stopped for the day. Avoid overexertion.

In most cases, the body's response to exercise in the water is like that on land, provided that the water is at an appropriate temperature. Cold water slows the heart rate and is a stress on the cardiovascular system. Water that is too warm may cause heat stress.

Cystic Fibrosis

Cystic fibrosis is an inherited disorder of the glands that causes abnormalities in respiration, perspiration and digestion, as well as hyperactivity of the autonomic nervous system. A person with cystic fibrosis can join an aquatic program during the early stages of the disease. Breathing exercises learned in aquatics can enhance air exchange in the lungs and help maintain health and fitness. The person may need a towel poolside to cough and spit phlegm into. As the disease progresses,

aquatic activity will become too physically stressful for the body and will eventually have to stop. Physical comfort and the person's desire to continue are the key factors in deciding how long to stay in a program.

Diabetes

No one should exercise alone in a pool, but persons with diabetes should be especially cautious because of the risk of a diabetic emergency, which may result in unconsciousness. The increased activity of water exercise may upset a diabetic person's insulin balance, leading to dizziness, drowsiness and confusion. Individuals with diabetes should have snacks on hand.

Fragile Bones

People with osteogenesis imperfecta (fragile bones) often find swimming an excellent form of exercise, because swimming helps build muscle mass, stimulate bone growth and maintain flexibility. Physical trauma, which could occur from such things as manipulating a body part, swimming in turbulent water or colliding with another person should be avoided because it could cause severe injury. People with osteogenesis imperfecta should always wear a life jacket for safety and use less strenuous strokes, such as the sidestroke or elementary backstroke. They should not dive or jump into the water.

Obesity

People who are overweight should exercise at a moderate level for the first few weeks. After that, they may extend the workout because the duration of the exercise is more important for weight management than intensity. Because people who are overweight can also be extremely buoyant, it is important that the limbs move with sufficient speed to make the exercise beneficial.

A person who is overweight is at some risk for coronary heart disease and may have other risk factors, such as high blood pressure, high blood sugar and high cholesterol. Aerobic exercise provides benefits that can counteract all these risk factors. However, changes in body composition occur slowly unless the diet is modified as well.

CHILDHOOD OBESITY

American children continue to gain weight. The number of children who are overweight rose at an alarming rate over the past several decades. Health experts worry about this disturbing trend for several reasons. Overweight children are more likely to face social problems. They are also at greater risk of developing serious health problems, including—

- High blood pressure.
- High cholesterol.
- Type II diabetes.
- Sleep apnea.
- Asthma.

In addition, overweight children and teens are more likely to become obese adults.

Health care providers usually do not recommend that most children diet or participate in weight-reduction programs because they are still growing and developing. Instead, parents can help their children from becoming overweight. The key to success is helping children balance the amount of calories they take in with the calories they use through normal growth and physical activity.

Healthy eating plays a major role in regulating the amount of calories a child consumes. Parents can help their children develop nutritious eating habits by—

- Teaching children about nutrition. Parents can help children become more aware of their eating habits and the relationship between eating habits, weight and activity level.

- Encouraging children to eat a variety of healthy foods. Vegetables, fruits, whole-grain products, low-fat or nonfat dairy products, lean meats, chicken, fish and beans are some good choices. It is also a good idea to help children limit the amount of saturated fats they consume.

- Controlling portion size. Parents should serve their children reasonably sized portions and avoid the large and super-sized meals available at many restaurants.

- Limiting high-calorie beverages. Children should drink plenty of water. Children should avoid sugary juices and carbonated beverages, which are full of empty calories.

- Making meals healthier. Parents do not have to give up favorite family meals. Instead, they can look for healthier ways to make the foods their family enjoys.

It is also important for children and teens to be active. Parents should set limits on the amount of time children spend on sedentary activities, such as watching television or playing computer or video games. Healthy children should engage in moderate-intensity activities for at least an hour on most days of the week. Swimming, playing tag, jumping rope, playing soccer or basketball and dancing are some activities that are fun and can help children stay healthy. Varied physical activity can help children manage their weight, strengthen their bones, reduce blood pressure, relieve stress and improve their self-esteem.

Weight-management programs that combine diet with exercise produce better results than diet or exercise alone. The key to successful weight management is to follow the program consistently. People with obesity may find it easier to stay with an aquatic exercise program because the environment is cool, comfortable and relaxing, as well as effective.

Safety

Hazards exist in any aquatic program, but these hazards are a greater risk for some people with disabilities and other health conditions. Differences in vision, balance, sense of direction, concept of space, depth perception and muscular control can all increase the risk of swimming for some individuals. For instance, a wet pool deck presents a modest hazard to an able-bodied person but the same hazard becomes significantly more dangerous to someone with limited mobility. Both the participant and the instructor of the program should be aware of the following special considerations:

- People with mobility, balance or motor-control impairments may need help moving on wet decks and ramps. A person using crutches or a walker or who has a prosthesis may need help. Devices to assist a person with a disability get into and out of the water should be available Most of these devices are portable and can be removed from the deck when not in use (**Fig. 9-14**).

- If an individual uses a wheelchair, it should be used between the locker room and pool. Brakes must be locked when the person is entering and leaving the chair. Children should also use their wheelchairs, as it is unsafe to carry anyone, even small children, on wet, slippery decks. Bathrooms should have private dressing rooms and designated dressing tables or areas designated for people who need to dress or be helped to dress lying down.

- People with limited control of their legs should not enter the water feetfirst from a diving board or from a height; twisting and injury to muscles are possible. Instead, people with limited control of their legs should learn entries from the deck.

- Safety signs and depth markings must be clearly marked. Signs should contain pictures and words.

Fig. 9-14

Other items that help make the pool area safer for individuals with disabilities include a contour line along a wall; clear indications of exits, water depth and location of emergency equipment; and a tape recording of pool rules. Handholds should be at or slightly above water level; if it is hard to hold on to the edge of the pool, a rope or railing can be added.

- In outdoor settings, temperature fluctuations and sun exposure should be closely monitored.

In addition, the following pool and facility features help provide safe access for individuals with disabilities:

- Designated parking near the entrance to the facility

- Doorways that are wide enough for wheelchairs (32-inch minimum width)

- Easily understood hallway access

- Accessible bathroom facilities

- Absence of stairs between entry and locker rooms

- Handheld or low-level showerheads and shower chairs or benches

- Hair dryers mounted at various heights

- Uncomplicated traffic pattern to pool area

Safety precautions for specific medical conditions should be followed carefully. When in doubt, check with the parents or health care provider for recommendations.

To ensure safety for individuals with visual impairments, decks should be kept free of clutter, doors should be kept either completely closed or wide open rather than ajar, possible hazards should be explained verbally, lifelines should be used to mark depth variance and people with visual disabilities should be instructed to alert the instructor or lifeguard when they need help.

Safety education is a vital part of every aquatic program. Everyone should learn personal safety skills, such as how to wear a life jacket, and take basic water safety courses. It is equally important that everyone learn land-based rescue skills that are consistent with their abilities. **Chapter 3**

Fig. 9-15

contains important information about what to do in an aquatic emergency.

Programming

People with disabilities and other health conditions have many different opportunities to participate in aquatic programs based on their abilities. On one end of the continuum, people with disabilities participate in the same lessons and activities with able-bodied peers while instructors and facility staff modify instruction or make accommodations to meet the needs of the participant (**Fig. 9-15**). This is called mainstreaming. On the other end is one-to-one instruction in an adapted aquatics program provided by a Water Safety instructor specially trained to teach people with disabilities. Between these two ends of the continuum is a variety of possibilities.

The selection of the right program is an important decision. People with disabilities or other health conditions should participate in programs that best meet their needs and physical abilities. They should also be able to move from program to program when their needs change. Everyone should have access to Red Cross aquatic programs. However, program administrators also have a responsibility to others in the class or program. At times, it is necessary to set up individualized programs for people with disabilities and other health conditions so that everyone can benefit from the classes they take.

People with disabilities and other health conditions have the following rights and responsibilities when they are applying for an aquatic program:

- The right to general information about the aquatics program, so they can determine if it suits their needs
- The right to apply for entry into the program
- The right to a specific explanation if the instructor believes the program is not suitable for the person
- The responsibility to give the instructor any pertinent information concerning their condition
- The responsibility to comply with an instructor's request for a pretest or trial lesson if needed
- The responsibility to provide one's own assistance, if needed, for dressing and for pool entry and exit

Expanding Opportunities in Aquatics

Competition

People with disabilities and other health conditions have opportunities in two types of competitive programs. The first is with able-bodied peers. Swim teams and swim clubs should be open to any person who makes the qualifying standards, despite any impairment. A disability should not be a barrier to successful competition against able-bodied peers.

Competition is also available through organizations geared to those with specific disabilities. Organizations, such as Special Olympics, offer athletes at all levels of ability the opportunity to train and compete in basic aquatic skills. Competition is also available at the elite level for athletes with disabilities, including the Paralympics Games, which are held in the same year and at the same venues as the Olympic Games, and the Fédération Internationale de Natation Amateur (FINA) World Swimming Championships.

Recreation

Recreational activity is important for everyone. Aquatic recreational activities include skin diving, scuba diving, boating, adventure recreation, water sports and visiting waterparks. All these are opportunities to develop additional aquatic skills. People with disabilities and other health conditions who are interested in any of these activities should do the following:

- Check with their health care provider before starting a new, active recreational activity, especially any that involve adventure or risk.

- Determine what swim skills are needed to begin the activity and learn those skills first.

- Take any needed lessons from a qualified or certified instructor.

- Advise the instructor, program director and lifeguard of any limitations. This knowledge will help them provide a safe environment.

- Participate with an able-bodied buddy. This can make learning more fun and ensures a person is there to help if needed.

CHAPTER 10
Lifetime Fitness and Training

Thanks to technology, most people use less physical effort in their daily lives than people in previous generations did. While technology has made life easier, there is a downside: many people do not exert themselves enough to maintain good physical health and fitness. Those with inactive lifestyles are more prone to serious health problems, including cardiovascular disease (disease of the heart and blood vessels), obesity, high blood pressure, diabetes and muscle and joint problems. Now, more than ever, people need physical activity in their daily lives.

The information in this chapter will be helpful for anyone wishing to use aquatics as part of a workout routine. Whether it is to start a training program to enhance fitness, add aquatics to an existing fitness program or improve performance at swimming competitions, this chapter outlines the basic knowledge necessary to enjoy aquatic programs for lifetime fitness and training.

Aquatic Fitness Programs

Aquatic programs are very effective forms of exercise for most people whether they are novices, physically fit or competitive swimmers. This chapter presents information on two basic types of aquatic fitness programs that may be appropriate for all fitness levels—fitness swimming and aquatic exercise. It also provides information on training programs for serious or competitive swimmers.

In fitness swimming workouts, swimming strokes are used to reach a specified level of intensity sustained for a set time (**Fig. 10-1**). Fitness swimming is an excellent way to improve overall physical fitness and especially the health of the cardiovascular system (the heart and blood vessels, which bring oxygen and nutrients to the body).

Aquatic exercise is an in-water fitness activity generally performed in a vertical position with the face out of the water (**Fig. 10-2**). Aquatic exercise workouts involve walking, jogging and jumping in shallow water or running in deeper water, sometimes using a flotation device (**Fig. 10-3**). These movements of the limbs through the water create resistance. Some aquatic exercise programs focus on cardiovascular fitness; others emphasize muscular strength and flexibility. An example of aquatic exercise is standing in neck-deep water and flexing the elbows to bring the palms toward the shoulder (bicep curls).

Before beginning any physical activity or fitness program, participants should see their health care

Fig. 10-2

provider for a thorough examination. This is especially true for those who have not exercised in a long time.

Training refers to a physical improvement program designed to prepare people for competition in sports. It is characterized by exercise of higher intensity than that used to

Fig. 10-1

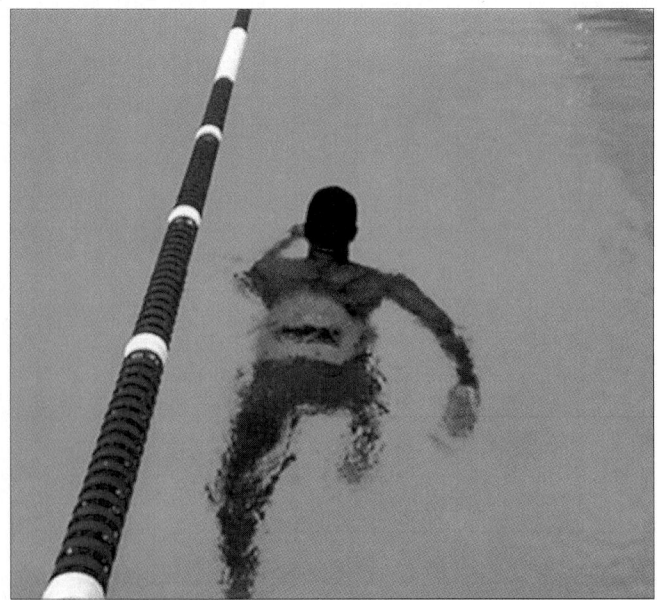

Fig. 10-3

improve health-related fitness. People who undertake training programs should already have a good level of fitness before the training begins.

Benefits of Aerobic Exercise

Aerobic exercise is rhythmic, physical exercise that requires additional effort by the heart and lungs to meet the body's increased demand for oxygen for a sustained period of time. When people perform aerobic exercises frequently enough, their bodies change in ways that improve their health. The benefits of regular aerobic exercise, also known as the training effect, include–

- Improved cardiovascular endurance.
- Increased muscular strength and endurance.
- Enhanced flexibility.
- Better weight management.

Cardiovascular Endurance

The cardiovascular, or circulatory, system supplies oxygen and nutrients to the body through the blood. Cardiovascular diseases cause more than half the deaths in the United States. The most common type of cardiovascular disease is coronary artery disease. This results from the narrowing and hardening of the coronary arteries, which carry oxygen-rich blood to the heart (**Fig. 10-4, A and B**). Risk factors that contribute to coronary artery disease include–

- Smoking.
- High blood pressure.

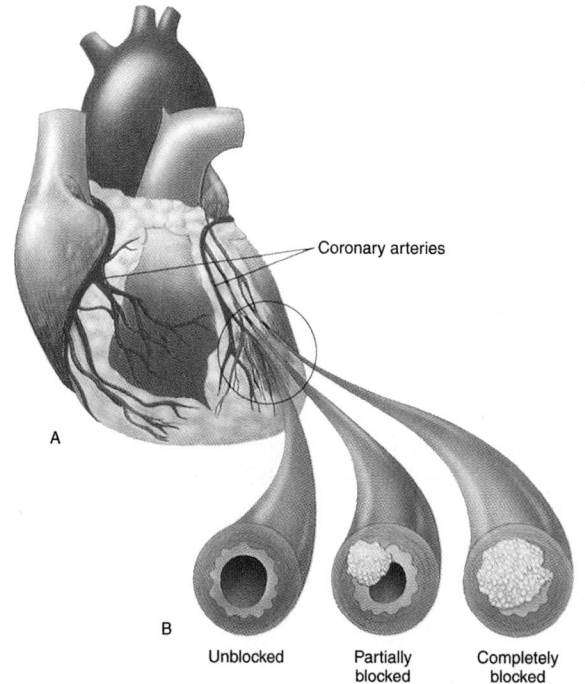

Coronary arteries

A

B   Unblocked   Partially blocked   Completely blocked

Fig. 10-4, A and B

- Obesity.
- High cholesterol.
- Diabetes.
- Lack of exercise.

With the right exercise, cardiovascular efficiency (also known as aerobic capacity) improves (**Fig. 10-5**). The heart becomes stronger and can pump more blood with each beat. Circulation

Fig. 10-5

improves and the blood vessels stay healthy. Other benefits include—

- Lower heart rate at rest and in moderate exercise.
- Shorter recovery time (the time it takes for the heart to resume its regular rate after exercise).
- Improved blood circulation to the heart.
- Increased capacity of the blood to carry oxygen.
- Increased ability of muscles to use oxygen.
- Decreased lactic acid, a byproduct of exercise that may cause muscle soreness and fatigue.
- Lower resting blood pressure (especially in people with high blood pressure).
- Lower cholesterol levels.

Muscular Strength and Endurance

Muscular performance involves both strength and endurance. Muscular strength is the ability of muscle to exert force. Strength leads to endurance, power and resistance to fatigue. Muscular strength protects against joint injury and helps maintain good posture.

Weakness in some muscles causes an imbalance that can impair normal movement and cause pain. For instance, a weak core (muscles in the abdomen, back and pelvis) combined with poor flexibility in the lower back and hamstring muscles (at the back of the thigh) can lead to lower back pain. Lower back pain is a major problem in the United States, costing millions of dollars a year in lost productivity. Muscular imbalances cause up to 80 percent of all lower back problems. Muscular strength is an important factor for staying healthy and avoiding or correcting muscular imbalances. Aquatic activity is a popular, effective way to develop this strength.

Muscular endurance is the ability of muscle to contract repeatedly with the same force over an extended period. Greater muscular strength often improves muscular endurance. For many people, muscular endurance, which helps to resist fatigue, is more important than strength for athletic activity.

Muscular strength and endurance generally decrease as people get older or become less active. Over time, the loss of strength and endurance may reduce the ability to do everyday chores and enjoy recreation. For this reason, the American College of Sports Medicine (ACSM) recommends muscular development exercises two or three times per week.

Aerobic exercise has the following benefits, especially when strength and flexibility exercises are included:

- Improves range of motion and function
- Increases strength and endurance
- Increases strength of tendons and ligaments
- Improves muscle tone
- Improves posture
- Reduces lower back pain and other disorders caused by inactivity

Flexibility

Flexibility is the range of motion of a joint or group of joints. Flexibility varies from joint to joint in the same person. Having flexibility in some joints does not translate to overall body flexibility. Sufficient flexibility helps prevent injuries to the bones, muscles, tendons and ligaments (**Fig. 10-6, A and B**). Ligaments are the strong elastic tissues that hold bones in place at the joints (**Fig. 10-7**). Tendons attach muscles to the bones. Although flexibility is partly determined by heredity, individual flexibility improves with stretching.

Weight Management

Up to half of the adults in the United States are thought to be overfat. Being overfat is not the same as being overweight. People who weigh more than the average based on their sex, height and frame size are considered overweight. People are considered to be overfat if the percentage of fat in their bodies is higher than recommended. These weight standards are published in tables with weight ranges for males and females of different heights and frame sizes. However, most of these tables do not account for body composition. Because muscle is heavier than fat, people with large muscles and a normal percentage of body fat may be classified as overweight. That is why it is important to consider actual body fat, as well as weight. People can

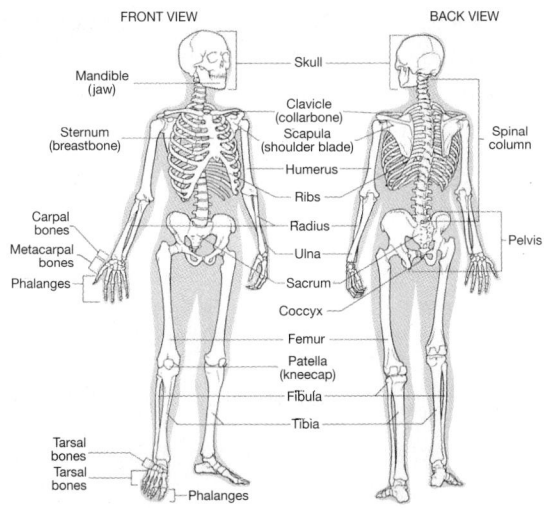

Fig. 10-6, A

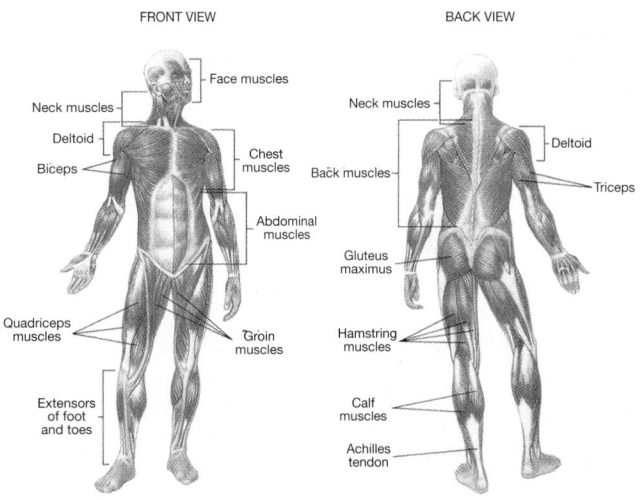

Fig. 10-6, B

ask their doctor or other health care provider for information about how to have their body fat measured.

Overfat individuals are at greater risk for many chronic health problems, such as diabetes, high blood pressure, coronary artery disease, stroke and some types of cancer. According to the Centers for Disease Control and Prevention (CDC), obese people are at an increased risk for many diseases and health conditions, including high blood pressure, Type II diabetes, stroke and coronary heart disease. The health consequences associated with obesity are so great that encouraging

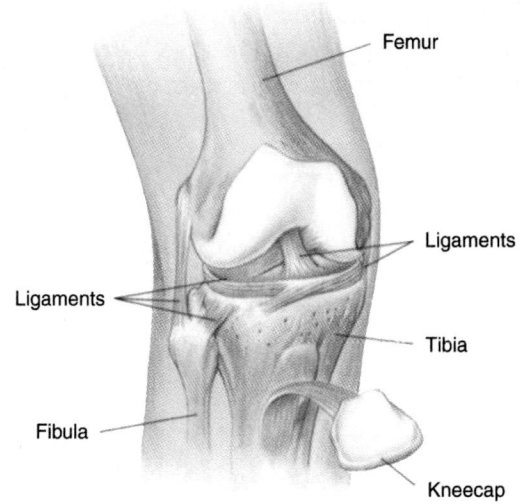

Fig. 10-7

people to achieve and maintain proper body weight and body fat percentages has become a national health priority.

Regular exercise is important for successful long-term weight control (**Fig. 10-8**). Exercise increases the basal metabolic rate (the amount of calories the body burns at rest). Moderately intense exercise also depresses appetite and improves mood. Most people who exercise regularly can eat more than inactive people can and still not gain weight.

Aerobic exercise helps control body weight in the following ways:

- Increases the rate at which the body burns calories

- Decreases body fat

- Maintains lean muscle tissue when losing weight or dieting

- Increases the body's ability to use fat as fuel

Specific Benefits of Exercising in Water

Whether engaging in aquatic exercise or fitness swimming, exercise in water has unique benefits. Buoyancy decreases the impact on the joints and the risk of injury. Because water helps cool the body during exercise, workouts in cool water are refreshing, a benefit for those prone to heat stress. On the other hand, exercise in warm water increases blood circulation and promotes

Fig. 10-8

healing of injured tissues. (See **Chapter 9** for recommended pool temperatures for different activities and conditions.) Warm water eases muscle spasms, relaxes tight muscles and increases joint motion.

Water resistance also helps improve muscular strength and endurance. Moving in and through the water helps maintain and improve flexibility. Because water resistance can be controlled or adjusted by speed or

MEASURING BODY COMPOSITION

Body composition can be tested to see the effect of a diet and training program on muscle and fat composition. The test breaks down body weight into the total lean weight and the total fat weight. When swimmers exercise and watch their diet, their muscle strength and capacity increase and their percentage of body fat declines. The body composition test allows monitoring of any changes.

There are many ways to measure body composition. Anthropometric tests measure the circumference of different body parts and then calculate body composition. Skinfold tests use a caliper to measure fat under the skin at different places, then make similar calculations. Bioimpedance tests measure electric currents through the body. Because the electrical properties of fat differ from those of muscle, the measurements can be used to calculate body composition.

A more accurate technique is underwater weighing, also known as *hydrostatic weighing*. This technique is based on the principle discovered by Archimedes, a mathematician and inventor who lived in ancient Greece. According to legend, Archimedes was looking for a way to determine the purity of the gold in King Hiero's crown when he discovered the physical principle of buoyancy. This is the basis for hydrostatic weighing. (For more details on buoyancy, see **Chapter 4.**)

Weighing a person in water provides the total body density (weight/volume). Because fat is less dense than bone and muscle, a person with a higher percentage of body fat will have a lower density. Thus, hydrostatic weighing can be used to determine the amount of body fat.

positioning, workouts can be designed to meet the needs of everyone, regardless of age and fitness level.

Adjusting Exercise Levels

The body is affected by any exertion. As the body exerts more energy, pulse and breathing rates speed up, sweat starts and additional calories are burned. Physical fitness comes from exerting the body beyond certain limits. To reach or maintain a level of fitness, exercise must put sufficient stress on the cardiovascular system to cause it to adapt beyond its current state. This stress must be achieved without too much or too little work, and it must be of sufficient duration. To become more fit, people must work harder than normal so the capacities of their muscular and cardiovascular systems increase. This is called overload.

Setting Up an Exercise Program

A person trying to achieve and maintain a healthy level of fitness needs to establish and follow an exercise program. A sound fitness program depends on the workout frequency, intensity, duration and type. Individuals who are striving for improvements in specific areas must include the particular exercises, activities or skills they wish to improve in their exercise programs.

Frequency refers to how often the exercise is done. The recommended frequency of exercise for most people is at least 3 days a week, for endurance exercises. The minimum frequency of exercise for strength building exercises is at least 2 days a week. Exercising more than 5 days a week usually does not lead to additional improvement and may lead to increased injury and fatigue. Specific exercise frequency depends on individual fitness goals. For example, to lose fat, it is better for people to exercise 5 days a week rather than 3.

Intensity refers to how hard people work when they exercise. This is the most difficult of the three factors to assess. People achieve better results if the intensity of their workouts stays within an optimum range. While very low-intensity exercise does have some benefits, cardiovascular improvement is slower when people exercise below the optimum range. Intensity above the target range can cause excessive fatigue and can lead to injuries. High-intensity exercise is difficult to sustain, so workouts usually are shorter, which may limit benefits to the cardiovascular system.

Duration, or the time spent during each exercise session, also affects the benefits. Muscular development sets should last for 20 minutes. Aerobic sets should last for at least 30 minutes at the recommended level of intensity. Warm-ups should last 5 to 10 minutes before starting the aerobic activity. At the end of workouts, people should gradually decrease the intensity of their workout followed by a cool-down period of 5 to 10 minutes and then move on to stretching exercises for 10 to 12 minutes.

Type refers to the kind of exercise performed. The principle of specificity is the most important factor in choosing what type of exercise to perform. For example, people wishing to improve their level of cardiovascular fitness should engage in cardiovascular types of exercises. The basic rule is that to improve performance, people must practice the particular exercise, activity or skill they want to improve.

Target Heart Rate Range

One way to determine proper exercise intensity is by measuring heart rate, which assesses physiological stress. The more intense the exercise, the higher the heart rate becomes. The ideal heart rate range needed to achieve the greatest cardiovascular benefit is called the target heart rate range (**Fig. 10-9**). This rate is calculated in several ways. One of the simplest methods for determining this rate involves calculating a percentage of the maximum heart rate, which depends on a person's age.

Fig. 10-9

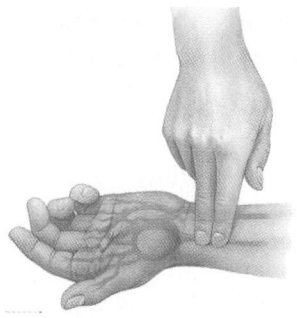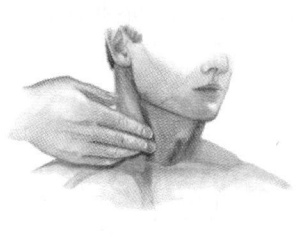

Fig. 10-10, A   **Fig. 10-10, B**

A moderate-intensity workout should raise the heart rate to between 50 and 70 percent of your maximum heart rate. A vigorous-intensity workout should raise the heart rate to between 70 and 85 percent of your maximum heart rate. To calculate your target heart rate, first subtract your age from 220 then multiply this figure by the percentage of the desired workout intensity.

The target heart rate for a 40 year old with a desired workout intensity of 50 percent can be calculated by following these steps:

1. $220 - 40$ years = 180 beats per minute (bpm)
2. 180×0.50 (50 percent) = 90 bpm (target heart rate)

The target heart rate for a 50 year old with a desired workout intensity of 80 percent can be calculated by following these steps:

1. $220 - 50$ years = 170 bpm
2. 170×0.80 (80 percent) = 136 bpm (target heart rate)

The heart rate can be measured during exercise with a pulse check (**Fig. 10-10, A and B**). To check the pulse, briefly stop exercising and find your pulse at the neck or wrist by pressing lightly with the index and middle finger at the carotid artery for the neck or, the radial artery for the wrist. Count the number of beats in 1 minute or count the number of beats in 30 seconds and multiply by 2. Because the pulse starts to slow down once you stop exercising, you can estimate the heart rate by counting the number of beats in 10 seconds and multiplying by 6. For those with a high level of fitness (those whose heart rate recovers very quickly) a more accurate measurement may be to count the number of beats in 6 seconds and multiply by 10.

The target heart rate range for swimming should be 10 to 13 beats per minute lower than the range for similar exercise on land. A swimmer's horizontal position along with the water pressure on the body prevents the heart rate from increasing as much as in vertical, dry-land exercise of the same intensity. The cooling effect of the water also helps with the task of cooling the body.

Although target heart rates for swimming are lower than for similar dry-land exercise, the issue is less clear for aquatic exercise. Some research shows that heart rates from vertical aquatic exercise are lower than rates on dry land. Other studies report that heart rates are the same as rates in dry-land programs with similar intensity. By subtracting 10 to 13 beats from the target heart rate range when doing aquatic exercise, it may be possible to underestimate the intensity and target heart rate range needed to reach exercise goals.

People should keep their heart rates within the target range for the type of exercise they are doing to achieve safe and consistent progress toward their fitness goals. The 50- to 85-percent range of moderate- and vigorous-intensity workouts is appropriate for most people. However, the cardiovascular health of sedentary people may begin to improve with an intensity level as low as 40 to 50 percent. In contrast, very fit athletes might not reach their training goals until they reach 90-percent intensity. Anyone who needs help determining appropriate intensity should talk with a health care provider.

If the heart rate is below the target range, increase the intensity of the workout. In aquatic exercise, making larger arm and leg motions or increasing water resistance helps raise the intensity of workouts. If the heart rate is above the target range, decrease the intensity of the workout by making smaller movements, slowing down or taking rest breaks more often.

This method of determining workout intensity might not work as well for some people. For example, some people may have a heart rate that is often above or below the target intensity even though they feel like the workout is at the right intensity range. People in this situation should consider using the rate of perceived exertion (RPE) to evaluate exercise intensity.

Rate of Perceived Exertion

Many factors, such as stress, illness and fatigue, can affect heart rates. In addition, because obtaining accurate exercise heart rates can be difficult while continuing vigorous exercise, an alternative method of monitoring intensity was developed, called the rate of perceived exertion (RPE). It is a valid and reliable method for determining the intensity of workouts based on how hard people feel they are working. Studies have shown that RPE correlates highly with other intensity indicators, such as heart rate and breathing rate (**Fig. 10-11**).

In the initial phase of an exercise program, RPE often is used with the heart rate to monitor intensity. To do this, identify a number on the RPE scale (with 0 feeling nothing at all to 10 feeling very, very strong) that corresponds with the perceived intensity, then check the heart rate to see how the two numbers relate. Once the relationship between heart rate and RPE is understood, rely less on heart rate and more on the how you feel.

Talk-Test Method

Like the RPE, the talk-test method is subjective and should be used in conjunction with taking a

Perceived Exertion	% Workload
20	100%
19-Very, Very Hard	90%
18	
17-Very Hard	80%
16	
15 Hard	70%
14	
13-Somewhat Hard	60%
12	
11-Fairly Light	50%
10	
9-Very Light	40%
8	
7-Very, Very light	
6	

Fig. 10-11

pulse. The talk test is quite useful in determining a person's comfort zone of aerobic intensity, especially for those just beginning an exercise program. People who are able to talk during a workout without a great deal of strain are most likely in the comfort zone. Working at an intensity that allows for rhythmic and comfortable breathing (being able to talk) throughout all phases of the workout ensures a safe and comfortable level of exercise.

Safety Considerations for Fitness Programs

Fitness programs are not risky for most healthy people. However, some people cannot start a program at 60-percent intensity and continue for 30 minutes. This intensity could even be dangerous for people who have not exercised in a long while.

People should always obtain a general health assessment from a health care provider to measure their level of fitness before beginning an exercise program. A health assessment can be a physical examination or an exercise stress test with blood testing. This information on initial fitness level helps determine an appropriate and safe beginning exercise intensity level.

Knowledge of current swimming skill levels also is very important. At lower skill levels, people may use more energy, even at slow speeds, because they swim less efficiently. Swimming even one length of the pool can be exhausting for novices. Swimmers who are just starting a program rest as often as needed and use resting strokes, like the sidestroke and the elementary backstroke. These swimmers should check their heart rate or monitor RPE at each break to make sure it is within the appropriate target range. The goal is to slowly raise intensity levels by gradually increasing the time spent continuously swimming while decreasing rest breaks.

Certain warning signals may require immediate medical attention to prevent serious injury and/or death. The following signals indicate the workout should be stopped:

- An abnormal heart action (such as a heart rate that stays high for some time after completing the exercise session)
- Pain or pressure in the chest, arm or throat

- Dizziness, light-headedness or confusion during or immediately following the workout
- Breathlessness or wheezing

If you notice any of these signals, tell the instructor or lifeguard. If you experience any of these signals during exercise and/or these signals persist, contact your health care provider.

Components of a Workout

A workout should meet individual fitness goals. A typical safe and effective workout includes a warm-up, stretching, an aerobic set (the main part of the workout) and a cool-down period. A muscular development set may be added to the aerobic activity.

Warm-Up

The warm-up prepares the body for exercise. It increases blood flow and helps adjust to the workout environment. Because pool water is often several degrees cooler than skin temperature, spend some time warming up on deck before entering the water. The warm-up should last 5 to 10 minutes and may consist of slow walking, jogging or low-intensity swimming.

Stretching

Stretching makes joints more flexible and improves range of motion (**Fig. 10-12**). There are two types of stretches: static and dynamic. Static stretches are movements where the muscle is passively stretched by holding it for an extended period, 10 to 30 seconds. Dynamic stretches

Fig. 10-12

involve exaggerated movements that replicate specific sports or exercise movements.

Current research suggests that static stretching before exercise may not prevent injury, except in sports that involve jumping and bouncing, such as basketball and volleyball, according to an ACSM position statement. However, dynamic stretching can be used during warm-ups or right after them. Static stretching should take place after exercise.

Aerobic Set

To benefit from an aerobic workout, it is important to keep the heart rate in the target range for at least 30 minutes (**Fig. 10-13**). At a lower level of intensity, fitness levels will likely not increase much. The aerobic set should make up 50 to 70 percent of the workout time and distance. Much of the following sections on fitness swimming and

Fig. 10-13

aquatic exercise apply to the aerobic sets for those exercise programs.

Muscular Development Set

The ACSM recommends that a fitness program include some exercise for muscular development. Probably the most popular form of exercise for muscular development is resistance training (weight lifting). The muscles are progressively overloaded by using barbells, dumbbells or weight machines (**Fig. 10-14**). Strength development for fitness should be general in nature. For most people, it is best to try to overload muscles from each major muscle group rather than focusing on a few muscle groups, using one or two exercises for each muscle group.

Anyone undertaking a muscular development exercise program should warm up thoroughly and learn the proper way of executing each exercise. The next step is to identify the appropriate weight for each exercise depending on an individual's current level of strength. Beginners should use weight they can lift 12 to 15 times in one set. If it is not possible to lift the weight at least 12 times without a break in the set, the weight is too heavy for that exercise.

Once the amount of weight for each exercise is selected, people can begin their weight-training

Fig. 10-14

program. A standard program for beginners is to lift the selected weight 10 times (repetitions) for two to three sets. The more often a person engages in resistance training, the easier it becomes to lift the selected weight. As it becomes easier to lift the selected weight, then more weight can be added. Strength training should be performed at least two times per week for 20 minutes as part of a regular fitness program. For more information on safe weight-training techniques, consult a coach or a trainer.

Strength training with aquatic exercise is another way for fitness swimmers to improve muscular strength and endurance (**Fig. 10-15**). In aquatic exercise, it is difficult to calculate the

Fig. 10-15

Fig. 10-16

Another way to cool-down is by simply slowing down (**Fig. 10-16**). Static stretching toward the end of the cool-down, but not immediately after strenuous activity in the aerobic set or the muscular development set, is also a good idea. A typical cool-down lasts 5 to 10 minutes.

Phases of a Fitness Program

Fitness improves as the exertion of the workout gradually increases. Once the body adapts to a workload, the work level should rise gradually. This is referred to as *progression*. People can increase their workload by raising the frequency, intensity or duration (time) of the workouts. In general, it is a good idea to increase the duration first, then the intensity or frequency.

The rate of improvement depends on individual fitness level at the beginning of the program and other individual factors. For safe and effective exercise, most people will want to increase the overload gradually in three phases: the initial phase, the improvement phase and the maintenance phase. Remember, fitness levels will not improve unless the stress of the exercise on the body is increased. In fact, fitness levels may decline if the workload decreases or stops.

Initial Phase

This phase should include lower-intensity exercise. For those who have not exercised in a long time, this phase helps increase their workload slowly and comfortably. They can move on to the improvement phase when they are able to comfortably maintain 60-percent intensity for at least 30 minutes. It is important to be patient during this phase. It may take up to 10 weeks to move from the initial phase to the improvement phase.

Improvement Phase

The improvement phase begins when a person reaches the minimum level to attain cardiovascular fitness. A person who has reached this threshold is exercising three times per week for at least 20 minutes at a level of at least 60-percent intensity. Fitness will improve by increasing frequency, intensity or duration. For example, exercising five times a week leads to improvements sooner than only three times a

resistance of the water so performing only three sets might not provide the overload needed to increase strength and endurance. The best way to determine overload in aquatic exercise is through perception. The overload for strength improvement may depend solely on increasing the speed of movement, number of sets or number of repetitions per set.

Cool-Down

The last part of the workout is a cool-down period. This is a time to taper off exercise and let the heart rate, blood pressure and metabolic rate return to their resting levels. A proper cool-down helps return the blood from the working muscles to the brain, lungs and internal organs. It also helps the body recover from fatigue and may reduce muscle soreness later.

Cool-down activities are like warm-up activities. One way to cool-down is by changing to a resting stroke to slow down the workout gradually and keep blood from collecting in the muscles.

week, if everything else is the same. Improvement comes more rapidly in this phase than in the initial phase. Anyone wishing to increase the duration must be sure to stay well within the target heart-rate range.

Maintenance Phase

The maintenance phase begins after a person has achieved his or her desired fitness level. The goal during this phase is to sustain fitness level rather than increase the workload. At this stage, individuals can exercise at a comfortable level and set different goals. For example, those with fit cardiovascular systems may consider working on learning a new stroke or exploring other activities to vary their program. This will help keep workouts interesting.

Reversibility of Training

The physical fitness gained from exercise can be lost. By stopping regular exercise, a person's fitness level will decrease and gradually return to the preexercise program level. It is better to maintain a current level of fitness than to let it decline and try to regain it. Having once been physically fit does not make it any easier to get back into shape, except that it may not be necessary to learn specific workout skills again. Fitness declines quickly but can be maintained with as few as two workouts a week. For most people, the key to a successful fitness program is developing fitness habits they can use for a lifetime.

Fitness Swimming

Fitness swimming programs require careful design. This means starting at the right level and following an effective progression in the exercise plan. This section illustrates how to design a program to progress from an inactive lifestyle to a desired fitness level. Moving through the initial phase quickly or even skipping it may be an option for some people depending on their current fitness level. Remember, the success of a program depends on a comfortable, practical plan that can be sustained through the future.

Always use a warm-up, stretching, an aerobic set and a cool-down in each workout and be sure to check your heart rate before, during and after

workouts to ensure the right intensity. Include a muscular development set in two or three workouts each week.

Initial Phase

The following are examples of specific exercises that can be included in a fitness program, with the following assumptions:

1. The pool is 25 yards long (a common length for pools in the United States). If the pool is longer or shorter, make adjustments.

2. The swimmer is able to swim one length of the pool using any stroke.

3. Workouts occur on three non-consecutive days per week.

4. A gradual warm-up and dynamic stretching exercises are completed before the aerobic set.

In the initial phase of the program, reaching 60-percent intensity is not necessary. Individuals who have not exercised in a long while should begin at 50 percent for the progression.

Between pool lengths, rest, walk or jog in the water for 15 to 30 seconds (**Fig. 10-17**). Try to keep a continuous effort without becoming too tired.

Fig. 10-17

Step 1	In chest-deep water, walk 5 minutes and exercise the upper body with an underwater arm stroke, such as the breaststroke. Check the heart rate after each length. If, after walking 5 minutes, the heart rate does not rise above the target heart-rate range, rest 15 to 30 seconds and do the 5-minute walk two more times. Gradually decrease the rest period until it is possible to do it for 15 minutes continuously. Be sure the heart rate does not go past the upper limit of the target range.
Step 2	In chest-deep water, walk one length using the arm stroke as is in Step 1, then jog one length. Rest 15 to 20 seconds after the jogging length. Continue for 15 minutes. Check the heart rate at each break. Gradually decrease the rest breaks until it is possible to walk or jog 15 minutes continuously. Check the heart rate every 5 minutes in the workout.
Step 3	Swim one length at a pace that takes more effort than jogging and then rest by walking or jogging one length. Continue for 5 minutes. Check the heart rate to be sure it is not too high. If it is, rest another minute. If the heart rate is within the target range, continue alternating swimming lengths with walking or jogging lengths. Check the heart rate every 5 minutes. Gradually decrease the rest breaks until it is possible to swim or jog continuously for 15 minutes.
Step 4	Swim one length with effort, rest 15 to 30 seconds, and swim another length. Use a resting stroke on the second length or swim slower. Check the heart rate after three laps. Continue this sequence for 15 minutes. Gradually decrease the rest break to 10 seconds.
Step 5	When it is possible to swim 15 minutes continuously or with minimum rest as in Step 4, recalculate the target heart rate at 60-percent intensity and repeat Step 4. When it is possible to swim continuously for 15 minutes at an intensity of 60 percent, the initial phase is complete. Move on to the improvement phase.

To find a safe level to start, swim one length and check the heart rate. If it is above the target range, start with Step 1. If your heart rate is well within the target range, start with Step 3. If the water is too deep for walking or jogging, use a life jacket or stay in water no deeper than the shoulders. Using a life jacket does not substitute for knowing how to swim.

Proceed with each step of the workout until it can be done easily, keeping the heart rate close to the lower limit of the target range. The initial phase

COOPER 12-MINUTE SWIMMING TEST

The 12-minute swimming test, devised by Kenneth Cooper, M.D., is an easy, inexpensive way for men and women of all ages to test their aerobic capacity (oxygen consumption) and to chart their fitness program.

The test encourages the swimmer to cover the greatest distance possible in 12 minutes, using whatever stroke is preferred, resting as necessary, but going as far as he or she can.

For instance, a woman between the ages of 30 and 39 is in excellent condition if she can swim 550 yards or more in the 12 minutes allowed for the test. However, a woman of the same age would be considered in very poor condition if she could not swim at least 250 yards in the same time.

The easiest way to take the test is to swim in a pool with known dimensions, and it helps to have someone there to record the number of laps and the time, preferably with a sweep secondhand.

Care must be taken with the 12-minute test, however. It is not recommended for anyone older than 35 years of age, unless he or she has already developed good aerobic capacity. The best way to determine this, of course, is to consult a health care provider.

The Cooper 12-Minute Swimming Test
Distance (Yards) Swam in 12 Minutes

Fitness Category		Age (Years)					
		13–19	20–29	30–39	40–49	50–59	>60*
I. Very poor	(men)	<500*	<400	<350	<300	<250	<250
	(women)	<400	<300	<250	<200	<150	<150
II. Poor	(men)	500–599	400–499	350–449	300–399	250–349	250–299
	(women)	400–499	300–399	250–349	200–299	150–249	150–199
III. Fair	(men)	600–699	500–599	450–549	400–499	350–449	300–399
	(women)	500–599	400–499	350–449	300–399	250–349	200–299
IV. Good	(men)	700–799	600–699	550–649	500–599	450–549	400–499
	(women)	600–699	500–599	450–549	400–499	350–449	300–399
V. Excellent	(men)	>800	>700	>650	>600	>550	>500
	(women)	>700	>600	>550	>500	>450	>400

* < means "less than"; > means "more than."
From Cooper K. H.: *The Aerobics Program for Total Well-Being*, New York: Bantam Books, 1982.

can take as long as 10 weeks, so do not try to rush through it at an uncomfortable pace.

There are several ways to check progress. One way is to check the resting heart rate every 3 to 4 weeks. As fitness level improves, the resting heart rate will drop. Many people may also notice that their heart rate returns to normal quicker as their fitness improves. This is another indication of progress.

Improvement Phase

Progress during the improvement phase varies greatly. Those who start out with a low level of fitness can expect to progress slower than someone who is more fit. Here are two options to consider when developing a fitness plan. Level 1 is for those progressing from the previous phase. Level 2 offers other training methods to add variety to the program. Both options use the same assumptions listed for the initial phase.

Level 1

These steps move in 2-week increments. Do not move to a more difficult step until it is possible to do the prior step easily. The full 2 weeks may not be necessary for some steps.

Weeks 1–2   Swim two lengths. Rest 15 to 30 seconds. Repeat for 15 minutes. Check the heart rate every few minutes during the breaks.

Weeks 3–4   Swim three lengths followed by a slow length or resting stroke. Rest 15 to 30 seconds. Continue for 20 minutes. With each successive workout, gradually decrease the rest breaks to 10 seconds.

Weeks 5–6   Swim five lengths followed by a slow length or resting stroke. Rest 15 to 30 seconds. Check the heart rate periodically. Continue for 20 minutes. With each successive workout, gradually decrease the rest breaks to 10 seconds.

Weeks 7–8   Swim continuously for 20 minutes. Rest only when needed but not longer than 10 seconds. If possible, use resting strokes instead of breaks. Check the heart rate every 10 minutes during the workout.

Weeks 9–10   Swim continuously for 20 minutes. With each successive workout, add one or two lengths until it is possible to swim continuously for 30 minutes.

Weeks 11–12   Swim 30 minutes continuously without rest. In the last week of this progression, test the progress by swimming a timed 12-minute swim.

Fig. 10-18

After reaching the 30-minute goal, continue to increase the overload by raising the frequency, intensity or duration of the workout. When doing this, change only one variable (frequency, intensity or duration) at a time to keep the progression gradual.

Level 2

Whatever the level of fitness, design the workout with various training methods. Refer to Training Techniques beginning on page 204 for descriptions of training methods that you can incorporate into your fitness plan. When planning the workout, remember the principles of frequency, intensity, duration and type and do not try to progress too fast.

Maintenance Phase

Once an individual has reached their personal fitness goals, they may not want to continue increasing their workload. They may want to review their original goals and either set new ones or maintain the current fitness level by continuing their present workout. Keep in mind that it is important to maintain at least a minimum level of fitness. Those who want to train for competition can use the methods described later in the chapter.

Swimming Etiquette

It may be frustrating to share the pool—or even a lane—with other swimmers during workouts. Cyclists do not have to share their bikes and runners can usually find a quiet road, but fitness swimmers rarely get a lane to themselves. Proper swimming etiquette helps ease this problem.

When sharing lanes, all swimmers should be organized and cooperative and know their swimming levels. First, swimmers should figure out their exercise speed. The workouts will be better in a lane where other swimmers are doing similar types of workouts (pulls, kicks, repeat short distances, long continuous swims) at similar speeds. Although many pools have lanes for fast, medium and slow swimmers, the speed within a lane can still vary.

Once the best lane is selected, circle swimming should be done so that all swimmers can enjoy the workout (**Fig. 10-18**). Circle swimming is swimming in a counterclockwise pattern around the center of the pool lane. With the correct etiquette, a faster swimmer overtaking a slower swimmer in the lane signals to pass by tapping the lead swimmer's foot. The lead swimmer should stop at the wall or pull over to the right to let the faster swimmer pass. It is common courtesy to allow the new lead swimmer at least a 5-second lead before following. Although this may seem to disrupt the workout, these short breaks will not affect the intensity.

Aquatic Exercise

People engage in aquatic exercise to manage weight, relieve stress, feel better and generally become more fit. Individuals with disabilities may get a special benefit from aquatic exercise. As discussed in **Chapter 9,** these individuals can improve their level of fitness, range of motion and muscular strength and endurance with aquatic activity.

In addition, aquatic exercise programs have grown in popularity in part because of other types of athletic programs. Water exercise is the perfect activity for coaches who want to rehabilitate injured athletes in a way that is safe but also good for cardiovascular conditioning. Aquatic exercise programs are a physical fitness avenue for health-conscious people and those with disabilities, as well as an effective method of rehabilitation (**Fig. 10-19**).

Aquatic exercise programs vary in many ways—from the water temperature and depth, to the style of aerobic exercises and the specific ranges of motion—and may be different from program to program.

Fig. 10-19

Fig. 10-20

Furthermore, many aquatic exercise programs do not require that people know how to swim.

Factors that Affect the Workout

In aquatic exercise, people can maintain the proper intensity by adjusting their body position and by moving in the water. The following factors have the greatest effect on the intensity of aquatic workouts:

- Buoyancy, as it relates to proper water depth and body position
- Resistance the working muscles must overcome (how much surface area swimmers present as they move through the water greatly impacts resistance)
- Speed of movement
- Type of movement

Buoyancy and Water Depth

Buoyancy reduces the apparent pull of gravity on the limbs and trunk. The closer the depth of the water is to a person's standing height, the more support the water gives. Exercising in water that is only ankle or knee deep does little to reduce the impact of the feet landing when jogging or jumping. Yet, in neck-deep water, it is difficult to stay balanced and in control because the body has more buoyancy. Increased buoyancy also reduces the workload so it may be difficult to get the heart rate up into the target range, although there are some types of effective deep-water workouts. Exercising in chest-deep water allows the arms to stay submerged (**Fig. 10-20**), which helps maintain

balance and proper body alignment. It can also enhance workouts. The effort of pushing the water improves upper body strength and endurance. Arm work underwater also affects the muscles that stabilize the trunk. These muscles, particularly the abdominal muscles, gain strength and help reduce stress on the lower back.

Obese people may need to adjust their workouts if their hips and thighs cause their center of buoyancy to be lower. Their legs will then tend to rise toward the surface, making it hard to keep balanced. Those who are obese may want to exercise in shallower water, but it should still be deep enough to support and protect their body from hard landings.

The manner of exercise also affects the intensity of the workout. With bouncing and bounding movements (such as those commonly associated with aerobic exercise done out of the water), the heart rate might not reach the target range because the body has a short rest while it drifts back to the bottom. However, movements involving walking, jogging or bouncing in the water can be of value as people progress toward workouts of higher intensity. People who do these exercises in the water typically avoid problems that are associated with the impact of landing.

Resistance

Exercise intensity is greater when the surface area of the body is larger, which creates more drag. People who exercise in the water can choose to move specific limbs in certain ways to adjust the resistance their bodies experience when pushing against the water. For example, a biceps curl uses more effort with an open hand than with a fist (**Fig. 10-21**). Moving a longer body segment, such as keeping the whole arm straight from the shoulder to the hand uses more effort than a shorter body segment, such as moving only the forearm during a biceps curl. Another way to adjust resistance is to use equipment designed for aquatic exercise.

Speed of Movement

The speed of movement in the exercise also affects the intensity of the workout. Faster movements result in greater resistance and require more effort. In aquatic exercise, this principle applies both to the speed of moving individual

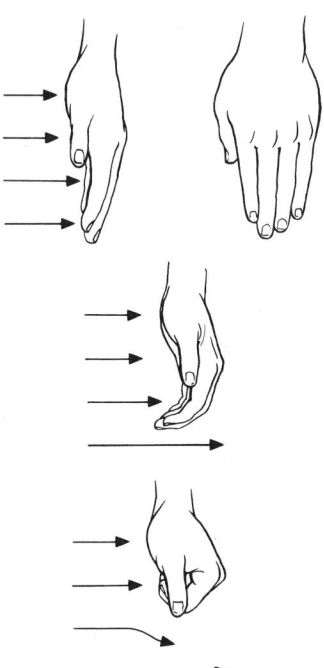
Fig. 10-21

limbs and to the speed of moving the whole body from one point in the pool to another.

Type of Movement

When limbs move through the water in aquatic exercise, the water is set in motion and stays in motion. If people continue moving with the water, they encounter less resistance. They can maintain resistance by accelerating their limbs (moving them faster and faster) or changing direction to move out of or against the flow of water.

Arm movements can be used in combination with leg movements to create a wide variety of exercise techniques. Bouncing, leaping, running and walking forward, backward and sideways are some of the movements that use the lower body. Scooping, lifting, punching and squeezing water are variations of upper body movements. People can adjust resistance by using cupped hands or slicing hands through the water. For instance, while jogging in shallow water, bursts of quick, short arm movements can increase workout intensity.

Workout Design

An aquatic exercise workout should have the same components as a fitness swimming workout. The warm-up lasts 5 to 10 minutes and consists of walking, slow jogging and slow aerobic activities. Warm-ups can be done in the water or on deck if the water is not warm enough. Stretching may be added after the warm-up. If there is a chill early in the workout, try stretching after the aerobic set.

The aerobic set should be rhythmic and continuous and use both arms and legs (**Fig. 10-22**). People should monitor their heart rate several times during this set to be sure it stays in the target range.

Two or thee times each week, the workout should include a muscular development set. This promotes flexibility, range of motion, strength and muscular endurance.

The cool-down in an aquatic workout should consist of slow, rhythmic activities. A good format for the cool-down is simply to reverse the warm-up activities.

Fig. 10-22

Aquatic Exercise for Muscular Development

The intensity of resistance training increases directly with the size of the surface area and the speed of movement. People effectively lift more weight if their movements are faster and the surface area meeting resistance is larger.

Equipment

Several products are available that provide greater overload during resistance training (**Fig. 10-23**). Wearing buoyant cuffs on wrists or ankles means that greater force must be used to move limbs deeper. Handheld paddles or buoyant dumbbells can add resistance for exercising the arms. Other devices increase the surface area of the limbs to provide resistance. Devices for aquatic resistance training are not recommended for beginners. For most people, the water alone provides an adequate overload for improvements in strength and muscular endurance. However, more advanced exercisers may want such equipment to help maintain the proper intensity for their workouts. Anyone who has a history of joint problems should check with a health care provider before using any equipment.

Safety Precautions

Follow these guidelines to keep aquatic exercises safe:

- Never exercise alone in a pool.
- Use the right equipment. It is important to use equipment specifically designed for aquatic exercise. Improvised equipment may cause injury.

Fig. 10-23

Always use equipment that can be controlled. Once a piece of equipment is in motion, it may continue to move, striking the body. Without enough strength to stop and reverse the motion or to stabilize the body during the movement, safety may be jeopardized.

- Keep the body centered. Body alignment is especially important when using equipment for resistance training. Choose exercises in which the movement is toward and away from the center of the body. Movements with limbs fully extended, such as leg or arm circles, may cause injury.

- Stabilize the trunk when lifting limbs and any equipment through the water. The larger surface area of these devices requires a greater degree of trunk stability for safe lifting technique. Stability throughout the lift is affected by the inertia of the equipment, and to a limited degree, by buoyancy. When performing lifting motions, the back should be flat, with the abdominal muscles tight, knees slightly bent and feet flat on the pool bottom.

- Isolate and work one muscle group at a time. This focuses attention on and helps improve individual muscle groups. Be sure to exercise opposing muscle groups equally.

- Work major muscle groups first. If people work the smaller, assisting muscle groups first, these muscles will fatigue early and limit the work possible with major muscle groups.

- Plan movements. First imagine where the piece of equipment will be at the end of the movement, and then perform the action. Use exercises that involve a full range of motion and be sure to return fully to the starting position. Make sure the equipment stays in the water. Passing the equipment into or out of the water can cause injuries to the joints and muscles.

- Use correct breathing. Do not hold the breath. This increases blood pressure and may increase feelings of stress. Instead, adjust the breathing to the rhythm of the exercise. Exhale during the work phase and inhale during the recovery phase.

- Stop any exercise that causes sharp pain, which can be a signal of a serious health condition. Seek immediate help for persistent pain in the chest or arm (pain that does not go away within 3–5 minutes and is not relieved by resting or changing position). Report any recurring pain to a health care provider.

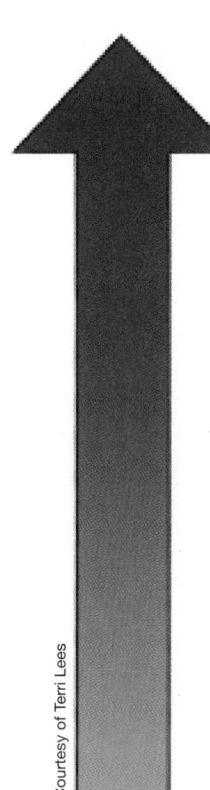

Progression Continuum

- Maintain speed
- Incorporate periods of longer levers and more angular motion

- Greater speed
- Short levers
- Curvilinear motion

- Maintain medium speed
- Incorporate periods of longer levers and more angular motion

- Medium speed movement
- Short levers
- Curvilinear motion

- Maintain slow speed of movement
- Incorporate periods with longer levers (more surface area) and alternate curvilinear and angular motion

- Slow speed of movement
- Small surface area (short levers)
- Curvilinear

Courtesy of Terri Lees

Fig. 10-24

Progressions for Aquatic Exercise

Progress can be easy in aquatic exercise because of the three factors—resistance due to surface area, speed of movement and type of

movement—used to reach the necessary level of intensity. If people are less fit, they can start with low-level exercises, such as walking in chest-deep water or slow jogging in waist-deep water. Use slow, rhythmic movements with small surface areas. People who are generally fit can exercise with larger surface areas, faster speeds and angular motion to reach the right intensity. The key to progressively overloading the system and maintaining target heart rates is to control how surface area, speed and type of movement interact (**Fig. 10-24**). It is possible to stay at the same intensity with a smaller surface area (for example, moving from chest-deep to waist-deep water) by increasing the speed of movement (such as walking or jogging faster). Exercisers also can change from angular motions to curved motions without losing intensity by increasing the surface area or the speed. Once exercisers are able to adjust the intensity of their workouts, they can participate in classes with others who are exercising at different intensities.

Principles of Training

Learning how to train to increase the strength or endurance of specific muscle groups or to improve skills can help swimmers prepare for competition

Mostly Aerobic (Low to Moderate Intensity, Long Duration)	Mixture of Aerobic and Anaerobic Exercise	Mostly Anaerobic (High Intensity, Short Duration)
■ Swimming	■ Water polo	■ Sprints of any kind (running, swimming, cycling)
■ Aerobics or aquatic exercise	■ Recreational basketball	■ Field events in track competition
■ Distance running or walking	■ Racquetball	■ Heavy weight lifting
■ Distance cycling	■ Weight training	■ Jumping rope
■ Cross-country skiing	■ Baseball or softball	■ Hill climbing
■ Rowing	■ Football	■ Isometrics (using resistance to increase strength and endurance)
■ Workouts on exercise equipment, such as bikes and treadmills	■ Tennis	

Competitive swimmers use various training techniques and tools to improve their performance. Equipment can play a significant role in the training process. Following are examples of basic and high-tech devices used by competitive swimmers:

- Kickboards. Experienced swimmers may use kickboards to increase their workload during the aerobic or strengthening portions of their workouts.

- Pull buoys. Swimmers hold these devices—usually made of two Styrofoam cylinders joined by a nylon cord—between their thighs or legs to prevent kicking. Pull buoys help swimmers isolate their arm action and strengthen their upper body.

- Hand paddles. Paddles are designed to increase the resistance the arms feel when pushing the water. Hand paddles require greater strength, so use should be limited to older swimmers.

- Fins. Accomplished swimmers may use fins to build their leg muscles and improve the flexibility of their ankles.

- Drag devices. Competitive swimmers often use devices—such as stationary trainers, drag boards, drag suits, training tubes and stretching tethers—that create drag or resistance to improve their performance.

- Dry-land resistance equipment. Swimmers use resistance equipment, such as free weights, barbells, dumbbells and stretch cords, out of the water to improve their strength and endurance. In addition, mini-gyms and isokinetic swim benches designed specifically for swimmers allow them to duplicate swimming motions on land. These isokinetic devices automatically adjust resistance based on the force applied by the muscles. The swim bench also measures the force of pull as swimmers simulate swimming movements.

- Pace clock. This large device on the pool deck works like a stop watch. It helps competitive swimmers maintain the appropriate pace during the different phases of their training programs.

(**Fig. 10-25**). Training differs from fitness exercise in several ways. The first difference is the intensity of workouts. The goal of fitness exercise is to stay within the target heart-rate range, usually at the lower end for those just starting a fitness program. People who are training are often at the upper end of the target heart-rate range and may even be above it for brief periods. The second difference is the amount of time spent in muscular development. In training programs, improved strength and endurance are critical goals. Therefore, muscular development sets are usually more frequent and more extensive in a training program. Competitive swimmers train nearly every day and often complete more than one session per day.

A training program should follow certain principles to help achieve goals. The following sections provide guidelines for any type of training program.

Specificity

The *principle of specificity* states that the benefits of exercise relate directly to the activity performed. Put another way, beyond the general benefits of

Fig. 10-25

exercise, there is very little transfer of effects from one kind of activity to another. For example, a runner who trains on the track will not have much improvement in swimming performance. Specific arm muscles do most of the work in swimming, whereas running uses specific leg muscles. Still, both activities improve aerobic capacity.

The principle of specificity is important in two areas: the energy system used and the nerves and muscles exercised in a given activity. The following sections explain the importance of these principles in any training program.

Energy Systems

Two major energy systems supply fuel to the muscles. The anaerobic (without oxygen) energy system uses the most rapidly available source of energy—sugars and carbohydrates stored in the body—for muscular activity. This system is the primary source of energy for anaerobic exercise (exercise at such an intensity that the skeletal muscles demand for oxygen is not consistently met). Fit individuals usually exercise anaerobically when their heart rate is above the 85-percent level of intensity. Exercise may be anaerobic at an intensity much less than 85 percent for those who are unfit or underfit.

For longer-lasting exercise, the aerobic (oxygen-using) energy system gives the muscles fuel. This system breaks down carbohydrates, fats

and proteins for energy when people engage in aerobic exercise (sustained, rhythmic, physical exercise that requires additional effort by the heart and lungs to meet the increased demand by the muscles for oxygen).

The specific energy system the body uses in an activity depends on the duration and intensity of the activity. The benefits of training depend on which energy system is being used. Improvements in the aerobic energy system need continuous, low- to moderate-intensity training. Improvements in the anaerobic energy system need high-intensity, short-duration training. For example, if you are training to improve your sprint performance, using swimming workouts that focus on repeated distances at high intensity are not effective. The benefits of various types of exercise can be located along the following continuum.

Overload

The principle of overload states that a body system improves only if the system is regularly worked at loads greater than normal. For example, muscular strength increases by lifting weights, but the amount of weight must gradually increase if the goal is to continue increasing strength. Muscular endurance, on the other hand, improves by increasing the number of repetitions rather than the load—for example, lifting the same weight more times.

Earlier sections of this chapter explained how to adjust three factors to overload the whole body or specific muscle groups or systems. These are frequency, intensity and duration. It also explained ways to monitor exercise intensity, including keeping track of heart rate or using the RPE, both of which indicate how hard people are working. Individual perceptions of workout intensity can be a reliable indicator of actual exercise intensity, especially for experienced swimmers.

Progression

As the body adapts to any workload, it gradually adjusts to that level of effort. Improvement will not occur unless the load is raised above the original overload. This principle also affects how a coach designs an athlete's workout during training season.

Stroke Length and Stroke Frequency

An obvious training goal for competitive swimmers is to improve their speed. To do this, they must consider two concepts—stroke length and stroke frequency. *Stroke length* is the distance traveled in one complete cycle of the arms (from the time the hand enters the water, through the pull phase, to exit and reentry). To determine stroke length, swimmers should count the cycles they take when swimming a known distance then divide that distance by the number of strokes. *Stroke frequency* is the number of complete arm cycles in a specified length of time. To determine stroke frequency, they can count the cycles swam in a known amount of time, and then divide the number of cycles by the number of seconds. For example, a swimmer who covers 50 meters in 25 seconds with 25 arm strokes would use the following calculations:

Stroke Length = distance stroked/number of cycles = 50 meters/25 cycles = 2.0 meters/cycle

Stroke Frequency = number of cycles/time = 25 cycles/25 seconds = 1 cycle/second

Speed is the product of stroke length and stroke frequency. Using the above example, speed would be:

Speed = stroke length × stroke frequency = 2 meters/cycle × 1 cycle/second = 2 meters/second

To increase speed, swimmers must make a corresponding increase in stroke length or stroke frequency. One way to increase speed efficiently is to gain greater distance from each stroke without increasing the number of cycles per second.

Training Techniques

The following are several training techniques that can be used in workouts to meet specific fitness and training goals either alone or in combination. The distances and speed swam and the duration of rest periods depend on various factors, such as the time set aside for training, training goals and the observations of any coaches or trainers who

are present. Using different techniques also adds variety to workouts.

Over Distance

Over-distance training involves swimming long distances with moderate exertion with short or no rest periods (**Fig. 10-26**). Over-distance training is used to improve endurance. The heart rate stays in the low to middle level of the target range for the whole swim. This is also an effective warm-up activity.

Fartlek

The *Fartlek method*, which gets its name from the Swedish word that means "speed play," was popularized by runners. It breaks swims into slow and fast lengths of the pool, using the same stroke. It can make long swims more interesting and is good for developing speed and endurance simultaneously.

Interval Sets

Interval sets are one of the most common training methods. *Intervals* are a series of repeat swims of the same distance and time interval (**Fig. 10- 27**). There is a specific rest period between the time spent swimming. The entire swim series is a set.

An example of an interval set is "8 × 100 on 1:30." The first number, 8, represents the number of times to repeat the distance. The second number, 100, is the distance of each swim in yards or meters, and the 1:30 is the total amount of time

Fig. 10-26

Fig. 10-27

for the swim and rest. In this example, a swimmer who swims the 100 in 1:15, has 15 seconds available for rest. This short rest period keeps the heart rate within the target range without dropping back to a resting heart rate. Used primarily in the main set of a workout, interval sets are the best all-around method to develop both speed and endurance.

Repetition

Repetition is a technique that uses swim sets of the same distance done at close to maximum effort (up to 90 percent of maximum) with rest periods as long as or longer than the swim time. Repetition sets develop speed and anaerobic capacity. Coaches use this training method after swimmers develop a good aerobic base. It is usually done after the aerobic set as a muscular development set.

Sprints

Sprints are short, fast swims (100-percent effort) to simulate race conditions. The rest between sprints is usually long enough to let the heart return to its resting heart rate. Like repetition swims, sprints improve anaerobic capacity.

Straight Sets

With the straight-set method, a steady speed is maintained throughout the set. Swimmers monitor their times to help keep an even pace. Distance swimmers often use this method.

Negative Split Sets

Negative splitting involves swimming the second half of each swim period faster than the first half. For example, if swimming 200 yards four times, the second 100 yards should be faster than the first 100 yards in each repetition.

Descending Sets

Often confused with negative splitting, *descending sets* refers to decreasing the time on successive swims. To swim 200 yards four times in a descending set, each 200 yards would be faster than the 200 yards preceding it.

Ladders

Ladders are several swims with regular increases or decreases in distance, for example, a swim of 25 yards, then 50 yards and finally 75 yards.

Pyramids

A *pyramid* is a swim of regular increases and decreases in distance, for example, a swim starting with 25 yards, then 50 yards, then 75 yards, then 50 yards and then ending with 25 yards. A variation of both pyramids and ladders is to increase the number of times the distance is repeated as the distances get shorter. For example, swimming one 500, then two 400s, then three 300s, then four 200s and five 100s.

Broken Swims

Broken swims divide a target distance into shorter intervals with a short rest in-between (for example, 10 seconds). The goal for swimmers is to perform each segment at a faster pace than they could maintain over the entire distance. Each segment is timed. Once the entire swim is complete, subtract the total time of rest from the total time to determine the swimming pace. Broken swims are a highly motivating method of training because they simulate stress conditions of competition but yield swimming times that may

TIPS FOR THE FIRST MEET

To find out about local meets, contact the local pool or swim team or get in touch with USA Swimming or US Masters Swimming (Appendix 1). They can help find a local organization that sponsors meets. Work with them to get a meet information sheet with lists of events, deadlines and other information, such as club membership.

Look over information about the meet carefully. Complete the entry form and include any entry fees. Do not forget any deadlines. For a club or team, the coach may send in all the registrations together. Swimmers should choose which events they feel comfortable entering and check that they are spaced far enough apart for rest in between. Make a list of entered events and when they occur in the meet. There will probably be enough anxiety without having to remember an exact schedule. If swimmers need more rest during the meet, they can change plans even after entering. They will need to let the officials know they will not be entering an event. This is called a *scratch*.

At the first meet, swimmers may feel some uncertainty. Almost everyone feels the jitters so swimmers should not be surprised if they feel "butterflies in the stomach" or have difficulty sleeping the night before the event. Keep in mind that meets are a way to evaluate training and performance that will help set new goals for the next season or meet.

When arriving at the pool, check in with the meet organizers to verify the events entered. This information should be listed on the heat sheet, which is usually posted in a window, on a bulletin board or on a table.

Some events are divided into heats. This is done when there are more competitors than there are lanes in the pool. When heats are used, entrants are organized into several groupings (for example, eight competitors at a time if the pool has eight lanes). Depending on the organization of the meet, the winners may be those who swim the fastest time in their heats or the fastest

swimmers from several heats may face each other in a final heat that determines the winner.

After checking in, swimmers should warm up. Look for published warm-up rules and safety procedures. Swimmers should find a lane with people who swim about the same speed as they do. They should ease into the pool from the edge or jump in feetfirst. They should not dive into the warm-up pool. Swimmers will want to pay attention to others in the lane. While swimming a few laps, they can loosen up and practice the strokes they will swim. The warm-up should safely raise the pulse rate.

While warming up, swimmers should orient themselves to the pool. For example, they can get used to the targets on the wall and find out if the wall is slippery. Those swimming the backstroke can check to see if the flags are the same number of strokes from the wall. Swimmers not used to starting blocks can get up on a block to judge the distance to the water. Some swimmers may be more comfortable starting from the deck or in the water.

During the race, swim at a constant pace. Use the first few strokes to establish a pace and stroke rhythm. Stay mentally alert during the race by focusing on whatever actions—such as turns—require hard work to master. If swimmers can get someone to time splits (segments of a race) during the race, they can use this information to analyze their race performance and set future goals.

After the race, swimmers should keep moving until their bodies cool down and their pulses returns to normal. If there is a cool-down area, they can stay in the water and do some easy laps, bob, scull or float. If there is no cool-down area, swimmers can walk around the pool area until their bodies recover.

Swimmers can later review the race. They may feel proud if their time improved, even slightly, or if their time was not as good as they hoped, they can look ahead to a future chance.

be faster than racing time for an actual event. Broken swims are often combined with other training variations, such as negative splits and descending swims.

Dry-Land Training

Dry-land training uses out-of-water training techniques to improve swimming skills. These techniques fall into two areas: flexibility and strength training. Done properly, strength training builds both strength and flexibility (**Fig. 10-28, A and B**). A half-hour of strength training, 3 days a week combined with 15 minutes of stretching can produce favorable results. When possible, swimmers may want to do their dry-land strength training after their water training so their training in the pool is not affected by fatigue from the dry-land training.

The Training Season

In general, there are two competitive swimming seasons. The short-course season for 25-yard pools usually runs from September to May; the long-course season for 50-meter pools usually runs from June to August.

For either season, training should follow three phases to culminate at the competitive event. These phases are individually set based on personal goals. The phase of training determines the type of workouts. The following is a description of each training phase of the swimming season, along with suggested workouts for effective training.

Early Season Phase

About 6 to 8 weeks long, the *early season phase* focuses on general conditioning to build a foundation for the whole season. Long, easy swims using various strokes help build endurance. Swim at a slower rate and make needed changes to stroke technique, flip turns and breathing patterns. Supplement swimming with dry-land training

Fig. 10-28, A

Fig. 10-28, B

Swimmers should remember to bring certain items to every swim meet. Here is a list that will help swimmers be fully prepared:

- Swimwear. It is not fun sitting around in a wet suit so bring more than one. Change into a dry suit after warm-ups and your events.

- Sun protection. Hat, sunscreen, sunglasses, protective clothing.

- Swim cap (if you wear one). An extra one is handy in case of rips.

- Goggles. A spare pair or strap is a good idea.

- Towels. Bring at least two, the larger the better.

- Extra clothes. To keep from getting chilled between events, wear a sweat suit, T-shirt and socks and shoes. If the meet is outdoors, bring a hat, sunglasses or umbrella for protection from the sun.

- Toiletries. Remember to bring shampoo, soap and lotions for cleaning up after the meet. For safety, use plastic bottles only.

- A lock. Keep belongings safe in a locker.

- Water.

- Snacks.

- Medicines. Necessary medications approved for swimming by the swimmers' health care providers and the swim competition rules or regulations committee.

Other items to have along are a pencil and paper to keep notes and records, a stopwatch, a beach chair, a cooler, cash and a camera.

to help improve strength, flexibility and cardiovascular conditioning.

Mid-Season Phase

In the *mid-season phase*, which is about 8 to 12 weeks long, swimmers can start to tailor their individual training based on specific goals (**Fig. 10-29**). Workouts can increase in distance so swimmers can pay more attention to fine-tuning strokes. Quality is the emphasis of the workout. Use dry-land training at maintenance level during this time.

Fig. 10-29

Taper Phase

The *taper phase* is the last and shortest part of training, usually lasting 1 to 3 weeks. As the set date for peak performance draws near, decrease the distances to swim but raise the intensity almost to racing speed. Do this by resting more between sets and by using broken swims and descending sets. Practice starts and turns to improve technique.

The specifics of the taper phase depend on the individual and the length and time of training in the earlier phases. For example, sprinters usually taper longer than distance swimmers and older athletes taper longer than younger athletes do.

Mental Training

Swimmers spend a lot of time training their bodies for competition, but it is also important for them to prepare their minds. They should think positively. Swimmers can help their bodies perform well by "rehearsing" their events mentally repeatedly. To build self-confidence, they can think about the things they have done well in the past.

Sample Training Workouts

The following workouts are divided into the three phases. They include samples of over-distance, Fartlek, interval and sprints training techniques.

Training for Open-Water Competition

Triathlons and cross-training techniques have led more and more people to open-water competitions

Early Season	Mid-Season	Taper Phase
Warm-up	Warm-up	Warm-up
4 × 200 swim/pull/kick/swim	8 × 100 alternating between	300 easy swim
Main set	swimming and kicking	Main set
800 maintain even pace at	Main set	6 × 50 descending set on 2:00
100s	5 × 200 broken swims on 4:00	4 × 100 broken swims on 3:00
1650 broken swim with 15	with 10 seconds rest at each	with 20 seconds rest at each
seconds rest after each	break	break
interval	1 × 100	2 × 50
1 × 500	2 × 50	Cool-down
1 × 400	5 × 300, swim first 200, kick	200 easy swim
1 × 300	last 100; rest 15 seconds	starts and turns
1 × 200	between swims	
1 × 100	Cool-down	
1 × 75	12 × 50 on 1:00	
1 × 50		
1 × 25		
Cool-down		
200 easy swim		

CROSS-TRAINING—TRIATHLON

Sports enthusiasts bring an additional meaning to the definition of cross-training. *Cross-training* is a method of exercising so that the effects of training in one sport enhance the effects in another. Simply put, it combines two or more aerobic endurance sports into one training program.

For today's fitness expert, cross-training means combining several fitness components to maintain optimum health. This includes stretching the musculoskeletal system, both as a warm-up and a cool-down, to reduce the risk of injury; using resistance and weight training to increase strength; and engaging in aerobic endurance activities to improve cardiovascular fitness. Also necessary is consuming a diet rich in nutrients to meet daily requirements.

The benefits of such a program are clear. Cross-training strengthens different muscle groups and can diminish the risk of injury. The stress on the bones, muscles and tendons used primarily in one sport is markedly reduced when a person uses different muscle groups while training in another sport. An added benefit of cross-training is the fun involved in participating in multiple sports.

Triathlons are increasingly popular cross-training competitions. In general, a triathlon could be a race combining any three sports done consecutively, such as kayaking, cycling and running. However, the most common configuration is swimming, bicycling and running, in that order. The best-known triathlon is the Ironman Triathlon World Championship held in Kona, Hawaii. It is a 2.4-mile swim, a 112-mile bike ride and a 26.2-mile run in which each contestant completes each event individually. Worldwide, it is considered the premier endurance event.

A triathlon can also be a relay competition. Three teammates compete, each doing one leg of the race. It can also be organized as a stage-event triathlon, in which each sport has a set start and finish time, possibly on different days.

Competing in an event such as a triathlon is an example of what can be achieved through cross-training: total body fitness. This requires full development of motor skills, muscular strength and cardiovascular fitness. It also involves all the ingredients for maintaining optimum health.

Photo courtesy of Jupiter Images

(Fig. 10-30). Open-water swimmers need to consider the psychological and physical differences of open water. Some may worry about becoming disoriented, about hazards in open water (e.g., rocks, sandbars or bites and stings from aquatic life) or about being overpowered by the water. The uncertainty is probably more threatening than the actual situation.

Staying calm, knowing personal limits and using the following techniques will help swimmers cope with tense moments.

Whenever swimming in open water, there may be a risk of hypothermia. This life-threatening situation happens when the body loses so much

Fig. 10-30

heat that the core temperature drops below normal. Be alert to the possibility of hypothermia if the water temperature is below 70° F (21° C). Temperatures below 60° F (15° C) pose an immediate threat of hypothermia. Shivering is an early warning signal. Shivering that stops without rewarming is a sign of deterioration and the need for immediate medical care.

Follow certain precautions to help prevent hypothermia. First, practice in moderately cold water. Repeated exposure to cold water helps the body acclimate to it. Second, wear insulation. Most heat is lost through the head. Wearing multiple swim caps or a neoprene swim cap helps hold in the heat (**Fig. 10-31**). Also, wear a racing wet suit or vest to insulate the body (**Fig. 10-32**).

Open-water swimmers need to study the various courses they race. They need to have an understanding of the open-water environment in which they will be swimming, practice how

Fig. 10-31

Fig. 10-32

to spot marker buoys and learn the transitions, starts and finishes. They should also check to see that race organizers have taken steps to ensure safety. Rescue personnel in small boats should accompany swimmers during open events. A system should be in place to ensure that everyone who enters the water is known to have exited.

Training in the Pool

Training for open water is much like training for long-distance swims. Train in the longest pool available or swim around the perimeter of the pool. The fewer turns taken, the more carryover there will be for the long-distance event. Practice taking the goggles off and putting them on in the deep end without the support of the pool bottom or sides.

Training in Open Water

For better or for worse, the best way to train for open-water swimming is by doing it. When swimming in open water, safety comes first—no one should ever swim alone. Swimmers should have a training partner or notify the lifeguard of their plans. They should also be aware of certain characteristics of open water and avoid dangerous weather conditions. For example, open water is rarely as calm as the roughest, most crowded pool. To manage the rougher water, swimmers should raise their elbows higher and roll their shoulders more to keep from catching them on the waves.

Getting off course can be a problem in open water. To swim in a straight line, look and lift the head after breathing and before putting the face back in the water. Practice this in the pool before venturing out into open water. Alternating breathing (breathing on each side) or having a friend paddle alongside in a boat also will help swimmers maintain a straight line.

The Event Itself

The start of any open-water event is usually chaotic (**Fig. 10-33**). Races with many swimmers often use staggered starts with swimmers positioning themselves. Be honest and smart. Swimmers unsure of their times should start among swimmers of moderate ability. Avoid being an obstacle that better swimmers need to climb over and go around. Staying to the side of the pack may mean swimming slightly farther to get on course, but participants will avoid the jumble of swimmers in a mass start. In most events, wearing a swimming cap may be required. For safety, many meets provide color-coded caps to all swimmers based on age or ability. Swimmers unsure of their abilities should request a cap color to alert the lifeguards. When dropping out of an open-water event, swimmers should immediately notify course officials so they can account for all swimmers at the end of the race.

Fig. 10-33

Opportunities in Aquatics

earning to swim opens doors to many different activities. This appendix provides a brief overview of organizations that provide additional knowledge and skills as well as opportunities to people who wish to continue to build on their love of the water.

Competition

People can engage in competitive aquatic sports in various settings, usually related to age, school affiliation or ability. Many organizations promote and conduct these events. One or more of the organizations described below offer programs that may meet most people's needs. Some organizations are more prominent in certain geographical regions than others.

USA Swimming

www.usaswimming.org

USA Swimming is the national governing body for amateur competitive swimming in the United States. USA Swimming was founded in 1980, based on the passage in 1978 of the Amateur Sports Act, which specified that all Olympic sports would be administered independently.

As the national governing body, USA Swimming conducts and administers competitive swimming in the United States. USA Swimming makes rules, implements policies and procedures, conducts national championships, gives out safety and sports medicine information and selects athletes to represent the United States in international competition. USA Swimming is organized on three levels:

- *International.* The international federation for amateur aquatic sports is the Fédération Internationale de Natation Amateur (FINA). USA Swimming is affiliated with FINA through United States Aquatic Sports (USAS), which regulates the four aquatic sports of swimming, synchronized swimming, diving and water polo.

- *National.* USA Swimming is a member of the United States Olympic Committee (USOC) and has voting representation in the USOC House of Delegates.

- *Local.* Within the United States, USA Swimming is divided into Local Swimming Committees (LSCs), each administering USA Swimming activities of local clubs in a specific geographical area. Each LSC has its own bylaws for local operations.

USA Swimming has the following classifications for competitions:

- Senior—for all registered swimmers

- Junior—for all registered swimmers 18 years of age and younger

- Age Group/Junior Olympic—for all registered swimmers grouped by ages 10 and under, 11–12, 13–14 and either 15–16 and 17–18 or 15–18. An 8-and-under age group competition may be conducted.

- Post Age Group—for all registered swimmers older than 18 years of age whom an LSC elects to include in its age group program

- Masters—for all swimmers 19 years of age and older who register with United States Masters Swimming

- Long Distance—for all registered swimmers

Open-Water Swimming

Open-water swimming is defined as any competition that takes place in rivers, lakes or oceans. In 1986, FINA, the world governing body of swimming, officially recognized open-water swimming. The first official competition was staged at the 1991 World Swimming Championships in Perth, Australia. Open-water swimming is now an Olympic event. Open-water swimming is roughly divided into long-distance swimming, with distances of less than 25 kilometers, and marathon swimming, with distances of more than 25 kilometers. Typically, events are held for both men and women at distances of 5, 10 and 25 kilometers.

USA Diving

www.usadiving.org

USA Diving, Inc. is the national governing body of diving. Also known as USA Diving, this organization is organized through Local Diving Associations (LDAs) encompassing clubs nationwide. USA Diving is organized into three programs:

- Junior Olympic–provides a developmental diving and physical fitness program for the youth of the United States and teaches fundamentals of diving and benefits of participation in competitions

- Senior–further develops and identifies U.S. divers of national and international caliber to compete in National Championships, Olympic Games, World Championships, Pan American Games and other national and international competition

- Masters–provides a continuing physical fitness program for diving enthusiasts 21 years of age and older who no longer compete in the Senior program

The mission of USA Diving is to conduct and promote the sport of diving in a manner that allows each participant to achieve the peak of excellence afforded by his or her ability, effort, desire and dedication. All divers have the opportunity to realize the poise, maturity, grace and strength inherent in diving and to reach their personal goals. Coaching and officiating opportunities are available at all levels of USA Diving.

USA Water Polo

www.usawaterpolo.org

USA Water Polo, Inc., (USWP) is the national governing body for water polo in the United States. Local clubs compete in matches and may progress to regional and zone competition. Qualifying teams from geographic zones compete in national championships. Teams compete in indoor and outdoor tournaments at the junior and senior levels. Age-group competition is organized as 13 and under, 15 and under and 17 and under, although many teams mix ages. Co-ed teams and leagues are sanctioned but do not have national competitions.

Water polo is a team sport that combines soccer and rugby skills and is played in deep water. It requires tremendous stamina and skill. It was made a sport in 1885 by the Swimming Association of Great Britain and became an official Olympic sport in 1908. Today, it is played as recreation and is a popular high school, college and Olympic sport. Even beginners who make their own rules can enjoy playing water polo.

United States Synchronized Swimming
www.usasynchro.org

United States Synchronized Swimming, Inc., (USSS) is the national governing body of synchronized swimming. USSS was founded in 1979 to promote and support all competitive and non-competitive levels of the sport. It also selects and trains athletes to represent the United States in international competition.

Registered members, who range in age from 6 to 80, belong to registered clubs. Masters swimming for USSS includes participants who are 20 years old and older. International Masters competition includes participants who are 25 years old and older and is based on rules set by FINA. There are clinics, camps and training programs for every level of swimming ability. There is also a training and certification program for coaches.

Three synchronized swimming events are recognized internationally: solo (one swimmer), duet (two swimmers) and team (up to eight swimmers). Synchronized swimming premiered at the 1984 Olympic Games in Los Angeles. The team event debuted in the 1996 Olympic Games in Atlanta—replacing the solo and duet events. The 2000 Olympic Games in Sydney included the team event, as well as the duet event. There are also compulsory figure competitions. USSS competitions also include the trio event (three swimmers) for junior national, age group, U.S. open and collegiate events.

Synchronized swimming combines skill, stamina and teamwork with the flair of music and drama.

Coaches, psychologists, physiologists, nutritionists, dance specialists and former champions all contribute their expertise. This sport is increasingly popular with both spectators and participants. Non-competitors can participate as coaches, volunteers and judges.

United States Masters Swimming
www.usms.org

United States Masters Swimming (USMS) is an umbrella organization with responsibility and authority over the Masters Swimming Program in the United States. Through its local Masters Swimming Committees and swim clubs, USMS offers competitive swimming to swimmers 19 years of age and older.

Competitions are organized by age groups of 5-year spans (and one 6-year span) (19–24, 25–29, 30–34 and so on, up to 95 and over). Events include 50, 100, 200, 500, 1000 and 1650 freestyle (400, 800 and 1500 in meters); 50, 100 and 200 backstroke, breaststroke and butterfly; and 100, 200 and 400 individual medley (an event in which each quarter of the total distance is swum using a different stroke in a prescribed order—butterfly, backstroke, breaststroke, freestyle). There are also freestyle and medley relays for men, women and mixed teams. In a medley relay, each member of a four-member team swims one quarter of the total distance and then is relieved by a teammate. Open-water swims are held in many locations in the summer, ranging from 1 to 10 miles.

Masters Swimming's credo is fun, fitness and competition. Masters swimmers enjoy the benefits of swimming with an organized group, participating in structured workouts and developing friendships with other adult swimmers. Members participate in a wide range of activities from non-competitive lap swimming to international competition. Socializing at meets is another reason that Masters Swimming is popular.

Coaching and officiating opportunities, paid and volunteer, are available at all levels of USMS. Contact a local Masters Swimming club or USMS for details.

YMCA of the USA Competitive Swimming and Masters Swimming

www.ymca.net

YMCA Competitive Swimming trains individuals of all ages to compete in YMCA programs that may lead to cluster, field and national championships. YMCA age group competition is organized in four age groups: 10 and under, 12 and under, 14 and under and senior. Competition is organized at four levels:

- Inter-association meets
- Cluster, league and district championships
- State or field championships
- National championships

YMCA Masters Swimming is an age-grouped competitive program for adults, starting at age 20. Groups are divided by 5-year spans 20–24, 25–29, 30–34 and so on, with no top age limit. Some YMCAs also sponsor competitive teams in springboard diving and synchronized swimming. YMCAs may register with U.S. Masters Swimming and represent the YMCA in regional and national competition.

National Collegiate Athletic Association

www.ncaa.org

The National Collegiate Athletic Association (NCAA) is the organization for U.S. colleges and universities to speak and act on athletic matters at the national level. The NCAA is also the national athletics accrediting agency for collegiate competition.

Founded in 1905 when 13 schools formed the Intercollegiate Athletic Association of the United States, the NCAA has grown to more than 1000 member institutions. The NCAA enacts legislation on nationwide issues, represents intercollegiate athletics before state and federal governments, compiles and distributes statistics, writes and interprets rules in 12 sports, conducts research on athletics problems and promotes and participates in international sports planning and competition (in part through membership in the U.S. Olympic Committee).

The NCAA sponsors the following national championships:

- Division I Men's Swimming and Diving Championships
- Division I Women's Swimming and Diving Championships
- Division II Men's Swimming and Diving Championships
- Division II Women's Swimming and Diving Championships
- Division III Men's Swimming and Diving Championships
- Division III Women's Swimming and Diving Championships

The National Junior College Athletic Association

www.njcaa.org

The National Junior College Athletic Association (NJCAA) was founded in 1937 to promote and supervise a national program of junior college sports and activities consistent with the educational objectives of junior colleges. The NJCAA interprets rules, sets standards for eligibility, promotes academics through the Academy All-American and Distinguished Academic All-American programs, publishes a monthly magazine, provides weekly polls and distributes sport guides.

There are member institutions throughout the United States, ranging in enrollment size from 500 to 25,000 students. The NJCAA sponsors 50 national championships, 25 for men and 25 for women. At the Men's and Women's National Swimming and Diving Championships each year, the NJCAA presents All-American Awards, Swimmer/Diver of the Year Award and Swimming/Diving Coach of the Year Award.

The National Federation of State High School Associations

www.nfhs.org

The National Federation of State High School Associations consists of the high school athletic associations of the 50 states and the District of Columbia. Also affiliated are 10 Canadian provinces, the Independent Interscholastic Athletic Association of Guam, the Saint Croix Interscholastic Athletic Association and the

St. Thomas–St. John Interscholastic Athletic Association.

The federation began in Illinois in 1920 and is a service and regulatory organization for its members. It provides central recordkeeping, publishes rule books and a journal and conducts conferences. It oversees more than 30 interscholastic sports and lists swimming and diving among the 10 most popular sports. Its goal is to promote the educational value of interscholastic sports.

Local Options

Many national caliber swimmers started as "summer" swimmers. As their love of the sport grew, they sought out more challenging teams. Finding a local competitive team to join is usually easy. The lifeguard or swim instructor at the local pool can often provide information. Local swim clubs and public recreation departments often sponsor teams or rent space to teams. Many locations have outdoor pools with seasonal teams that welcome beginning competitors. Leagues group swimmers by skill level and often provide instruction.

USA Triathlon

www.usatriathlon.org

USA Triathlon is the national governing body for the multisport disciplines of triathlon, duathlon, aquathlon and winter triathlon in the United States. USA Triathlon is a member federation of the U.S. Olympic Committee and the International Triathlon Union. USA Triathlon's membership is comprised of athletes of all ages, coaches, officials, parents and fans striving together to strengthen multisport. USA Triathlon recognizes four distance categories:

- *Sprint.* These events vary greatly, depending on local organizers, and are often called training triathlons. The national championship event is a 0.5-mile swim, 13.5-mile bike race and 3-mile run.

- *International and Olympic.* This category, also called "short course," uses the distances proposed for an Olympic event: 1.5-kilometer swim, 40-kilometer bike race and 10-kilometer run.

- *Long course.* With a 1.2-mile swim, 56-mile bike race and 13.1-mile run, this category is half the ultra distance.

- *Ultra.* This category includes the world-famous Ironman race, first held in Hawaii, comprised of a 2.4-mile swim, a 112-mile bike race and a full 26.2-mile marathon.

Participants from age 15 to over 70 compete in 5-year-age groups at regional, zone and national levels. Some triathlons are team efforts. For beginners, completing the course is seen as a tremendous personal achievement. Fitness enthusiasts engage in the sport to gain the benefits of cross-training. Some career triathletes compete as often as 25 times a year.

More than 2000 triathlons are held in the United States each year. Three-quarters are in the International distance category.

Competition for People with Disabilities

Phil Cole/ALLSPORT

Swimming competition for people with disabilities has a long history. In 1924, the Comite International des Sports des Sourds (CISS [the International Committee for Sports for the Deaf]) held the first Summer World Games for men and women who were deaf. Athletes with cognitive disabilities first joined in international swimming competition in 1968 with the International Summer Special Olympics. At the 2003 Special Olympic World Games, more than 600 athletes participated in aquatic events.

In 1948, Sir Ludwig Guttmann organized a sports competition in Stoke Mandeville, England, involving World War II veterans with spinal cord injuries. Four years later, competitors from Holland joined the games and the international movement, now known as the Paralympics, was born. Olympic-style games for athletes with a disability were organized for the first time in Rome in 1960. In the 1960 Games, there were nine swimming events each for men and women.

Special Olympics

www.specialolympics.org

Special Olympics is an international nonprofit organization dedicated to empowering individuals with intellectual disabilities to become physically fit, productive and respected members of society through sports training and competition. Special Olympics offers children and adults with intellectual disabilities year-round training and competition in 30 Olympic-type summer and winter sports, including swimming.

Because of the wide array of swimming events offered, aquatics is appropriate for a range of ages and ability levels. Aquatics competition events are based on a variety of strokes. Special Olympics also offers events for lower ability level athletes to train and compete in basic aquatics skills. The development of these key skills is necessary prior to advancing to longer competitive events.

Athletes are grouped in competition divisions according to ability level, age and gender.

- Freestyle events: 50, 100, 200, 400, 800 and 1500 meter
- Backstroke, breaststroke and butterfly events: 25 meter (breaststroke, butterfly), 50, 100 and 200 meter
- Individual medley events: 200 and 400 meter
- Freestyle and medley relay events: 4×25, 4×50, 4×100 meter and 4×200 meter freestyle relay

The following aquatics events provide meaningful competition for athletes with lower ability levels:

- 25-meter freestyle and backstroke
- 15-meter walk
- 15- and 25-meter flotation race
- 10-meter assisted swim
- 15-meter unassisted swim

United States Paralympics

www.paralympics.teamusa.org

Formed in 2001, U.S. Paralympics is a division of the U.S. Olympic Committee, the organization responsible for underwriting the expenses of U.S. teams in the Olympic, Pan American, Parapan American and Paralympic Games. The Paralympic and Parapan American Games are elite sport events for athletes from different disability groups. As in the Olympic and Pan American Games, competitors in the Paralympic and Parapan American Games compete in freestyle, backstroke, butterfly, breaststroke and medley events.

Through education, sports programs and community partnerships, U.S. Paralympics strives to make a difference in the lives of individuals with physical disabilities. U.S. Paralympics operates community, academy, military and elite programs to provide individuals with physical disabilities opportunities to participate in sports.

Fitness

Many people enjoy the water as a means to get and stay fit. The following organizations can motivate people toward fitness or take it to the next level by teaching others to get fit.

The President's Council on Physical Fitness and Sports—President's Challenge
www.fitness.gov

The President's Challenge is a program that encourages all Americans to make being active part of their everyday lives. People of all activity and fitness levels are able to participate in the President's Challenge. People can win Presidential awards for daily physical activity and fitness efforts, including swimming. Requirements for

awards are categorized by the following age groups: kids, teens, adults and seniors.

Aquatic Exercise Association
www.aeawave.com

Aquatic Exercise Association (AEA) is an internationally recognized organization of aquatic fitness education for professionals conducting aquatic exercise programs. AEA offers certifications and numerous continuing education programs throughout the world. Certifications are currently offered in eight languages and have been presented in 30 countries. AEA currently offers two certification programs in the United States and two international certifications as well as in-depth educational programs designed to enhance leadership knowledge and skills in the aquatic fitness industry.

United States Water Fitness Association
www.uswfa.com

The United States Water Fitness Association (USWFA) is a nonprofit, educational organization committed to excellence in education and promoting aquatics including water exercise. The USWFA offers the following National Certifications:

- Primary Water Fitness Instructor
- Master Water Fitness Instructor
- Aquatic Fitness Personal Trainer
- Masters Aquatic Fitness Personal Trainer
- Water Walking Instructor
- Aquatic Director
- Water Fitness Coordinator

Employment

Aquatics offers a wide array of employment opportunities. Listed below are only a few job opportunities for people who want to stay on or in the water.

Lifeguard
www.redcross.org

Lifeguarding is a challenging and important job. The American Red Cross trains more than 170,000 lifeguards each year. Through classroom learning and hands-on practice, people learn–

- Surveillance skills to help recognize and prevent injuries.
- Rescue skills–in the water and on land.
- First aid training and professional rescuer cardiopulmonary resuscitation (CPR) and automated external defibrillation (AED) to help prepare for any emergency.
- Professional lifeguard responsibilities like interacting with the public and addressing uncooperative patrons.

Course lengths vary from 30 to 37 hours and options include–

- Lifeguarding–for lifeguards working at traditional pools.
- Waterfront Lifeguarding–for lifeguards at nonsurf, open-water environments, such as lakes and rivers, as well as traditional pools.
- Waterpark Lifeguarding–for lifeguards at waterparks, multiattraction facilities and traditional pools.
- Shallow Water Attendant–for lifeguards that will work only in areas with water attractions up to 4-feet deep.

United States Navy
www.navy.mil

Swimming and aquatic skills are an integral part of the U.S. Navy. All naval personnel must meet minimum swim qualifications. Successful completion of a higher-level swim test is required for naval duties, which require increased exposure to water hazards. The most arduous swimming and aquatics programs include special warfare schools, dive schools, rescue swimmer schools and aviation water survival training.

Water Safety Instructor
www.redcross.org

The Red Cross Water Safety Instructors course provides instructor candidates the training needed to teach courses in the Red Cross Swimming and Water Safety program by developing their understanding of how to use the course materials, how to conduct training sessions and how to evaluate participants' progress.

Water Safety instructors teach people of different abilities and needs–infants and preschoolers, children and youth, people with disabilities, adult beginners and older adults–how to be safe in, on and around the water and how to swim.

Youth Service Organizations

Youth who are involved in aquatics and participate in youth service organizations, such as Boy Scouts of America and Girl Scouts of the USA, can earn merit badges and interest project patches.

Boy Scouts of America
www.scouting.org

Boy Scouting is a year-round program available to boys between ages 11 to 18 years old. Core objectives of the Boy Scout program include developing character, citizenship and personal fitness. Aquatics-related merit badges for Boy Scouts of America include Swimming, Lifesaving and Sports.

Girl Scouts of the USA
www.girlscouts.org

Girl Scouts of the USA is dedicated solely to girls where they build character and skills for success in the real world. In partnership with committed adult volunteers, girls develop qualities that will serve them all their lives, like leadership, strong values, social conscience and conviction about their own potential and self-worth. Interest projects that can be completed with aquatics as the emphasis include Leadership and Water Sports.

Recreation

Scuba

www.padi.com

Some 3 to 4 million scuba divers enjoy the beauty and excitement of the underwater world. Scuba divers wear a mask and fins and carry a compressed air supply and regulator for breathing underwater for extended periods. Scuba divers also use buoyancy control devices, weights, wet suits and a variety of instruments to monitor depth, time and direction underwater. Divers enjoy a variety of underwater activities, such as shore diving, boat diving, reef diving, night diving, underwater photography and underwater archeology.

Recreational scuba diving by certified divers has a good safety record because of the comprehensive training required. At least 40 hours of instruction in the pool and the classroom are required before students start supervised training in open water. A medical examination and a swim test are strongly recommended and often required before learning scuba. The Professional Association of Diving Instructors (PADI) offers certification in scuba diving.

Boating Safety—United States Coast Guard

www.uscgboating.org

As an agency of the Federal government and a servant of the public, the U.S. Coast Guard is a leader in improving the boating experience of the maritime public. It is the mission of the Coast Guard to minimize the loss of life, personal injury, property damage and environmental impact associated with the use of recreational boats, through preventive means, to maximize safe use and enjoyment of America's waterways by the public.

The Coast Guard offers boating safety education to teach people to prevent accidents, injuries and fatalities while boating.

Glossary

Aboveground pool: A portable pool of limited depth that sits on the ground.

Active drowning victim: A person exhibiting universal behavior that includes struggling at the surface in a vertical position and being unable to move forward or tread water.

Adipose tissue: Body tissue that stores fat.

Aerobic exercise: Sustained, rhythmic, physical exercise that requires additional effort by the heart and lungs to meet the increased demand by the skeletal muscles for oxygen.

Anaerobic exercise: Exercise at an intensity such that oxygen demand by skeletal muscles is not consistently met. Anaerobic exercise involves high-intensity events that last 1 minute or less.

Aphasia: The absence or impairment of the ability to communicate through speech, writing or other nonverbal methods.

Approach: The move toward the end of a diving board before the takeoff. It can be a walk or series of jumps.

Aquatic exercise: Fitness activities conducted in water; generally performed in a vertical position with the face out of the water.

Atlantoaxial instability: A weakness in the ligaments between the first two vertebrae.

Back glide: Coasting through the water in a horizontal, face-up position after pushing off from a solid surface.

Basal metabolic rate: The amount of calories the body burns at rest.

Bobbing: The skill of repeatedly submerging and pushing off from the bottom to return to the surface.

Body position: Dives in which the body is in a tuck, pike, straight or free position.

Body roll: A rotating movement of the body around the midline.

Breakpoint: The area of the pool where the depth changes from shallow to deep.

Broken swims: A swimming method that divides a target distance into shorter intervals with a short rest in-between (for example, 10 seconds). The goal for swimmers is to perform each segment at a faster pace than they could maintain over the entire distance.

Buoyancy: The upward force that water exerts on an object.

Cardiovascular endurance: The ability of the heart, lungs and circulatory system to sustain vigorous activity.

Cardiovascular system: The heart and blood vessels, which bring oxygen and nutrients to the body through the circulation of blood.

Catch: The stage in an arm stroke when the swimmer first engages the water in a way that starts movement; the start of the power phase.

Center of buoyancy: A theoretical point in a body where the entire buoyancy of that body can be considered to be concentrated.

Center of mass: A theoretical point in a body where the entire mass of that body can be considered to be concentrated.

Cross-training: A method of exercising so that the effects of training in one sport enhance the effects in another. It combines two or more aerobic endurance sports into one training program.

Descending sets: Decreasing the time on successive swims.

Disability: A physical or mental impairment that significantly limits one or more life activities.

Diving board: A diving apparatus that consists of a flexible board secured at one end and a fulcrum below the board. Also called a springboard.

Diving equipment: Pool structures used to make dives from a 1-meter or 3-meter springboard or from a platform that is 1, 3, 5, 7 ½ or 10 meters high.

Diving platform: An elevated stationary platform structure for diving.

Diving tower: An elevated structure used for diving that includes diving platforms at several heights. Towers used for competitive diving often have platforms that are 1 meter, 3 meters, 5 meters, 7 ½ meters and 10 meters high.

Down Syndrome: A congenital disorder that usually causes delays in physical and cognitive development.

Drag: The resistance of water on a body moving through it.

Drowning: Death by suffocation in water.

Dry-land training: The use of out-of-water training techniques to improve swimming skills. These techniques fall into two areas: flexibility and strength training.

Duration: The amount of time spent during each exercise session.

Early season phase: Lasting about 6 to 8 weeks long, a training method in which swimmers focus on general conditioning to build a foundation for the whole season. Long, easy swims are peformed using various strokes to help build endurance. Swimmers proceed at a slower rate and make needed changes to stroke technique, flip turns and breathing patterns. This phase is often done in conjunction with dry-land training to help improve strength, flexibility and cardiovascular conditioning.

Emergency medical services (EMS) personnel: Trained and equipped community-based personnel dispatched through a local emergency number to provide emergency care for injured or ill people.

Emergency medical services (EMS) system: A network of community resources and medical personnel that provides emergency care to victims of injury or sudden illness.

Entry: The part of a dive in which the body passes through the surface of the water.

Epilepsy: A person who has recurring seizures, also known as *seizure disorder.*

Equilibrium: A state of balance between opposing forces.

Fartlek method: From the Swedish word that means "speed play," it breaks swims into slow and fast lengths of the pool, using the same stroke.

Feetfirst surface dive: A technique for descending underwater from the surface with the feet leading.

Finning: A technique for moving through the water on the back using a pushing motion with the arms underwater.

Fitness swimming: A swimming program in which the workouts have a specified level of intensity and are sustained for a set duration.

Flexibility: The range of motion in a joint or group of joints.

Flight: The movement of the body through the air during a dive.

Flip turn: A fast and efficient turn done in a tuck position; used in lap swimming and in the freestyle and backstroke events in competition.

Floodproofing: Remodeling or rebuilding a home using materials and methods that will prevent or minimize damage from future floods.

Footfirst scull: A sculling technique for moving the body feetfirst through the water in a horizontal position using only back and forth movements of the arms and hands.

Form drag: The resistance related to a swimmer's shape and body position when moving through the water.

Freestyle: A competitive event that allows any stroke, although the front crawl is generally used.

Freestyle relay: A common competitive event in which each member of a four-member team swims any stroke one quarter of the total distance.

Frequency: The number of occurrences of exercise sessions.

Frictional drag: The resistance force caused by an object's surface texture as it moves through a fluid.

Fulcrum: A pivot point near the center of a diving board that lets the board bend. Many fulcrums are adjustable to alter the amount of spring.

Glide: The stage of a stroke after the power phase when the body keeps moving without additional swimmer effort.

Grab start: A competitive start in which the hands grasp the front of the starting blocks for a fast takeoff.

Headfirst scull: A sculling technique for moving the body headfirst in a horizontal position on the surface of the water using only back and forth movements of the arms and hands.

Hearing impairment: Partial or total loss of hearing.

Heat: A race in which times are compared with those from other races to determine overall ranking. A heat is used when there are more entrants in a swimming event than there are lanes in the pool.

Hopper-bottom pool: A pool with a bottom that angles sharply up on all four sides from the deepest point.

Hydraulic: Whirlpools created as water flows over a ledge, such as a low-head dam or waterfall; an unwary swimmer may be trapped in the circulation.

Hydrodynamics: The science that studies the physics of fluids.

Hydrostatic weighing: A technique based on the principle discovered by Archimedes, an ancient Greek mathematician and inventor, it involves being weighed underwater.

Hyperventilation: A dangerous technique some swimmers use to stay underwater longer by taking several deep breaths followed by forceful exhalations, then inhaling deeply before swimming underwater.

Hypothermia: A life-threatening condition in which cold or cool temperatures cause the body to lose heat faster than it can produce it.

Individual medley: An event in which the competitor swims each quarter of the total distance using a different competitive stroke in a prescribed order (butterfly, backstroke, breaststroke, front crawl).

In-line stabilization: A technique used to minimize movement of a victim's head and neck while providing care.

Intensity: How hard one works out when exercising.

Intervals: A series of repeat swims of the same distance and time interval. There is a specific rest period between the time spent swimming. The entire swim series is a set.

Kinesthetic awareness: The conscious sense of where the body or its parts are positioned or how they are moving at any given moment.

Ladders: Several swims with regular increases or decreases in distance, for example, a swim of 25 yards, then 50 yards and finally 75 yards.

Law of acceleration: The principle by which the change in speed of a body depends on how much force is applied to it and the direction of that force.

Law of action and reaction: The principle that for every action there is an equal and opposite reaction.

Law of inertia: The principle that a force must be applied to change the motion of a body.

Law of levers: The principle that movement of levers is the product of the force and force arm is equal to the product of the resistance and resistance arms.

Leading arm: When arms work in opposition, the arm reaching farthest beyond the head. In the sidestroke, this is also called the bottom arm.

Lever: A mechanism that has a pivot point and one or two rigid parts called arms.

Lift: The principle that as fluid moves around an object, the individual particles within the fluid speed up or slow down to stay parallel with the particles on either side of the object.

Longshore currents: Currents that move parallel to the shore.

Mainstreaming: The process of including people with disabilities in the same programs as able-bodied peers.

Masters: A classification in some organizations for swimmers 19 years old and older and divers 21 years old and older.

Medley relay: A competitive event in which each member of a four-member team swims one quarter of the total distance and then is relieved by a teammate. The first uses a backstroke start and swims the backstroke, the second swims the breaststroke, the third swims the butterfly and the fourth swims freestyle.

Metabolic rate: The amount of energy produced by the body in a given period.

Midline: An imaginary line from head to feet that divides the body equally into left and right parts.

Mid-season phase: Lasting about 8 to 12 weeks long, a training method in which swimmers start to tailor their individual training based on specific goals. Workouts can increase in distance so swimmers can pay more attention to fine-tuning strokes. Quality is the emphasis of the workout. This phase is often done in conjunction with dry-land training at maintenance level during this time.

Motor function: The brain's ability to direct both reflexive and voluntary movements.

Negative splitting: Swimming the second half of each swim period faster than the first half.

Open turn: A simple turn used in non-competitive situations.

Open-water swimming: Any competition that takes place in rivers, lakes or oceans.

Over-distance training: Swimming long distances with moderate exertion with short or no rest periods.

Overload: A fitness principle based on working somewhat harder than normal so that the muscles and cardiovascular system must adapt.

Passive drowning victim: An unconscious victim face-down, submerged or near the surface.

Physics: The science that studies matter and energy.

Physiological: Relating to the physical processes and functions of the human body.

Pike position: A basic diving position during flight with the body bent at the hips and the legs straight.

Pike surface dive: A technique for moving underwater from the surface by bending at the hips and descending headfirst with legs kept straight.

Power phase: The stage when the arm or leg stroke is moving the body in the desired direction.

Power safety cover: A motor powered barrier that can be placed over the water area and can also be used to secure the pool area. The space under a pool barrier should not exceed 4 inches.

Press: The diver's final downward push on the diving board caused by the landing from the approach.

Principle of specificity: The benefits of exercise relate directly to the activity performed.

Progression: An ordered set of steps, from the simplest to the most complex, for learning a skill; in an exercise program, gradually increasing frequency, intensity or time so that an overload is produced.

Prone: On the front, face-down.

Propulsive: Causing motion in the desired direction.

Psychological: Referring to the way the mind works and the attitudes, behaviors and beliefs reflecting a person's state of mind.

Pyramid: A swim of regular increases and decreases in distance, for example, a swim starting with 25 yards, then 50 yards, then 75 yards, then 50 yards and then ending with 25 yards.

Racing start: A long, shallow entry from starting blocks used by competitive swimmers.

Recovery: The phase of a stroke when the arms or legs relax and return to the starting position.

Rehabilitation: Process of providing and directing selected tasks to enhance, restore and reinforce performance.

Repetition: A technique that uses swim sets of the same distance done at close to maximum effort (up to 90 percent of maximum) with rest periods as long as or longer than the swim time.

Rip currents: Currents that move water away from the shore or beach and out to sea beyond the breaking waves.

Rotary kick: A kicking technique used for treading water; sometimes called the eggbeater kick.

Safe diving envelope: The area of water in front of, below and to the sides of a diving board that is deep enough that a diver will not strike the bottom, regardless of the depth of the water or the design of the pool.

Scratch: When swimmers inform meet officials they will not be entering an event for which they were previously registered.

Sculling: A propulsion technique for moving through the water or staying horizontal using only the arms and hands to manipulate the flow of water.

Sensory functions: Sight, touch, taste, smell and hearing.

Set: A prescribed series of swims in a particular pattern or sequence.

Shallow angle dive: A low-projecting headfirst entry with a streamlined body position.

Somersaults: A movement in which a person turns forward or backward in a complete revolution bringing the feet over the head.

Specific gravity: The ratio of the weight of a body to the weight of the water it displaces.

Specificity: The principle that states that the benefits of exercise relate directly to the activity performed.

Spinal cord: The bundle of nerves from the brain at the base of the skull to the lower back, inside the spinal column.

Spoon-shaped pool: A pool with a bottom that is rounded upward from the deepest point to all the sides.

Sprints: Short, fast swims (100-percent effort) to simulate race conditions. The rest between sprints is usually long enough to let the heart return to its resting heart rate.

Standard scull: A sculling technique using only back and forth movements of the arms and hands to remain floating in a horizontal, face-up position on the surface of the water.

Starting block: A raised platform from which competitive swimmers begin a race. A bar or handhold is usually attached for backstroke starts.

Straight position: A basic diving position of the body during flight with the body straight or arched slightly backward and the legs straight and together.

Streamlined position: A body positioned so that as it moves through the water, it pushes the least amount of water, receiving the least amount of resistance.

Stroke frequency: The number of complete arm cycles in a set period.

Stroke length: Distance traveled in one complete cycle of the arms.

Stroke mechanics: The application of the hydrodynamic principles to understand and improve swimmer performance.

Supine: On the back, face-up.

Swim meet: A competitive event in swimming; may be a contest between teams or between individuals.

Synchronized swimming: Rhythmical water activity of one or more people performed in a pattern synchronized to music.

Tactile impairment: Partial or total loss of the sense of touch.

Takeoff: The propulsive part of a dive in which a diver's feet leave the deck or the end of a diving board or platform.

Taper phase: The 1- to 3-week period in a training season before a peak performance, in which the person in training decreases distances but raises the intensity almost to racing speed.

Target heart rate range: The ideal heart rate range for an individual to maintain during exercise for greatest cardiovascular benefit.

Track start: A competitive start often used from starting blocks for a fast takeoff. Differs from grab start in initial foot placement.

Trailing arm: The arm that rests on the hip in the glide phase of the sidestroke. Also called the top arm.

Training effect: An improvement in functional capacity of a system (cardiovascular, respiratory, muscular) that results from an overload of that system.

Treading water: A skill using arm and leg movements to stay vertical in the same location with the head out of the water.

Triathlon: A sporting event made up of three different activities, usually swimming, biking and running, in that order. Triathlons often start with an open-water swim.

Tuck position: A basic diving position during flight with the body pulled into a tight ball, the knees drawn up to the chest and the heels drawn to the buttocks.

Tuck surface dive: A technique for moving headfirst from the surface with the hips and knees flexed to under the water with the hips and knees extending.

Twists: A twist is a rotation along the mid-line of the body, which is held straight during the twist.

Vision impairment: Partial or total loss of sight.

Wave drag: Energy loss due to generation of waves as a body moves along the surface of the water.

Sources

American Academy of Pediatrics. *Water Safety.* Available at http://www.medem.com/MedLB/article_detaillb. cfm?article_ID=ZZZ7IV4O97C&sub_cat=104. Accessed July 2008.

American Alliance for Health, Physical Education, Recreation and Dance. *Safety Aquatics.* Sports Safety Series, Monograph #5. American Alliance for Health, Physical Education, Recreation and Dance, 1977.

American College of Sports Medicine. *Fit Society Page Newsletter, January-March 2001.* Available at http://www.acsm. org/pdf/01fitsoc.pdf. Accessed July 2008.

American College of Sports Medicine. *Physical Activity and Public Health Guidelines.* Available at http://www.acsm.org. Accessed July 2008.

American National Red Cross. *Adapted Aquatics: Swimming for Persons with Physical or Mental Impairments.* Washington, D.C.: The American National Red Cross, 1977.

American National Red Cross. *Basic Water Rescue.* Yardley, Pennsylvania: StayWell, 1998.

American National Red Cross. *Community Water Safety.* Yardley, Pennsylvania: StayWell, 1995.

American National Red Cross. *Lifeguarding.* Yardley, Pennsylvania: StayWell, 2007.

American National Red Cross. *Responding to Emergencies.* Yardley, Pennsylvania: StayWell, 2007.

American National Red Cross. *Small Craft Safety.* Yardley, Pennsylvania: StayWell, 1998.

American National Red Cross. *Swimming and Water Safety.* Yardley, Pennsylvania: StayWell, 2004.

Anderson, B. *Stretching.* Bolinas, California: Shelter Publications, Inc., 1980.

Armbruster, D.A.; Allen, R.H.; and Billingsley, H.S. *Swimming and Diving.* St. Louis: The C.V. Mosby Company, 1968.

Auerbach, P.S. *A Medical Guide to Hazardous Marine Life.* Jacksonville, Florida: Progressive Printing Co., Inc., 1987.

Besford, P. *Encyclopedia of Swimming.* New York: St. Martins Press, 1971.

Brems, M. *The Fit Swimmer: 120 Workouts & Training Tips.* Chicago, Illinois: Contemporary Books, 1984.

Brems, M. *Swim for Fitness.* San Francisco: Chronicle Books, 1979.

Burgess, G.H. "Shark Attack and the International Shark Attack File," in Gruber, S.H., editor. *Discovering Sharks.* Highlands, New Jersey: American Littoral Society, 1991.

California State Parks. *Types of Disabilities.* Available at http://www.parks.ca.gov/pages/735/files/avw-02-types%20of%20di sabilities.pdf. Accessed July 2008.

Canadian Red Cross. *Drown-Proofing Toddlers: Safe Practice or False Security?* Available at http://www.redcross.ca/article. asp?id=025216&tid=024. Accessed July 2008.

Centers for Disease Control and Prevention Data and Statistics. *WISQARS: Web-based Injury Statistics Query and Reporting System.* Accessed July 2008.

Centers for Disease Control and Prevention Injury Center. *Water-Related Injuries: Fact Sheet.* Available at http://www.cdc. gov/ncipc/factsheets/drown.htm. Accessed July 2008.

Centers for Disease Control and Prevention Physical Activity. *Target Heart Rate and Estimated Maximum Heart Rate.* Available at http://www.cdc.gov/nccdphp/dnpa/physical/measuring/ target_heart_rate.htm. Accessed July 2008.

Clayton, R.D., and Thomas, D.G. *Professional Aquatic Management.* Champaign, Illinois: Human Kinetics, 1989.

Clayton, R.D., and Tourney, J.A. *Teaching Aquatics.* Minneapolis: Burgess Publishing Company, 1981.

Collis, M., and Kirchoff, B. *Swimming.* Boston: Allyn and Bacon, Inc., 1974.

Colwin, C.M. *Swimming Into the 21st Century.* Champaign, Illinois: Leisure Press, 1991.

Cooper, K.H. *The Aerobics Program for Total Well-Being.* New York: Bantam Books, 1982.

Counsilman, J.E. *Competitive Swimming Manual.* Bloomington, Indiana: Counsilman Co., Inc., 1977.

Counsilman, J.E. *The Science of Swimming.* Englewood Cliffs, New Jersey: Prentice-Hall, Inc., 1968.

Edwards, S. *Triathlon: A Triple Fitness Sport.* Chicago: Contemporary Books, Inc., 1983.

Environmental Protection Agency, Office of Water. *Before You Go to the Beach.* Available at http://www.cdc.gov/healthyswimming/pdf/epa_beachbro.pdf. Accessed July 2008.

Federal Emergency Management Agency. *Are You Ready? Floods.* Available at http://www.fema.gov/areyouready/flood.shtm. Accessed July 2008.

Firby, H. *Howard Firby on Swimming.* London: Pelham, 1975.

Flewwelling, H. "Sparging System," in Gabriel, J.L., editor. *U.S. Diving Safety Manual.* Indianapolis: U.S. Diving Publications, 1990.

Forbes, M.S. *Coaching Synchronized Swimming Effectively.* Champaign, Illinois: Human Kinetics Publishers, Inc., 1988.

Gabrielsen, M.A. *Diving Injuries: A Critical Insight and Recommendation.* Clayton, R.D., editor. Indianapolis: Council for National Cooperation in Aquatics, 1984.

Gabrielsen, M.A. *Diving Injuries: Prevention of the Most Catastrophic Sport Related Injuries.* Presented to the Council for National Cooperation in Aquatics, Indianapolis, 1981.

Hay, J.G. *The Biomechanics of Sports Techniques.* Englewood Cliffs, New Jersey: Prentice-Hall, 1985.

Ichthyology at the Florida Museum of Natural History. *Reducing the Risk of Shark Attacks.* Available at http://www.flmnh.ufl.edu/fish/Sharks/Attacks/relariskreduce.htm. Accessed July 2008.

Jonas, S. *Triathloning For Ordinary Mortals.* New York: W.W. Norton & Co. Inc., 1986.

Katz, J. *Swimming for Total Fitness: A Progressive Aerobic Program (2nd edition),* New York: Bantam Doubleday Dell Publishing Group, 1993.

Katz, J. *The W.E.T Workout.* New York: Facts on File Publications, 1985.

Knopf, K.; Fleck, L.; and Martin, M.M. *Water Workouts.* Winston-Salem: Hunter Textbooks, Inc., 1988.

Krasevec, J.A., and Grimes, D.C. *HydroRobics.* New York: Leisure Press, 1984.

Leonard, J., editor. *Science of Coaching Swimming.* Champaign, Illinois: Leisure Press, 1992.

Maglischo, E.W. *Swimming Faster.* Palo Alto, California: Mayfield Publishing Company, 1982.

Maglischo, E.W., and Brennan, C.F. *Swim for the Health of It.* Palo Alto, California: Mayfield Publishing Co., 1985.

Malina, R.M., and Gabriel, J.L., editors. *USA Diving Coach Development Reference Manual.* Indianapolis, Indiana: USA Diving Publications, 2007.

McArdle, W; Katch, F.; and Katch, V. *Exercise Physiology: Energy, Nutrition and Human Performance (2nd edition).* Philadelphia: Lea & Febiger, 1986.

McEvoy, J.E. *Fitness Swimming: Lifetime Programs.* Princeton: Princeton Book Company Publishers, 1985.

Medline Plus. *Health Topics–Disabilities.* Available at http://www.nlm.nih.gov/medlineplus/disabilities.html. Accessed July 2008.

Medline Plus. *Health Topics–Water Safety (Recreational).* Available at http://www.nlm.nih.gov/medlineplus/watersafetyrecreational.html#cat22. Accessed July 2008.

Messner, Y.J., and Assmann, N.A. *Swimming Everyone.* Winston-Salem: Hunter Textbooks, Inc., 1989.

Montoye, H.J.; Christian, J.L.; Nagle, F.J.; and Levin, S.M. *Living Fit.* Menlo Park, California: The Benjamin/Cummings Publishing Company, Inc., 1988.

National Association of the Deaf. *Info and FAQs.* Available at http://www.nad.org/site/pp.asp?c=foINKQMBF&b=99567. Accessed July 2008.

National Heart, Lung, and Blood Institute. *What is Cystic Fibrosis?* Available at http://www.nhlbi.nih.gov/health/dci/Diseases/cf/cf_what.html. Accessed July 2008.

National Institute of Neurological Disorders and Stroke. *Amyotrophic Lateral Sclerosis Information Page.* Available at http://www.ninds.nih.gov/disorders/amyotrophiclateralsclerosis/amyotrophiclateralsclerosis.htm. Accessed July 2008.

National Institute of Neurological Disorders and Stroke. *NINDS Cerebral Palsy Information Page.* Available at http://

www.ninds.nih.gov/health_and_medical/disorders/cerebral_palsy.htm. Accessed October 2003.

National Institute of Neurological Disorders and Stroke. *NINDS Multiple Sclerosis Information Page.* Available at http://www.ninds.nih.gov/disorders/multiple_sclerosis/multiple_sclerosis.htm. Accessed July 2008.

National Institute of Neurological Disorders and Stroke. *NINDS Stroke Information Page.* Available at http://www.ninds.nih.gov/disorders/stroke/stroke.htm. Accessed July 2008.

National Oceanic and Atmospheric Administration. *NOAA Ocean Service Education.* Available at http://oceanservice.noaa.gov/education/welcome.html. Accessed July 2008.

National Safety Council. *Injury Facts.* Chicago, Illinois: National Safety Council, 2002.

Office of Special Education and Rehabilitative Services. *IDEA '97.* Available at http://www.ed.gov/offices/OSERS/Policy/IDEA/the_law.html. Accessed July 2008.

Paralympic Games. *Paralympic Games.* Available at http://www.paralympic.org. Accessed July 2008.

President's Council on Physical Fitness and Sports. *Guidelines for Personal Exercise Programs.* Available at http://www.fitness.gov/publications/council/fitness_pdf.pdf. Accessed July 2008.

Report of the 16th Annual Meeting, Council For National Cooperation in Aquatics, 1966.

Safe Kids USA. *Clear Danger: A National Study of Childhood Drowning and Related Attitudes and Behaviors.* Available at http://www.usa.safekids.org/NSKW.cfm. Accessed July 2008.

Special Olympics. *Special Olympics Official General Rules.* Available at http://www.specialolympics.org. Accessed July 2008.

Swimming Pools: A Guide to Their Planning, Design, and Operation. Champaign, Illinois: Human Kinetics Publishers, Inc., 1987.

United States Army Corps of Engineers, National Water Safety Program. *Safety Tips.* Available at http://watersafety.usace.army.mil/safetytips.htm. Accessed July 2008.

United States Coast Guard, Boating Safety Division. *The Main Channel.* Available at http://www.uscgboating.org/index.aspx. Accessed July 2008.

United States Coast Guard. *Boating Statistics 2006.* Available at http://www.uscgboating.org/statistics/Boating_Statistics_2006.pdf. Accessed July 2008.

United States Coast Guard, Office of Boating Safety. *Children and Personal Watercraft.* Available at http://www.uscgboating. org/articles/pdf/Children%20&%20PWC.pdf. Accessed July 2008.

United States Consumer Product Safety Commission. *Guidelines for Entrapment Hazards: Making Pools and Spas Safer.* Available at http://www.cpsc.gov/CPSCPUB/PUBS/363.pdf. Accessed July 2008.

United States Consumer Product Safety Commission. *Safety Barrier Guidelines for Home Pools.* Available at http://www.cpsc.gov/cpscpub/pubs/pool.pdf. Accessed July 2008.

United States Department of Health and Human Services, Physical Activity Guidelines Advisory Committee. *Physical Activity Guidelines Advisory Committee Report.* Available at http://www.health.gov/paguidelines/Report/Default.aspx. Accessed July 2008.

United States Department of Justice, Americans with Disabilities Act ADA Home Page. *Americans with Disabilities Act of 1990.* Available at http://www.ada.gov/pubs/ada.htm. Accessed July 2008.

United States Lifesaving Association. *International Life Saving Federation International Standards for Beach Safety and Information Flags.* Available at http://www.usla.org/PublicInfo/library/FlagWarningStandardsILSFinal20FEB04.pdf. Accessed July 2008.

United States Paralympics. *About U.S. Paralympic Team.* Available at http://paralympics.teamusa.org/content/index/71. Accessed August 2008.

United States Synchronized Swimming. *About USA Synchro.* Available at http://www.usasynchro.org/#. Accessed July 2008.

USA Diving. *About USA Diving.* Available at http://www.usadiving.org/USD_03redesign/about/about.htm. Accessed July 2008.

USA Swimming. *About USA Swimming.* Available at http://www.usaswimming.org/usasweb/DesktopDefault.aspx?TabId=21&Alias=Rainbow&Lang=en. Accessed September 2003.

USA Triathlon. *About USAT.* Available at http://triathlon.teamusa.org/content/index/56. Accessed July 2008.

USA Water Polo. *Inside USA Water Polo.* Available at http://www.usawaterpolo.com/InsideUSAWaterPolo.aspx. Accessed July 2008.

Ward, A.W.; Trent, W.P.; et al. *The Cambridge History of English and American Literature.* New York: G.P. Putnam's Sons, 1907–21; New York: Bartleby.com, 2000. Available at http://www.bartleby.com/cambridge/. Accessed July 2008.

Williams, M. H., *Nutrition for Fitness and Sport.* Dubuque, Iowa: William C. Brown Company Publishers, 1983.

YMCA of the USA. *The Parent/Child and Preschool Aquatic Program Manual.* Champaign, Illinois: Human Kinetics Publishers, Inc., 1999.

YMCA of the USA. *Principles of YMCA Competitive Swimming and Diving (2nd Edition),* Champaign, Illinois: Human Kinetics Publishers, Inc., 2000.

YMCA of the USA. *The Youth and Adult Aquatic Program Manual.* Champaign, Illinois: Human Kinetics Publishers, Inc., 1999.